COLLECTED POEMS

C.H. SISSON

COLLECTED POEMS

CARCANET

First published in 1998 by
Carcanet Press Limited
4th Floor, Conavon Court
12-16 Blackfriars Street
Manchester M3 5BQ

A CIP catalogue record for this book
is available from the British Library
ISBN 1 85754 379 3

The publisher acknowledges financial assistance
from the Arts Council of England

Set in 10pt Palatino by Bryan Williamson, Frome
Printed and bound in England by SRP Ltd, Exeter

Contents

vii

The new poems from *In the Trojan Ditch* (1974)

Miscellaneous poems since *Exactions* (1980-83)

Antidotes (1991)

Poems since *What and Who* (1994-98)

Appendix: Poems 1931-5

Early poems and
The London Zoo

On a Troopship

They are already made
Why should they go
Into boring society
Among the soldiery?
But I, whose imperfection
Is evident and admitted
Needing further assurance
Must year-long be pitted
Against fool and trooper
Practising my integrity
In awkward places,
Walking till I walk easily
Among uncomprehended faces
Extracting the root
Of the matter from the diverse engines
That in an oath, a gesture or a song
Inadequately approximate to the human norm.

In Time of Famine: Bengal

I do not say this child
This child with grey mud
Plastering her rounded body
I do not say this child
For she walks poised and happy
But I say this   .
Who looks in at the carriage window
Her eyes are big
Too big
Her hair is touzled and her mouth is doubtful
And I say this
Who lies with open eyes upon the pavement
Can you hurt her?
Tread on those frightened eyes
Why should it frighten her to die?
This is a fault
This is a fault in which I have a part.

In the Hills

Whereas I wander here among
Stone outcrops, rocks and roots
Below me tapers the peninsula
All India going to the sea.

Below, summer is a disease
Which seas surround whose glassy blue
Nothing can cool and nothing cure
But seize my heart

The jackal wandering in the woods
For I have speech and nothing said
The jackal sniffing in the plains
The vulture and the carrion crow

O jackal, howl about my bed.
O howl around my sleeping head.

The Body in Asia

Despite the mountains at my doorstep
This is a hollow, hollow life.
The mist blows clear and shows the snow
Among the dark green firs, but here
Upon the cold, scorched, dusty grass
The camels looped together raise
Their supercilious noses.
Upon the road the donkeys trot
And mule-teams with their muleteers pace.
The country lies before me like
A map I carry in my mind –
A wall built by the Hindu Kush
A plain that falls away to sea
I on the foothills here between
Sniffing the cold and dusty air.

Too long of longing makes me cold
The heart a tight and burning fistful
Hangs like a cold sun in my chest
A hollow kind of firmament.

I can imagine my exterior
The body, and the limbs that run off from it
But there is nothing in it I am sure
Except the ball of heart that weighs one side
Like the lead ballast in a celluloid duck.
And in my head a quarter-incher's brain
Looks out as best it can from my two eyes:
It can imagine how the country lies
To left and right, extensions of the limbs
But has no thoughts that I can understand.
Not only in this land I have felt it so
But on the Brahmaputra where
Bits of the jungle floated down
Black heaps upon the coloured river
When night fell and the sun
A red and geometric disk
Above its square reflection stood
For half a moment and then dipped:
I heard it sizzle in the water.
The flat and muddy banks, remote
Beyond the miles of plashing water
Diminished me
Till, smaller than the skin I stood in
I leaned against the rails and watched
The searchlights on the licking water.
The secret of diminishment
Is in this sad peninsula
Where the inflated body struts
Shouting its wants, but lacks conviction.
Conviction joins the muscles up
But here the body flaps and flutters
A flapping sail in a fitful wind.

Beyond the River

Jungle, scrub and paddy-field
And, looking up, I see
O shower of leaves in the sky
On the thinly-peopled tree

Ce pays où, à l'improviste . . .

Dust gets upon its feet behind the gharry
That starts, and leaves me standing in the roadway.

The Hills again: with a Horse

The terraced and eroded country
Makes shadows in the evening sunlight
My horse trots smoothly and then falls

Courage is of no use against
The dust and falling mountains
The body feels its weakness and
Measures its tiny pace against
The Asiatic distances
In mind like Christ walks on the waters.

The Writer

The bitter wind that blows against
The windows of my squalid cell
Re-assures me, if need were,
In all this world nothing is well.

The liar with the microphone
The liar with the printer's ink
The vain with their stupid fantasies
Are shouting what they hope they think.

A rustling pendulum of bones
Parades as the traditional spook
But, hung from an observant skull,
It writes its thoughts down in a book.

In a Dark Wood

Now I am forty I must lick my bruises
What has been suffered cannot be repaired
I have chosen what whoever grows up chooses
A sickening garbage that could not be shared.

My errors have been written in my senses
The body is a record of the mind
My touch is crusted with my past defences
Because my wit was dull my eye grows blind.

There is no credit in a long defection
And defect and defection are the same
I have no person fit for resurrection
Destroy then rather my half-eaten frame.

But that you will not do, for that were pardon
The bodies that you pardon you replace
And that you keep for those whom you will harden
To suffer in the hard rule of your Grace.

Christians on earth may have their bodies mended
By premonition of a heavenly state
But I, by grosser flesh from Grace defended,
Can never see, never communicate.

Fellfoot

They live in a solid cottage by the stream
And I know this of what is in their skin
It grows to hope but does not seed to dreams
They are the sort of country they live in.

Their limbs lie on these boards, heavy with sap
The eyes they close are grey and green as stone
They are not happier than trees perhaps
When they are sad, then like the wind they moan.

The pot upon the hearth cooks simmering food
Logs will not burn to ash in a whole day
Their cankers are kept numb by a slow blood
Slowly they twist, and turn from brown to grey.

Epitaph

These two in life did not discourage death
But oh! it was like amber in their hearts
Growing, at last it left no room for breath
And they are hard and clear in all their parts.

In London

I float between the banks of Maida Vale
Where half is dark and half is yellow light
In creeks and catches flecks of flesh look pale
And over all our grief depends the night.

I turn beside the shining black canal
And tree-tops close like lids upon my eyes
A milk-maid laughs beside a coffee-stall
I pray to heaven, favour my enterprise.

But whether there is answer to my prayer
When with my host at last I redescend
After delicious talk the squalid stair
I do not know the answer in the end.

Sparrows seen from an Office Window

You should not bicker while the sparrows fall
In chasing pairs from underneath the eaves
And yet you should not let this enraged fool
Win what he will because you fear his grief.

About your table three or four who beg
Bully or trade because those are the passions
Strong enough in them to hide all other lack
Sent to corrupt your heart or try your patience.

If you are gentle, it is because you are weak
If bold, it is the courage of a clown
And your smart enemies and you both seek
Ratiocination without love or reason.

O fell like lust, birds of morality
O sparrows, sparrows, sparrows whom none regards
Where men inhabit, look in here and see
The fury and cupidity of the heart.

In Kent

Although there may be treacherous men
Who in the churchyard swing their mattocks
Within they sing the *Nunc Dimittis*

And villagers who find that building
A place to go to of a Sunday
May accidentally be absolved

For on a hill, upon a gibbet . . .
And this is Saint Augustine's county.

A Death

We dare not mourn
And will not look upon the face of the dead
Our inattention turns
Away the head
Our inattention spurns
Grief, love and death.

The Attic

Why should two animals inhabit there?
– He, small and dark, made like the root of a tree
She with the round flesh of considering kine –
Why should they crouch above that gaslit stair?

Is it because a city is a forest
Which to escape is to be less than beast?
And to be open is to be encaged
Where there is neither sacrifice nor priest?

Out of a farm-house built upon a Roman's
Hearth, girdled with leaf and Druid stone
He could not die but in a hidden city
Nor would she proudly have her death less fine.

So he will dance before Saul, and in his attic
Work all his glittering jewels to savage shapes
And therefore we must drink the cup he offers
Before his hand is wrenched aside by fame.

The Retreat

For quiet, quiet is the world
I by divining seek to know
A vase of flowers is good for that

What I indeed have proved upon
The practical intelligence
Is, two pursuits alone make whole
To touch the flesh in love, to pray.

A Duckling

I almost prayed for its departing
The tiny bird with sodden feathers
The Christian faith forbids such pity

The duckling weaker than her sisters
Crouching in straw within the hen-coop
Recedes from the immeasurable time.

So small a life with beady eye
Comfort cannot come at and none accompany
Entering among threshed ears the darkening shades.

The Night Ferry

The turning and deceits of time
Do not allow to catch full face
Even the face of agony
But all is mixed and wrought to nought
In those evading corridors

Love is the light by which we see
The heart can hardly hold it still.

Vienna

The heavy waters of the Danube
Flow eastward now away from me
The steppe creeps upon the city

I turn towards the distant seaboard

> O island standing in the breakers
> God keep you from this grief of empires
> And may June see
> The dog-rose open in the hedge.

An Old Man

How empty one can be
The evil gone
Blind with forgetfulness
The eye
Fingers clutched on the knee
Alone expect.

Stockholm

The dissipated lauds
Of crowds on a glad morning
They have cast clouts
And their skins are a little nearer the sun
Men ordinarily wrapt in care
Feel themselves closer to the off-the-shoulder girls.

And in the church
Clear Nordic voices
                Allena Gud
Under twelve candles and a gold pulpit
Like birds singing
                Tense
Himmelrik
                tillhöra
In narrow pews.

A Girl

A fragile moment of her life
She stands upon the sunlit grass

Cancer may eat her or age bend her
Her mind may grow of weevils full
But one spring morning she will have stood there
Virgin, naked, eighteen and in the sunlight
The distant elms about the level of her nipples.

A Monument in Milan

Liberty is a great killer
All the *caduti*
Died in her name.
At every street corner
Someone crossed over in front of a machine-gun.
It is not only for the life that she promises
That liberty is loved.

The Poet

To make a poem out of nothing
Would pass the time
But heart four paws and swollen liver
And what else I am furnished with
Will not allow my small poetic factory
To work without them.
The price of every poem is a twist of the knife.

Maurras Young and Old

1

Est allé à Londres
Monsieur Maurras jeune
From a land of olives, grapes and almonds
His mind full of Greek.
Under the shadow of the British Museum
He reflected on the many and foolish
Discourses of the Athenians
And on the Elgin marbles.

The fog settled
Chokingly around the Latin head
Of the eloquent scholar.
Quick like a ferret
He tore his way through
Scurrying past the red brick of Bloomsbury
To the mock antique portals.

The Latin light
Showed on the Mediterranean hills
A frugal culture of wine and oil.
Unobserved in their fog the British
toto divisos orbe
Propounded a mystery of steam
In France they corrected the menus

Writing for *biftec*: beefsteak.
Monsieur Maurras noted the linguistic symptoms
He noted, beyond the Drachenfels
The armies gathering.

2

The light fell
Across the sand-dunes and the wide *étang*.
In their autochthonous boats
The fishermen put out
And came back to the linear village
Among the vineyards and the olive groves
Place de la République
Rue Zola
In which names the enemy celebrated his triumphs.

Twenty-five years:
Beyond the Drachenfels
The armies gathered again
irruptio barbarorum
The boats are moored on the *étang*
For Monsieur Maurras
The last harvest is gathered.

A Latin scorn
For all that is not indelibly Latin
A fortiori for the Teutonic captain
Passing him on the terrace of the Chemin de Paradis
Enemy and barbarian.
Inutile, Monsieur, de me saluer
His eyes looked out towards the middle sea
He heard not even that murmur
But an interior music.

Paludes

I pass my bitter life within
The stinking marshes of despair
Waist deep in glutinous days
I part the rushes
To see the gnats dance like hopes before me
While in fact the bog
Encases me more juicily at every moment
And squelch soon
Will stop my mouth.

La Plage, la Nuit

The lights in all the windows show
Everybody eating
The children
Stuffing their mouths or running round the table screaming

The young women
Their midriffs no longer bare
Leaning over a domestic bottle of wine
Or reproving their younger cousins.

In the darkness on the beach two odd people
Embrace in an individual love
Such as the others have not even the time to dream of.

In Sloane Square

May she not think, the naked bronze
Suspended in the autumn air
Without a thought are fallen leaves
And women blown about the square?

Her solid metal, quietly,
Reposes in a single thought
They clutch their skirts, and squint at her
As miscellaneously distraught,

Not one leaf falls to hide her shame
And they are muffled cosily
Yet the veiled tenderness is hers
And theirs the brazen nudity.

Dialogue between a Knight and a Lady

SHE: Nothing that is not intent
Moves my mind: my pursed lips
Place every word to whip and will

HE: The narrow grange that you inhabit
You bar further against assault
Retreating to one room of it

SHE: Do not expect me again to issue
Into the sunlight, though green spring
Invite to copulation under the trees

HE: Locks hold you, which you have tightened
So that, in a dark squalid corner
You may without interruption suffer the embrace of fear.

Astronomy

There is no reply from outer space
Where the astronomers calculate God to be
No wonder therefore
If they and the world they advise tire
Of their insipid prayers.

Under the arc of the world
Looking inwards at its quartzes and crystals
It is possible to see
The address of all prayer
The small dimensions
Having become infinite.

On the Way Home

Like questing hounds
The lechers run through London
From all the alley-ways
Into all the thoroughfares

Until, shoulder to shoulder, they vanish
Into the main line stations
Or the Underground traps them.

A moment of promiscuity at nightfall
Their feet go homewards but their attentions
Are on the nape of a neck or the cut of a thigh
Almost any woman

As Schopenhauer noted
Being more interesting to them than those
Who made their beds that morning.

Silence

Let not my words have meaning
And let not my bitter heart
Be expressed, like a rotten
Pomegranate. Guts full of pus
And a brain uncertain as a thunderstorm
Do not, I think, amuse the muses.

Moriturus

The carcase that awaits the undertaker
But will not give up its small voice lies
Hollow and grim upon the bed.

What stirs in it is hardly life but a morosity
Which when this skipped as a child was already under the lids
Rebellious and parting from the flesh.

What drunken fury in adolescence pretended
Merely to possess the flesh and drove onwards
The blind soul to issue in the lap of Venus?

The hope of fatherhood, watching the babe sucking
(Ah, he will grow, hurled headlong into the tomb!)
Gives way to a tenderness split into amnesia.

The last chat of corruption reasonable as a syllogism
The image of God is clear, his love wordless
Untie my ligaments, let my bones disperse.

The Aeroplane

High over the alps
In what seems to be a stationary aeroplane
It is possible to hold
That each of our lives is a metallic nullity
Or a biological wriggle.

Below
Gathered around the Easter cup may be
Those who think of themselves as the children of God
But up here is empty
He is not here, and below
Are only emptinesses with a taste for precedence.

La Biologie

The full creature dressed in her skin from top to toe
Is *La Biologie*, the famous beauty

The child, dancing and jumping to be or to possess this
The old, who scarcely knew when they passed this zenith

Claim separate minds in hope or in desperation
But blackness covers all, and the wind blows.

Thirty-five

You preserve under a trim office dress
Erotic surfaces which you value as a resource
Not to be expended but in necessity
Or on the throw of a dice
Which might for a prize bring luxury

The contrast between the soft declensions
And the hard calculations
It is difficult not to believe
In the acid corruption of the mind
And in the permanence of the body a boon of nature.

The Shape of Life

The shape of life
Is ejaculation
What aspiration
The old men have, sitting toothless at their meetings
Is recollection

The function done
The body waits to stiffen
Into a waxen log

The residual feelers
Not yet stilled
Wave and exacerbate themselves

Governing the world
Doing its businesses and arrangements
Who shall not say, praying.

Ightham Woods

The few syllables of a horse's scuffle at the edge of the road
Reach me in the green light of the beeches
Les seuls vrais plaisirs
Selon moy
Are those of one patch between the feet and the throat.
Maybe, but the beeches
And that half clop on the gravel
Indicate a world into which I can dissolve.

Family Fortunes

I

I was born in Bristol, and it is possible
To live harshly in that city

Quiet voices possess it, but the boy
Torn from the womb, cowers

Under a ceiling of cloud. Tramcars
Crash by or enter the mind

A barred room bore him, the backyard
Smooth as a snake-skin, yielded nothing

In the fringes of the town parsley and honey-suckle
Drenched the hedges.

II

My mother was born in West Kington
Where ford and bridge cross the river together

John Worlock farmed there, my grandfather
Within sight of the square church-tower

The rounded cart-horses shone like metal
My mother remembered their fine ribbons

She lies in the north now where the hills
Are pale green, and I

Whose hand never steadied a plough
Wish I had finished my long journey.

III

South of the march parts my father
Lies also, and the fell town

That cradles him now sheltered also
His first unconsciousness

He walked from farm to farm with a kit of tools
From clock to clock, and at the end

Only they spoke to him, he
Having tuned his youth to their hammers.

IV

I had two sisters, one I cannot speak of
For she died a child, and the sky was blue that day

The other lived to meet blindness
Groping upon the stairs, not admitting she could not see

Felled at last under a surgeon's hammer
Then left to rot, surgically

And I have a brother who, being alive
Does not need to be put in a poem.

Victoria Station

The man with nothing to say
May walk in a crowd
His assumed occasions
Will give him reason.

Those therefore whose tacit purposes
Do not allow of apology
Accept the plausible context
Of Victoria Station.

And my verse
Sidles like a child between categories
Instead of poetry I have
Only a location.

The Origin of Species

O let me die in a dark corner
For what is called the heart
Is only a tropism that any scorner
May name as he will, assigning whatever part

His own corruption suggests to this pain
Borne in my changing shape with changing lies
One aches towards God: he is called the saint
The lecher leans over a girl and sighs.

Whom I address from darkness: This mutation
Has failed, before I AM I hide my face
Gather in without numbering this lost nation
And let a new creation succeed this race.

At the Airport

Out of blue air
You descend like light
Child, not mine but me
Your heart in my mouth

But what seems similar
Across age, sex and size
Is no such matter
My look in your eyes
Brighter than in my own
My grief beside yours
Minute
And when I seem to burn
With a like flame I am
Cold ash beside you.

Versailles

In an avenue of Versailles
Where the limes clasp their fingers above
She sat on a stone bench and I
Did not have to declare my love.

Haunt of old lechers, to the goat also
Comes this serenity, to watch the kid
She comes for a moment to drink at this pool
Then she may go, and others must follow and plead.

Commuters

The slack faces
Of those in the train
Watch the bum-paper
In their sweaty hands.

Like folk in privies
They lean forward, each alone
Their visceral lives
Sagging within the skeleton.

If this is hope, they have it
The carriage will defecate
On the usual platform
They will find the amorous night.

In Honour of J.H. Fabre

My first trick was to clutch
At my mother and suck
Soon there was nothing to catch
But darkness and a lack.

My next trick was to know
Dividing the visible
Into shapes which now
Are no longer definable.

My third trick was to love
With the pretence of identity
Accepting without proof
The objects 'her' and 'me'.

My last trick was to believe
When I have the air
Of praying I at least
Join the mantis its prayers.

Ide Hill

He sits with his gun across his knees
His fair wife beside him, with high cheek-bones
They are amorous without seeking to please
And fit to make their home among stones.

History does not remember enough to recount
Their ancestry, which is with ape and ant
Their manners are from the greenwood, the ground
Of their affections is patent as the sex of a plant.

Epictetus

I want to die creditably and with permission
Or I would long since have ended my days
The moon rises and the vast elms
Stand black at the edge of the haze.

Whether I live or die there is no I
Only the multifarious skelter of nature
Nothing except pride in this crowd
Marks out the rational (as they call him) creature.

The Art of Living

The child can grow
Only by being blind
He owes his greatness
To his fumbling.

The mind askew
From the appetite that drives him
The youth gives reasons
And has destinations.

The old man's waltzing nerves
Misdirect his hand
Aphasia, medicine, hope
Obscure his end.

Nude Studies

They are separate as to arms and legs
Though occasionally joined in one place
As to what identity gives
You may question the opacity of the face.

Either man is made in the image of God
Or there is no such creature, only a cluster of cells
Which of these improbabilities is the less
You cannot, by the study of nudity, tell.

At a Cocktail Party

They are machines with few surprises
Circulating with little ado
On plottable courses, asking each other
What make are you?

At an International Conference

These are not words
In which a heart is expressed
You cannot catch in their rhythm
Which way the nerves twist.

This is not the lean orator
With palm touching the sky
It is not the beggar
Defining what is due.

This is not the actor
With tragic or comic mask
Nor the astringent Terpsichore
With whips for muscles.

This is the pot-bellied bankrupt
Naked upon the stage
With a porridge of news-talk
Obscuring his grimace.

Tintagel

The clear water ripples between crags
And the Atlantic reaches our island
A clout on the outer headland.

A small band gathered God into this fastness
Singing and praying men; while others
Climbed up the perilous stairway shod in iron.

In every clearing a mad hermit
Draws his stinking rags about him and smoke rises
From thatches lately hurt by rape or pillage.

Cynadoc, Gennys, names as clear as water
Each hill unfolds, and the sheep
Pass numerous through the narrow gate.

St Gennys

In the granite church the wry priest
Handles the bread and the cup: and outside
Is a small windswept oak.

The mistletoe is cut down, but we creep
Naked as cats and dogs to this altar
Licking the blood upon the chancel steps.

To Walter Savage Landor

No poet uses a chisel in quite the same way
You do, or lays the marble chips together
In the sunlight, chip by chip.

If you had this girl before you, you
Would make her excel in some way by mere words
But I have only my pity and little to show
For forty-five years. Memoranda
Are strictly not to be memorised. It is the fleeting moments
Sunlit leaf upon leaf, your speech
That remains.

In Autumn

The sap is going out of my fingers
And the tune that my father used to drum
Comes readily to them.

Nothing that I could plead to young beauty
Could secure that my cold hand would be forgiven
Or the tears I cannot shed.

Well might Augustine pray that the ebb be not too fast
Holm-oak and myrtle and the treacherous bay-tree
Could not comfort him.

So turn me home towards God, and my last sunlight
Fall on no child of woman but on ash and chestnut
When the leaf falls.

Cranmer

Cranmer was parson of this parish
And said Our Father beside barns
Where my grandfather worked without praying.

From the valley came the ring of metal
And the horses clopped down the track by the stream
As my mother saw them.

The Wiltshire voices floated up to him
How should they not overcome his proud Latin
With We depart answering his *Nunc Dimittis*?

One evening he came over the hillock
To the edge of the church-yard already filled with bones
And saw in the smithy his own fire burning.

The Conversation of Age

Understanding is easiest between limbs
That run with the sap in them and have need
Of one another.

Longing may even appear in the eyes
And intelligence flicker for a moment in looks
Appealing for compassion.

When truth has been found and the curled garden
Sown out of measure and loved beyond all reason
The faces are averted.

Understanding is hardest between heads
Jigging away like machines in public loneliness
In the conversation of age.

Knole

The white hill-side is prickled with antlers
And the deer wade to me through the snow.
From John Donne's church the muffled and galoshed
Patiently to their holy dinners go.

And never do those antlered heads reflect
On the gentle flanks where in autumn they put their seed
Nor Christians on the word which, that very hour,
Their upturned faces or their hearts received.

But spring will bring the heavy doe to bed;
The fawn will wobble and soon after leap.
Those others will die at this or the next year's turn
And find the resurrection encased in sleep.

The Luxembourg

It must be admitted that they are historic,
These ladies – young ladies I mean – walking in the Luxembourg:
How else distinguished from Marie de Medici,
This girl bending over the edge of the *bassin*?
She is whatever she would be doing
Which she would because she comes from where she does –
Out of this *appartement* half way up the cliff of that building
With a childhood in this or that *ville de province* –
Not undetermined, resting in the hand of God
Who broods menacingly over all our fornications.

The Leopard and the Lynx

The lynx and the leopard stand
At the entrance of the forest
They paw and sniff.
Enter if you can
Pass their muzzles softly
If you would be safe.

Their eyes are on the ground
Dust rises out of it
As their soft pads strike.
What in their behaviour
Makes you invisible
As velvet in the night?

Go then, naked one,
Into the forest
Where the flat leaves breathe
Like a sleeper and
Fingers for all your dress
Cannot give security.

The leopard laughs like a drain
And the lynx too
Now you have crept by.
Why should they not be gay,
He or he, so
Patient till you would try?

Wander though you do
With all your skin on
Yet be not proud:
He or he, no longer demure,
The leopard or the lynx
Will eat you when you come out.

Two Shepherds

A: Now let us walk together, knowing
There is nothing to sing.
Winter and summer have been over us
More than enough times, and spring
Will not come unless we are envious,
Which we no longer are.
B: All the fleeces are now in one place,
Real or imagined the black faces
Have one thought. My ram
Climbs on the back of what is.
This is full of promise.

The Ragman

Well, it was wife or mother by
The cold fire.
The ragman at the door.
'He has come, in the night, I am alone
As he might think.'
A heavy tread
Comes down the stairs.
'Ragman, what are you?'
'I will force an entry.'
Two sides of the door.
The grandfather clock
Spoke.   .
Which would away?
Cool day, and no offence.
The breakfast things
Laid on a perfect table.
'Ragman eat your eggs.
It is a long way to go
And no reprieve.'

On a Civil Servant

Here lies a civil servant. He was civil
To everyone, and servant to the devil.

Money

I was led into captivity by the bitch business
Not in love but in what seemed a physical necessity
And now I cannot even watch the spring
The itch for subsistence having become responsibility.

Money the she-devil comes to us under many veils
Tactful at first, calling herself beauty
Tear away this disguise, she proposes paternal solicitude
Assuming the dishonest face of duty.

Suddenly you are in bed with a screeching tear-sheet
This is money at last without her night-dress
Clutching you against her fallen udders and sharp bones
In an unscrupulous and deserved embrace.

Ellick Farm

The larks flew up like jack-in-the-boxes
From my moors, and the fields were edged with foxgloves.

The farm lay neatly within the hollow
The gables climbing, the barn beside the doorway.

If I had climbed into the loft I should have found a boy
Forty years back, among the bales of hay.

He would have known certainly all that I know
Seeing it in the muck-strewn cobbles below.

(Under the dark rim of the near wood
The tears gathered as under an eyelid.)

It would have surprised him to see a tall man
Who had travelled far, pretending to be him.

But that he should have been turning verses, half dumb
After half a lifetime, would least have surprised him.

Heroes

The heroism of the hunter
Is in his prey, is in his prey
The leaping animal
Always ahead of him.

The heroism of the fisher
Is in his catch, is in his catch
Which he examines
Like snot in his handkerchief.

The heroism of the aviator
Falling through space is the
        fall through space
A little moist jelly
Under a barrow.

The Deer-Park

In this bracken Diana
Of a surety is concealed.
Ah, huntress, the wonder to us
Is no longer the naked goddess
But the deer bounding
Of a surety from the brake.

Ah, little machines, like bounding
Shuttles above the bracken,
Like gnats on a fine evening,
Be pleased to represent for us
The universal machinery
Which else were intolerable.

We also are turning
In this fine evening
As parts of the vanquished world;
Your companionable fate
Is more now to the hunter
Than the girl's pretensions.

And the horn sounding at the death
Of the torn Actaeon
Echoes for similar deaths
In identical forests
For in this machine world
No one can die lonely.

The hounds bear down upon
No individual sorrow
Or even identified pain
The certainty of reproduction
Is no longer the promise of life
But a co-terminous repetition.

It is possible that the musk ox
Descending the glacial valley
Enters the dying vision
Of the effete hunter, or the bell
Of the emerging church-tower marks
A point in the gathering mists.

The Un-Red Deer

The un-red deer
In the un-green forest

The antlers which do not appear
And are not like branches

The hounds which do not bay
With tails which do not swish

The heather beyond and the insignificant stumble
Of the horse not pulled up

By the rider who does not see all this
Nor hear nor smell it

Or does so but it does not matter
The horn sounds Gone away

Or, if it does not, is there hunter,
Hunted, or the broken tree

Swept by the wind from the channel?

The London Zoo

From one of the cages on the periphery
He is brought to London, but only for duty.
As if radio-controlled he comes without a keeper,
Without any resistance, five times in the week.
See him as he rises in his ordered household,
Docile each morning before he is expelled,
Take his bath when he is told, use the right towel,
Reliable as an ant, meticulous as an owl.
His wife, until he is gone, is anxiously protective
In case after all one morning he should resist,
But all is well each day, he hasn't the spirit
– He is edged out of the door without even a murmur.

The road to the station is reassuring
For other black hats are doing the same thing
Some striding blithely who were never athletic,
Others, who were, now encased in Cadillacs,
Snug and still belching from their breakfast bacon,
All, halt and well, keen to be on the train.

Each sits by other whom a long acquaintance
Has made familiar as a chronic complaint,
Although the carapaces they wear are so thick
That the tender souls inside are far to seek.
First there is *The Times* newspaper, held before the eyes
As an outer defence and a guarantee of propriety,
Then the clothes which are not entirely uniform
So as to give the appearance of a personal epidermis,
But most resistant of all is the layer of language;
Swathed around their senses like a mile of bandage;
Almost nothing gets in through that, but when something does,
The answering thought squelches out like pus.

These are agreeable companions. At this hour
The people travelling are certainly superior
To those you would have the misfortune to see
If you came up one morning by the eight fifteen
– Typists and secretaries talkative and amorous
With breasts like pears plopping out of their bodices.
Mr Axeter's companions do not distract him:
Carefully he spreads out his copy of *The Times*,
Not unwilling to be stimulated by disasters
Less likely to happen to him than sex,
Disappointed when he finds so boring a centre page
That this morning his mind is not going to be raped.
As an alternative he begins to eavesdrop
On the holidays and car which a lot
Of people have larger and more expensive than he does.
He computes their incomes and their intelligences,
The one larger, the other smaller than his own,
Though his intelligence has shrunk and his income grown
– A not unsatisfactory bit of co-ordination
Which comforts him as his train enters the terminal station.

Out on the platform like money from a cashier's shovel
The responsible people fall at the end of their travel.
Some are indignant that their well-known faces
Are not accepted instead of railway passes;
Others faithfully produce the card by which the authorities
Regulate the movement of animals in great cities.
With growing consciousness of important function
Each man sets out for where he is admired most,
The one room in London where everything is arranged
To enlarge his importance and deaden his senses.
The secretary who awaits him has corrected her bosom;
His papers are in the disorder he has chosen.
Anxieties enough to blot out consciousness
Are waiting satisfactorily upon his desk.

Mr Axeter's office is designed theologically;
Upstairs there is one greater than he;
Downstairs there are several he must keep in submission
Who smoothly profess they are doing what should be done.
Yet the conflict here is no simplified battle,
As you might think, between God and the Devil.
Swords go ping on helmets in every direction
– It is not the fault of God if there is not confusion.
Every man may speak according to his conscience
If he has had it regulated in advance.
A man who goes out to meet a bullet
Is after all some sort of serious character,
For it is him the bullet goes through all right, though he
    wishes
For an MC or a *Croix de Guerre* or loves spit and polish,
But the man who makes money or who gives wise counsel
Is prostitute or pimp to more live originals
– Still, this is what he takes his money for;
He wouldn't be more honest if he were less of a whore.

Meanwhile from the same train Professor Tortilus
Has gone where they allow him to profess.
Already his zealous students are reading their comics
In the library of the School of Economics
– Judicious journals where those who think thoughts
For a living lay out their unappetising corpses.
The long-haired, the beautiful and the black

Learn that to be intelligent is to be dull
And that to be perfect you should be statistical as well.
To these hopefuls Professor Tortilus
Will explain the maxims of his own mysterious
Speciality which is nothing less than the complete science
Of correctly conducting human government.
The morning papers, which to many brought only diversion,
To him brought irrefutable demonstration
That all who exercise power will certainly fail
Simply through not following his principles.
All round the School is utter confusion
– The city, Whitehall, industry in ruins –
Only Professor Tortilus, as in a calm season
Still swimming happily in a pool of reason.

There are many others, of course, in the same trainload
As Mr Axeter and Professor Tortilus.
Each has his pretensions and his importance,
Worth good money at the price of utter dependence.
The happiest are convinced by their own rackets,
And there is no racket that does not provide a pretext
For those who are willing to be convinced: one
Incidentally produces something useful as well as money;
Another can be shown, although itself despicable,
To prevent what can be thought of as a worse evil.
Each actor thinks of the particular part he acts
As producing only beneficial effects;
He does harm and picks up his money as unobtrusively
As a physician taking a tip or a waiter a fee.
This lawyer, a vehement defender of the rich against the poor,
Pays no attention to that part of his behaviour,
But advertises himself as a kind of John Hampden
As, without risk to himself, he becomes eloquent
On the inalterable right of the poorest he
That is in England to have an advocate, for a fee
To be paid for by the public out of those taxes
The evasion of which is the object of his main practice.
Many who, in a more rational system,
Would be thought mad if they behaved as they do in this one
Are obsessed by the more insidious forms of property:
They buy and sell merchandise they will never see,
Hawking among Wren's churches, and, if they say their prayers,

Say them, without a doubt, to stocks and shares.
– One an barely imagine what scandal would be caused
If they were to be found on their knees in Saint Paul's.
For everything is turned from its right use, so that
Even the lobster that climbs on the business man's plate
Is there less for its colour or its marine taste
Than to impress a customer, or conclude a bargain
– A species of harlotry in edible materials
As the tax-free limousine is a harlot on wheels.

And who am I, you may ask, thus to belly-ache
At my betters? I tell you, I am one of the same lot
– Without lobster and limousine, but, like the rest,
Expending my best energies on the second-best.
There are those who do not, who accept no pay
For work they know would better be done otherwise
– Not the scabs of culture for whom any talk of the arts
Brings money to their purses and a throb to their silly hearts,
But the few still remaining who have decided to live
Without taking account of what is remunerative.
You will hardly believe it, but it is those few
Who are the only spectators in this zoo
– And yet to call it a zoo is certainly an injustice
To the family of hyenas, apes and bustards
Who have no difficulty in speaking with their own voice
And do not look to be respected for their price.

It is rather as a somewhat extravagant machine
That the managerial classes should be seen,
Whose only animal activity is when
Mr Cog returns at the end of the day to his hen.

Numbers

My Life and Times

I would not waste this paper for
(I hope) a merely personal bore
But write about the singular
Because 'I am' may read 'We are.'
So damn the individual touch
Of which the critics make so much;
Remember that the human race
Grins more or less in every face.

My mind unfocussed like my eyes,
When young I showed, not felt, surprise.
Perhaps. But what comes from the womb
Is all that goes into the tomb
Or more than all. And what we mean
Or may imagine in between
Is trivial by comparison.
It is the gloss that we put òn.

My elders recognised my shape.
Thereafter there was no escape
For parents do the best they can
To capture us and make us Man.
So I became subjective too
And what was hopeful now is true.

As my especial mode of thought
Was finding where I had not sought,
When Love at last possessed my mind
It was exactly of that kind.
There was no exercise of will;
It came, I saw it and stood still.
It was a blaze and I was dark.
The grief that scorched me left the mark.

No money and much time to spend.
I walked the streets for hours on end
Then lay upon my iron bed.
Some have their youth. This was instead.
What mattered when I left this shore
And found the classic world of war?

I understood the natural hate
Of man and cruelty of state
And the Schutz Staffel was to me
The natural heart of Germany.

War happened like a second birth
Upon an even blinder earth:
Some happy to increase the rate
At which they drink and fornicate
But exile and anxiety
For others. This included me.
From this excitement then I come
To settle soberly at home
And, blindly occupied with work,
I live completely in the dark.
For I have reached that slippery place
Where Nisus fell upon his face
While his young friend ran on. The truth
Took over from the hopes of youth.
Rather, I saw the limits of
Even the promises of love.
This moment comes, early or late.
Rather, you slide into a state
In which the heart is running on
Perhaps, but expectation's gone.
For the first part of life we move
To get to where we came from – love.
Then time is moving and we stand.
Something descends and is at hand.
There are innumerable ways
Of marking the *nel mezzo* phase
But all men understand that breath
Grows shorter long before our death.
So I, improvident, looked round
And saw that I was losing ground
And that it did not matter for
To win would also be a bore.
I could say, like some wily man
I had thought out a clever plan.
In fact, it worked the other way;
I did what offered day by day.
Small children climbed upon my face

Or ran in front to set the pace.
The only secret of 'I go'
Is following what you do not know.
I burrow in an office where
There is no purpose in despair.
This is, indeed, the last descent.
But how await the sure event?
For time will wave his arms about
Until he gives his final shout.

Good-day, Citizen

My life is given over to follies
More than I can exaggerate:
If I told you half you would imagine
That I am a very respectable person.

First, there is the folly of earning money
In order to have what is called independence:
You can admire that quality if you will,
I know what it is and do not admire it.

Secondly, there is the folly of spending it wisely,
So much for insurance, so much for the house,
Suitable provision for the children's education
Which for the most part they would rather not have.

Thirdly there would be, if that were not in fact all,
The supervening graces of domestic virtue
Everything paid up, honest as the day
But I am nearest to my own language in sleep.

The Nature of Man

It is the nature of man that puzzles me
As I walk from Saint James's Square to Charing Cross;
The polite mechanicals are going home,
I understand their condition and their loss.

Ape-like in that their box of wires
Is shut behind a face of human resemblance,
They favour a comic hat between their ears
And their monkey's tube is tucked inside their pants.

Language which is all our lies has us on a skewer,
Inept, weak, the grinning devil of comprehension; but sleep
Knows us for plants or undiscovered worlds;
If we have reasons, they lie deep.

A and B

A
I was in the lane and saw the car pass.
The white face of the girl showed through the windscreen,
Beside her a youth with a tight grip on the wheel.

B
There was a blue Anglia; I remember.

A
I caught the girl's eyes as she passed;
They were in deepest contentment.
She communicated in perfect freedom to me
The candour with which she would undress when they reached
        the wood.
It was a point that had been troubling the boy.

B
And what has their pleasure to do with us?

A

You think a philosopher should stick to his port.
That is not my opinion.
What is enacted in these hills
Is a sacrifice as certainly as any propounded
Under the shadow of the Giant of Cerne
And sacrifice is not for the actors.

B

What nonsense is this about a sacrifice?
This is what two people did, and that is all.

A

What they did in a flurry of consciousness,
Their hands upon one another's sides,
Was trivial enough. But what were their intentions?
Some hope perhaps of giving or taking pleasure.

B

I should think they might have been partially successful.

A

I met an old man on a tall horse
He had ridden for thirty years. It was his intention
When he had seen the last of it, to bury it
Out in that field beside his dead mare.
Do you think he had planned that harmony?
Did not a spirit seize him by the throat
And tell him what to do: there, under the old church
Rising there on that mound above the groin?

B

I am afraid, A, you are not a philosopher.
You are merely an inconsiderate fool who loves his country
At the very moment when love has become vain.

A

See there where a party of picnickers
Trace their way over the springy turf
And the world proceeds without understanding.
Perhaps all will be well.

A Letter to John Donne

On 27 July 1617, Donne preached at the parish church at Sevenoaks, of which he was rector, and was entertained at Knole, then the country residence of Richard Sackville, third Earl of Dorset.

I understand you well enough, John Donne
First, that you were a man of ability
Eaten by lust and by the love of God
Then, that you crossed the Sevenoaks High Street
As rector of Saint Nicholas:
I am of that parish.

To be a man of ability is not much
You may see them on the Sevenoaks platform any day
Eager men with despatch cases
Whom ambition drives as they drive the machine
Whom the certainty of meticulous operation
Pleasures as a morbid sex a heart of stone.

That you should have spent your time in the corruption of courts
As these in that of cities, gives you no place among us:
Ability is not even the game of a fool
But the click of a computer operating in a waste
Your cleverness is dismissed from the suit
Bring out your genitals and your theology.

What makes you familiar is this dual obsession;
Lust is not what the rutting stag knows
It is to take Eve's apple and to lose
The stag's paradisal look:
The love of God comes readily
To those who have most need.

You brought body and soul to this church
Walking there through the park alive with deer
But now what animal has climbed into your pulpit?
One whose pretension is that the fear
Of God has heated him into a spirit
An evaporated man no physical ill can hurt.

Well might you hesitate at the Latin gate
Seeing such apes denying the church of God:
I am grateful particularly that you were not a saint
But extravagant whether in bed or in your shroud.
You would understand that in the presence of folly
I am not sanctified but angry.

Come down and speak to the men of ability
On the Sevenoaks platform and tell them
That at your Saint Nicholas the faith
Is not exclusive in the fools it chooses
That the vain, the ambitious and the highly sexed
Are the natural prey of the incarnate Christ.

Act Munday

(See Anthony à Wood, July 11, 1692)

A body that was stubbornly dead
They carried out and brought him to All Hallows,
Under the upper window in the north churchyard.
Young men carried him, maids at his funeral
Extended a white sheet over his stiff corpse,
Reluctant, as they might be, to let him depart.

Words

I have noticed that words are not understood.
Where the dappled fawns walk in the sunlight
In contrast with their sisters dark against the sky-line
The beeches crack.

At First

Nothing that is said or done
Can equal in the end
The first apprehension of love.
And so it is at last.
Speak, God, to the encumbered
Servant I am. It will be news
If you tell me I am saved.

Eros

One must be blind if there shall be love.
The grey-haired woman running with a small child
Feeds on a hope she can no longer enjoy:
The lunacy makes her straggling hair wild,
I expect no hope but what comes from without
If there were not a blind god I should be in doubt.

Of two walking in arms along the pavement
– There are her buttocks through her summer frock –
One at least will repent.
It is the one that understands now
The passion of the god; when contemplation
Drives to a madness that should be doing.

Oh, I have stood appalled before beauty
With no speech but gratitude; who will not betray that?
Understanding was too far in my heart:
None could make sense of me. Is not
That the delirious impotence of youth
For those who later are to take refuge in truth?

Now I seek daily for my own blindness
In the assertion reason cannot mitigate
And now an impotent old man comes running:
It is him I go to meet.
Will you not cut me one tress for tenderness,
Eros, because I acknowledge the blind?

An Old Man

Old man with white hair falling
Over your eyes, my experience
Will be very ripe when I am like you.
You could stand on one leg and sing,
Having little of what is called sense
– Little also left of your senses it is true.

Your eyes decayed, you cannot see the sparrow
Unless he perches on top of your spade
More of a flutter than a seen thing;
You cannot smell the invisible rose
Only your body odours and the general autumn,
The acrid smoke of the bonfire that makes you spit.

In and out of the trees you go to die in the jungle
Scratching among the leaves you find no grave.
It is a worm you turn up
There is no reed you do not mistake for Syrinx.
These are unsuitable favours for you to crave
But you have no objection to being a fool.

The ambition not to be one is still too strong for me;
It is this which makes you wiser than I
But your alarmed features declare
That you have not altogether found peace.
Are you still aware of the passing time?
Your mouth has failed but your eyes try to remember.

While your amnesia is only partial
You grope round reality like a mathematician:
There are degrees of folly.
It is not odd to find the world unintelligible
So, until merciful death comes
Creep round your garden, all the town protects you.

The Thrush

You do not see your speckled breast and bright eye;
What you eat is what interests you. I do not eat
You but I am interested and have the name beauty
For your feathered and energetic stand and sharp beak.

This is what it is to be the image of God:
I am it because I reflect your image,
Loving without eating. But eating
Is the end of loving. No wonder if I am confused.

And this young beauty is aware of herself
From shoulder to shank she is for discovery
By herself as well as by the hungry who would eat her.
Her mind is out of the order of nature.

It is puzzling that the form of natural good
Is a little different from the specifically human.
Those who out of congress invented lechery
Were the first inventors of man and woman.

Adam and Eve

They must be shown as about to taste of the tree.
If they had already done so they would be like us;
If they were not about to do so they would be
Not our first parents but monsters.

You must show that they were the first who contrived
An act which has since become common,
With head held high when it is conceived
And, when it is repented of, dangling.

There must be not one Adam but two,
The second nailed upon the tree:
He came down in order to go up
Although he hangs so limply.

The first Adam, you will recall, gave birth
To a woman out of his side;
For the second the process was reversed
And that one was without pride.

Easter

One good crucifixion and he rose from the dead
He knew better than to wait for age
To nibble his intellect
And depress his love.

Out in the desert the sun beats and the cactus
Prickles more fiercely than any in his wilderness
And his forty days
Were merely monastic.

What he did on the cross was no more
Than others have done for less reason
And the resurrection you could take for granted.

What is astonishing is that he came here at all
Where no one ever came voluntarily before.

Nuptials

The clever ape with the hyaena laugh
Wishes to obscure the image of man.
His teeth walk out of him, he leans back in his chair
And reason vibrates in him like a humming-top.

Behind closed doors he laughs his trousers off,
Advances with wide hands upon his prey,
Who at one time thought that a superlative love
Must lurk in a character so coaxed and combed.

The complications of his logic-board
Are no help to his tender victim;
Nothing can be said and the brilliant mind
Falls on her like a heap of scaffolding.

By the Lift Gate

Well I can understand your contraction
The lines by your eyes and your pointed nose:
You pull your coat about you (but I can guess)
Advancing one foot with suspended toes.

The melancholy at the approach of winter
Is not for the season but the summer lost,
Your juices retracted, but not yet gone
The moment, you would probably say, passed.

But whether you reached for that moment
And so fell headlong into the abyss
Or waited on the brink, all is one in the end:
You are approaching forty and no peace.

I have hunted your eyes like weasels among the ferns:
Who can say when there is an end of hope
Or what peace there would have been in satisfaction?
Close the lift gate and go up on the end of a rope.

Great Down

With the great book of nature open upon your knees
You sit like a comptometer on the hill-side,
Reckoning the church-spires. Is what the machine
Records a proper object of pride?
Is it more than the animal can scent?
Is there also human consent?

The naked Bororo divides his village
And without this geometry loses his faith:
Others have trudged in the course of the sun.
Mechanical compulsions are not of this age.
The best rule is that you should seek to please;
Go down on your back or on your knees.

How were you taught when young to be you?
You had not been invented before, there was no pattern.
Your parents invented you as you grew;
They gave you a name and your love and you learned
That there was no alternative to being a person,
Never suspecting the sense of that tradition.

You will deny that you were born to ask
That your few feet of flesh should have hope.
Proud fool! You think you are degraded by asking
And yet, of all the mind's movements, this is the top:
First, for what I may give you in your womb,
And then, for what you will find for yourself in the tomb.

A Young Woman

You straddle in the street like Atalanta.
You were somebody's daughter not long ago,
Now mother to this brood.
You extend one hand to a straw-haired child;
Another trips over your long back leg
As you run laughing towards a third.

There is a cave in your athletic belly
From which these made their way to the fragrant world.
Now they are like petals but the lines gather
Already about your eyes;
The flesh you took into your bridal bed
Is already such that the boys no longer whistle.

Soon you will understand that hope
Which you at present pursue
Has to be carried like water in a cup.
At last you will hold it so,
The race having turned to mere knowledge
And you by the fire or fingering the turned-down sheet.

Grandmother

Grandmother wheeling a perambulator
With outstretched arms and senescent leer,
What reason for hope have you here?
Shame on the body at fourscore!

Only Christ can have mercy on you now;
You can look for none from Venus or Lucina.
The boy's stout finger admonishes you
What a danger to women he intends to be.

Turn up the pram and let him tumble upon
The flat silk front that covers your dugs.
You are glad to feel the strength of his legs;
He is harmless in your lap as others were not.

Once you gave your body to the poor.
That will sustain you now more than any prudence.
Now you may give it to this young impotent
As he laughs and kicks but you know more.

Grandmother you may perambulate
With broken spokes and distorted frame;
You are cheerful and it may be half crazed
Not for what you have but for what you gave.

Loquitur Senex

I return to the horror of truth
After a life of business:
I was happy to be employed
But now my hunger is extreme.

The swans drift by and the bridge
Is pendulous over the profound stream:
The water is habitable by the mind
And the stationary fish are swimming against it.

Where were the fish when I,
Flurried by consultation,
Laboured to distinguish myself
In vanity and discursive reason?

Now, with the fish, nose pressed
Against reality,
I look through the watery glass
At weeds standing on stone.

The age is lost that had
Laughter hidden under the hand
But in the peace that remains
There is still what lives in the eye.

Gracious God, when the tension gives
And I am swept below the weir
Do as Berkeley says
Hold this world in your mind.

The Nature-Lover

Where the hare with her slight thoughts
Passes and the badger leaves his bones
My eyes fill with them and the fields,
But this boy with the gun has the right idea:
It is by killing that we join in their fun.

Things Seen

When the bomb has fallen
And the land is scored
With burns over its once delicious green
Time will be erased from these walls
And not even the written word
Call back things seen.

Look your fill while you may,
Burying your face in woods as among the dew
And turn home at night-fall
Where the children's voices promise no posterity
Or as much as a cat where they grew
And the only certainty is that night will fall.

The Lion Man

It is a mud-cracked world. A scaly sun
Has frowned on it since day began.
Picking them from the floor Imo has thrown
Komo's arrows out of the house.
I do not know what it means; it is an insult.

Imo has a niece.
One day when this child
Walks into the scrub to leave her turd out of sight
The women release the lion man, I suppose by a word.
There is nothing more to this story: a few entrails,
A few bones, a few rags left in the jungle.
Imo should not have thrown those arrows out of the house.

The Temple

Who are they talking to in the big temple?
If there were a reply it would be a conversation:
It is because there is none that they are fascinated.
What does not reply is the answer to prayer.

Eclogue

CORYDON, DAPHNIS

Put the buggers under the wall.
No-one will notice that you have strangled the bastards.
Thus Corydon, regardful of his flock.
Daphnis took a bunch of *parfum chèvre*
In his great mit and, having adjusted his jock-strap,
Set out to dazzle or woo the incomparable Chloe.
I suppose she was lying on her back
With legs wide open, pretending to snore.
At any rate Daphnis made short work of her.
Back with his mates, Corydon took up the pipe:
All things were made for the violent and the greedy.
Thank you, Pan, for your inclination towards us.

STREPHON, DORINDA

STREPHON: So, Dorinda, you will not take my garland
Although I am an educated shepherd;
I pipe all day but you cannot hear me.
DORINDA: Too apt a replica of human life
Is apt to distress those for whom it is intended.
STREPHON: You know a trick better than distress;
You sit all day with your knees hunched,
Your mind concentrated on counting your lambs.
If you took our country pleasures
You might suddenly become endowed with understanding.
DORINDA: That is a fantasy of the adolescent
And really only a pun on carnal knowledge.
The shepherd who seeks to move me with his pipe
Does not thereby acquire a right to my conversation.

STREPHON: But if the understanding is not carnal
It is no more than your tallies without your sheep.
DORINDA: Do not press me to accept that argument.
I will bathe myself in the clear stream
But do not join me, Strephon.

DORINDA, DAPHNIS, CORYDON

DAPHNIS: Hey, Corry, that tart is taking her clothes off.
CORYDON: Leave her; she don't need no help from you.
DAPHNIS: Watch me. Daphnis is the boy for this.
DORINDA: Daphnis, you are deceived by your own name.
DAPHNIS: I never heard of a tart who spoke like that before.
DORINDA: Which of your two tongues is the more eloquent
I have, I assure you, not the slightest doubt.
Even with a voice of full-throated melody
It is hard enough to say what is being expressed,
A fortiori with a tongue which merely licks.
DAPHNIS: Lie down over there and I will show you.
If Strephon can't manage you well then I can.
DORINDA: It is not in the management but in what is managed
Or rather in whether what is distinguished from who
That the problem lies
And if that is the limit of your invention
You will really get us no nearer a solution.
Corydon, taking his pipe, induced this song:
Charm without thinking, calf-deep in the splashing water
Under the green shadow that makes your flesh a thought.

DAPHNIS, STREPHON

DAPHNIS: Shepherds without identity is a good lark
– Dorinda and me copulating like flies.
To be nothing but an objective buzz!
STREPHON: For you that is a comprehensible ambition
Because you are not aware that being an object
Is different in kind from observing what is.
Even the pleasure you took with Chloe,
Vigorous and unreflective though it was,
Did not succeed in reaching annihilation
Nor can you forget her foul breath
Or the way her teeth met you.
DAPHNIS: Chloe was all right though she stank a bit

But what I should like is to get Dorinda
When she has stopped being a naiad.
STREPHON: Corydon's song was meant to warn you against that
As much as to silence Dorinda.
It was only an echo from the philosophers
Came through her lips and reverberated through the grotto
And philosophy is harmless enough.
But for you to suppose you could achieve brutality
And become like a May-bug driven against a pane
By uniting yourself with one so rational
Is to misunderstand the nature of love.

DAPHNIS, STREPHON, DORINDA

DORINDA: Indeed it is the nature of love which is in question
But why either of you should think he can be united
Merely by favour of a ridiculous pipe
With someone conceived of as an entity
Of a different kind, is more than I can say.
STREPHON: Dorinda, you are a monster of vanity.
You understand well enough that the problem
Is not the penetration of your superb self
But how we come to be talking of it.
If you in fact had been that slight figure,
More gracious than I can say, among the rushes
I need have been no more than my eyes.
It was in that moment that Corydon made his song.
That was no sooner ended, however, than this lout
Daphnis, forever with his mind on the bacon,
Comes up with his unremunerative plans for action
And you quickly lay claim to an identity
Which means you must not be touched.

DAPHNIS, STREPHON, DORINDA, CORYDON

CORYDON: My verse also was a deception.
It is time we came to the sheep-shearing.
Here, Daphnis, take hold of this crook.
Go and collect the flock from the long meadow.
Strephon, you get the antiseptic shears
And grind them on the stone behind the dairy.
I will look after Dorinda.

DORINDA, CORYDON

CORYDON: Put on your clothes and come and eat a posset
Of curds and whey under the great oak.
Perhaps you would care to be my secretary;
I need a girl with brains to count my sheep.
DORINDA: Well, that would certainly be better than love;
I am rather fed up with being admired.
I should like instead to be useful.
CORYDON: You could be doubly so if you came with me.
I have employment enough for your intelligence
And at night, when we have counted our money,
We will play at natural objects.
DORINDA: I cannot too much praise your invention.
Midas was embarrassed by his golden touch
But you turn gold to nature.
CORYDON: So that is fixed?
DORINDA: I will accept you if you make it legal.

DAPHNIS, STREPHON, CORYDON, DORINDA

DAPHNIS AND STREPHON: Everything is ready for the sheep-
    shearing.
DORINDA: Boys, I shall enjoy watching you work.

In Memoriam Cecil De Vall

   late garrison chaplain, Barrackpore

You can count me as one who has hated
Out of spoiled love rather than malice.
Let me lie now between tufts of heather,
My head in the grass.

The sky is too high, I prefer to be far under it
The road is happily distant.
No angel shall catch me here, nor tourist
Abase me with his talk.

Out from this patch of dust the flat plain
Extends like Asia under a blue sky.
It is no misanthropy that binds me here
But recognition of my own failure.

I ask no better than that
The long convolvulus shall grow over me
And prickling gorse
Keep the children away.

Soon the fallen flesh will begin to crawl
Making off in the worm's belly
Into the undergrowth, and the polished flies
Will riddle me like hat-pins.

I bid their rising lives welcome because
It is better to be many than one;
The mirrors of blue-bottle and worm
May reflect to more purpose than I.

Curl my fin where the shark
Lurches in the blue Mediterranean;
Open my wizened eye
Like a lizard under a tropical leaf.

As I bite the dust of this flat land
For the last time, with dissolving chaps,
Keep me free from all such reflection
Lest the mind dazzle as it goes out.

I do not wish to recognise Christ
As I enter the shades.
What other company could I have
In darkness of my own choosing?

Perhaps it is no more than a recollection
– The banks of a river,
The heavy vegetation wet with the monsoon,
My friend on the verandah?

He brought out the long whiskies and proved
That God hated nothing that He had made:
At no time did I take at his hands
Any but his own hospitality.

Fill my mouth with sand, let the passer's boot
Unwittingly fold my skull.
I have resigned the pretensions
Of the individual will.

From the darkened shores of the river
The dogs howled;
I was alone with the famished and the dead.
Whatever stirred in those shadows was not God.

The Death of a City Man

Quantum meruit was what he got
When he hung by his braces on the door.
He had often – had he not? –
Looked on the lift-shaft with desire.

Well, he could have loved another way
But all falling is one.
See him with his burning eyes
Up and down in the lift, John.

How much for his sagging flesh
Laid out in the bath-room?
With black tights and a gold chain
Quantum meruit has gone home.

No Title

I will tell you the story of my success:
I had lived in great obscurity before,
The room was literally dark, I came and went
As a person without mystery, gifted with reason.
It was a hell and an obscure one,
But the more specious hell I live in now
Full of light and colours, and predestination
Moving my arms like windmills and my legs like a treadmill.
My nature is not what I am
But what these manipulations appear to be.
It is not the world that is reflected in my eye
But the dark interior of my face.
There are two kinds of being, recognition
Making the larger out of the dust
Which composed the meaner and more exact person.
It is as if I had become somebody else
Not by becoming another person but by becoming
Some of the things one person may seem to another.
As if, by pretending, I had become a stone,
Not as something inert but a seen thing
Instead of a seeing thing, and the corruption
Which should wait to seize the body till death
Already begins to eat at my living carcase.

Being is not necessarily at one with person;
It is rare indeed for the conception
To fit in the body or even the manner of walking.
This person who conceives ideas
Carries a tangle drawn from all quarters
His own mind is unexpressed
It is the last of those that find voice.
This hair, these toes, and these excreta
Walk in the form of fashion, not their own.
The body is not more clad than the mind:
The bowler hat and the supporting stick
Give courage to the unadmitted nude.
It is this lie and this silence
Which comprise the excellence of the world.
I have that excellence now;
It is certainly a splendid thing to be successful.

On a Favourite Death

Useless to plead it is for pay
You hug the office day by day.
Ça va sans dire. Is there not still
Some love, deny it how you will?
The deep affections of the womb
Are found in your familiar room.
O faint love but persistent, for
Upon the handle of your door
You grope with a dull, amorous hand
And what you touch you understand.
It is an image of the mind
– Reason in front, passion behind.
An argument I want to win
Entices me as I go in
While several others that I must
Discourage me and dull my lust.
The tarts of logic and pretence
Parade their flouncy evidence.
There is no exercise of mind
Quite comprehending human kind.
The game we play at here denies
What reason cannot analyse
Much that it can. And it is well
Here, to ignore the visible.
The passion that consumed my youth
Was for a different kind of truth.
When I am quiet I am free.
Here the great winds blow over me.
This is the world, where none may say
The thing he will in his own way;
Happy at last if he can find
A service in the common mind.
So let me leave my unmarked bones
Under the miscellaneous stones.

Thomas de Quincey

Thomas de Quincey lying on the hearth-rug
With a finished manuscript at his side,
His bare feet in slippers and, tied up with ribbon,
There was his mind.

Of course it was stupor that he wanted
But his mind would work.
He followed the eloquence whose end is silence
Into the dark.

To Brian Higgins on First Reading
Notes While Travelling

I could not understand your book
Although I had read some poems before,
So I tried holding it upside down
And read it sitting on the floor.

This worked marvellously, at first
I received several bizarre impressions.
It was a good laugh, and that is something
For a man in my position.

Then I noticed that while I was reading
You were working on the floor below.
If that is his game, I said to myself,
I'm damned if I will follow!

So I turned the book the right way up
And read it by the light of reason.
Damn this fellow, I said,
Who thinks he can live under his own legislation!

Damn that for a cock-eyed idea
– Doing away with civil servants!
Someone has to hold up the post
For Brian Higgins to lean upon.

The Beach

Sad slaves on holiday! 'I'll clout your head!
I'll slap your bottom! Send you home to bed!'
This is Love speaking at her festival
If she indeed express herself at all.
And this bald man runs up and down all day;
He has the logic of his holiday.
He knows it is his duty to be fit,
Persist and stultify his natural wit.
His wife waits for him with the sandwiches;
She is the one that makes this pleasure his.
'You go back to your work on Monday dear.'
Lucky it only happens once a year.

The Theology of Fitness

This is what I call mind:
Your behind,
That patch of hair in front,
Your navel, your cunt,
Your nipples, your lips;
The hair in your arm-pits
(If a depilatory
Have rased that memory
The hair on your head
Will do instead).
Starting at the nape
I examine your shape;
It is intellectual
And accordingly small.

There is the line
As I descend your spine
To your two legs
Split like a clothes peg.
Quelle heureuse pensée!
You will probably say
If I want a ewe to tup

I should start higher up
And, for example, surprise
Your intellect in your eyes.
Wishing merely to understand,
Lady, I kiss your hand.

Consider, since that is you
Who I am, who
Address these courtesies
And seek to please.
Shall I admit my mind
Starts in my behind
Or that my balls and hair
Gives my verse its air?
(Less pleasant to dwell upon
I find, it is all one.)
This is my fund of wit
And cavity for shit.
Oh, there is much else
Still, when I see myself
I do not over-emphasise
The intelligence of my eyes.

So, when we resurrect
That which was once erect
(Although, in paradise
The suits are without flies)
Your spirit and your bum
Will certainly be one;
Every orifice
Will receive a kiss;
The lowly heart
Will trumpet out a fart;
There will be hosannas
From long bananas.

That being so
What shall we do now?

What a Piece of Work is Man

The man of quality is not quite what he was
In the days when that was a technical term
But there are, happily, a number of qualities
You can be a man of, and it is hard if there is not one
In which you can claim distinction.
Like speaks only to like, and without quality
Which you cannot communicate because you have it by blood
Or some subtler misfortune known as intelligence
There can be no speech.
It is by quality that you are not alone.
Those gathered around the bar, as they lift their beer-mugs
Tremble to break the enchantment of what is common:
It is so by the well or the dhobi-ghat
Or the club where charm may not exceed a pattern.
Pray do not address me in Japanese
In which language my hopes express themselves ill.
Yet what I have in common with the cat
Suffices for a very short conversation
Each time we meet.

Love is of opposites, they say: but the opposite
Is by way of being a philosophical refinement
And what wedges itself in the female slot
Though apposite enough, is hardly that.
If what goes on there is understanding
Then understanding is something different.
Do not imagine the body cannot lie;
What else have we for lying or for truth?

We talk by species and genus.
God who created us made himself understood
First in the thunder, then in the cloud and then in us.
I wish I did not hear him in the thunder.

How does it happen that the table leg
Has this curve in one age, that in another?
Or that the carved figures of men
Differ more than the men themselves?
Conception rules the art.
How then can one man speak to another?

Is it not the conception
Past any man's thinking, that is expressed
Even in the voice that seems to speak clearly?
And in the million voices that chatter together
Over this peninsula or that continent
A peculiar god looms
And what seems to be said between two people
Is only part of a complex conversation
Which they cannot hear and could not understand.
Yet it is only by taking part in that conversation
That they can give names to their own movements.
I lift my hand: there is a hand, certainly.
I touch your cheek: a hand touches a cheek.
In the name of what god? I have no name of my own.
Can I see my own movement except in conception?
What art has the heart, how does it understand
Its own beat?
The heart opened and the body chilled
Or the mind unneeded because the body is perfect.
The leaves of the jungle are parted. There comes out
One who moves like a deer.
And in the city the tapes record the prices,
Which is also a mode of understanding.

Words are not necessary between bodies.
O admirable attempt to forget to be human.
But you are clothed in words
Less of your own devising than your own body
And of which nothing can strip you but death.
Age and forgetfulness may leave you mumbling,
The words eating your toes or soft belly:
How are you speaking now?

A Girl

You speak of love, as if there were
Some certainty that it is here.
I see you coming and avert
My eyes lest they should do you hurt.
Your gentle limbs are confident
It is a woman that was meant
And yet, the very eyes you please
Destroy you with analyses.
It is not merely that my mind
Alas, is lecherous more than kind
And so distinguishes a part
It could not fairly call your heart,
Though I admit that, in the end,
The piston may destroy the friend.
My aching doubt is worse than that.
The human tasks that you are at
Neither begin nor end in you
Though in your mind you think they do.
With admiration you admire
What pulls you like a puppet wire.
How dare you claim a special you
Invented by the way you grew?
How can it be the words you use
Are really there for you to choose?
No mind, no error; but the grace
I worship in your holy face
Could hardly be without a mind.
How did you guess at human kind?
You walk by faith. If there is love
You see it pouring from above.

The Reckoning

My life dates from the day of my father's death
When I lay weeping and it was not for him.
Now I am to continue the degenerescence
Until I enter his dream.

There is nothing a drink cannot settle at forty
Or money at fifty, the cure of all is death.
But all lovers can remember a moment
When they were not alone.

From a Train

Two on a railway bank
They do not need their own thoughts
Their organs hanging on the verge.

The hanging gardens of Babylon
Flower in vast space between their legs
They crouch with great knees side by side.

Hands laced across the shoulders O
The light electrical touch of reason
O need they give each other names?

Go home at last to parents' eyes
The spirit unscaling as you go
Unlace those arms and be alone.

What you will not believe as you lie down
And call on God for the fornication you did not dare
Is that by chastity you have begun your age.

This loneliness will become your natural condition
When everything has been added and taken away
You will be left with a small grit which is yourself.

Amour Propre

Are there twenty-five
Fingers to one mind?
Are there seventy-three
An eye-lash and some teeth?
Does one skin make a whole
Remarkable soul?
Does anything prove
The mind is made of love?
Is it more in the bub
Than in the tunnelling grub?
Is the sword that makes a wife
Replaced by a knife?
So hard it is to know
What love should do.

Consequences

Why should I not allow myself to speak?
After his face changed and his mouth grew weak
I first understood mortality.
Then it took root in me
Now all I look upon
Turns to dissolution.

Numbers

1
Now you have left that face I am perplexed
To find no-one where I have loved best.
That is why, in the High Street, I stare
Wondering whether there is anyone anywhere.

2
Nothing that is remembered is true
– And what precisely does that make of you?

3
Please now leave indignation alone.
It is enough if you are a stone.
There are the mountains, the waving trees, and you
Flat on the open ground from which they grew.

4
If there were time it would be time to go
– It is the lack of it makes me rage so.
Yet you may say, laughter would do as well
Since for the eternal all things are possible.

5
I said this man would fall and he fell.
With power dreams become terrible.
The power is nothing and the dream is all.

6
Let me escape the burning wheel of time.
There is no other purpose in rhyme
– As if a man could be identified
At least for his folly after he had died.

7
You come from sleep like a body from the womb
A moist wisp, and straggle into bloom.
There is an instant of delicacy, then
You strumpet unnoticed through a world of men.

8
Lechery in age is not kind.
It is the last exercise of the mind.

9
Do not burn, my heart
– That would be to exaggerate your part.
It would not do for you to reduce to tears
One who has carried you for fifty years.

10

If there were not air what would there be?
The voice passed my ear musically
Yet somehow I managed to be aware
Of what she was talking about – the air.
There were spirits in it, not least her own.
They are a substance immediately known
So there was no trouble about using the body
And that, for the moment, satisfied me completely.

11

Clifford says the mind is destroyed by work
And I agree my mind is destroyed by work.

12

Age, you have reached others before me.
They do not again expect to see me.
As they say good-bye they do not even have tears
Lest they seem to acknowledge their fears.

13

They do not know whether they are going to rest
Or a long recession from what they have loved best.
The truth in those old eyes and in my own
Is all that was said in that conversation.

14

He says good-bye from his wooden chair.
We go out and he is left there.
But which of us sees most vividly in the street
The boys and girls passing on featherweight feet?

15

I saw five hares playing in the snow.
That was only a winter ago
Yet they dance in my eyes and are as wild
As if I were old and had seen them as a child.

The Shortest Day

How can you tell whether a man is human?
Surely Christ must have mercy on the souls of animals
How else could I know who is my neighbour?

I met a man running across a plain
With taut cheeks and movements like an engine
There is need of mercy for me who encountered him.

Is it arms and legs, the long hands
The armoury of sex and the spoken word
Or what little the premature foetus is born with?

It cannot be only those I can speak to
It is those who are answerable to God
– May I be content not to identify them.

Badger my friend on the periphery of the city
The snow covers the time of the Incarnation
And I cannot understand the hard mind of God.

Christmas at the Greyhound

'All strangers now; there is nobody that I know.'
Draw near to the hearth; there is one nature of fire.

Metamorphoses

To the Queen

It is long, Elizabeth,
Since the crown you wear
Was justly celebrated.

The dogs bay in the streets
And those that call you Queen
Understand less than they.

Monarch, but under God,
Your sceptre cannot fall
Or, if it does, your son

Will hold it in your stead
And will, until this realm
Is covered by the sea

Or worse democracy.
But now the people's voice
Still conjures jackanapes

Out of its throngs, while you
Brood on the restless whole.
Your scorn is justified.

Though you must hold the rein
Loose on the errant back,
Express no sympathy.

Gather your force until
We all are of one mind;
Then let the pagans go,

Deride the Scots and send
The Welsh back to their holes.
Drive out those Irish priests.

O first Elizabeth,
Your membrane now untie
And bring this one to birth.

NOTE: *The penultimate line refers, rather indelicately, to the gossip Ben Jonson reported to Drummond, that Queen Elizabeth I 'had a membrane on her, which made her uncapable of man, though for her delight she tryed many.'*

Human Relations

My mind is so evil and unjust
I smile in deprecation when I am flattered
But inside the palace of my smile
Is the grovelling worm that eats its own tail
And concealed under the threshold of my lips
Is the trustless word that will wrong you if it can.
Come nearer to me therefore, my friend,
And be impressed by the truth of my explanation.
No less, lady, take my chaste hand
While the other imaginatively rifles your drawers.

Virgini Senescens

I

Do you consider that I lied
Because I offered silent hands?

And are my lips no use at all
Unless they have a lie to tell?

Because my eyes look doubtfully
Must they not look on you at all?

And if my hands drop to my sides
Are they then empty of desire?

And are my legs unusable
Because the linked bones of my feet

Rest where they are upon the floor?
I could have used them otherwise

And brought my legs across the room,
Lifted my arms and caught you up

And housed my eyes under your brows
And fixed my lips upon your own.

Or would you then have said that I
Performed but did not speak the truth?

II
Although the body is your truth
The mind may have some part in it

As, mine that holds your body fast
And yours, said to keep house inside

Perhaps the yawning mind of God
Which folds us in his universe.

The mind that holds you is my eye
The quicksilver inside your own

Which, seeing me, collects and runs;
It is the mucus in my skull

And your intestines tight with fear
Our several secret, hirsute parts

Our finger-nails which dig the flesh;
It is our flushed or dented skin

The toes we clench inside our shoes.
Or do you think it less than that?

The spidery numbers you can read?
The tricks they play among themselves?

The art by which you hope to draw
A self from chaos, and be pleased?

A reputation? Who admires?
Oh, I am old and sly, I twist

A way through ribs and weeds and trees
And mark my body as I go:

While you are young, and hardly dare
Moisten your lips upon a stone,

Your fluttering look is hardly out
And does not reach your nearest parts.

Do not imagine I am bold.
It is this terror I admire:

It is the shaking universe
I too inhabit, but in me

Age has reformed the hope of love.
The *quia impossibile*

Drifts with me as, I make no doubt,
It travels with the astronaut.

III

I turn myself from you, to think
Upon the gravity of age

Which bears upon me now until
My weightless body floats in space.

I want it anchored where I live
Why should I bother with the mind?

It is an old excuse for death
Or else a young man's sleight-of-hand:

Attend to that and he will grow
And, silent as a savage, steal

Upon the world of sex and war.
He will grow up while I grow down

And hold you firmly in his arms
Still talking of the intellect

And, turning to me, will pretend
That we are equals in our minds

Although my body will shrink until
He well could throw me out of doors

Or push my huddled frame against
The fender, while he pokes the fire.

It has not come to that, but I
Must plan now my civilities

While I can give him knock for knock.
I will accept his gambit and

Use all my thin and polished words
To make him feel my harmless ease

Whereas my burning heart prepares
To snatch you from him if I can.

It can do you no good, this war
In which you gain by my defeat.

Do not suppose I shall give up
Till I have hurt you if I can.

Iago was an honest man;
I have that reputation too.

IV
The honest thing for you to do
Is take your clothes off while you can

And let me look upon your mind.
I had intended this request

The day I asked you for a kiss
And now the truth is out I give

The comprehensive reason why.
But you will not be taken in:

The complication is in me.
The history riddled in my brain

Protects me now against the world
But does not hide the man I am

And you see clear the face of lust,
The last dance of an ageing man.

I would not have you think I lied.

In Preparation for an Epitaph

Letters have been the passion of my life
Habit the habit and affairs the bane:
If by passion you mean a continuous attention
Intermitted for everything more important
And by a bane what only partially kills
That is it. Now I am nearly fifty
It is the habit which shrouds me as I go down to death
(For in my sense the bane is working at last).
It is only the tombstone that I shall regret
For which I might have written a noble inscription.

Catullus

Catullus walked in the Campus Martius.
He had seen all he needed to see,
Lain on his bed at noon, and got up to his whore.
His heart had been driven out of his side
By a young bitch – well, she was beautiful,
Even, while the illusion was with him, tender.
She had resolved herself into splayed legs
And lubricity in the most popular places.
He had seen Caesar who – had he not been, once,
The drunken pathic of the King of Bithynia? –
Returning in triumph from the western isles:
Nothing was too good for this unique emperor.
Against these fortunes he had nothing to offer
– Possibly the remains of his indignation,
A few verses that would outlive the century.
His mind was a clear lake in which he had swum:
There was nothing but to await a new cloud.
We have seen it. But Catullus did not;
He had already hovered his thirty years
On the edge of the Mediterranean basin.
The other, rising like a whirlwind in a remote province,
Was of a character he would have ignored.
And yet the body burst out by lechery,
Turning to its tomb, was awaiting this,
Forerunning as surely as John the Baptist
An impossible love pincered from a human form.

VALEDICTION
Catullus my friend across twenty centuries,
Anxious to complete your lechery before Christ came.

The Queen of Lydia

Candaules, King of Lydia,
Whose mouth was bigger than his prick

Boasted about the Queen his wife:
'You ought to see her in her bath;

She is a smasher.' Gyges said
He thought it inappropriate.

He was a soldier and he knew
The elements of discipline.

He also knew you did not trust
A master with an outsized mouth.

The King insisted, and arranged
Gyges should stand behind the door

While she came in and got undressed.
And this he did. Candaules lay

Discreetly in his double bed,
His nose above the counterpane.

He liked the Queen to take her time
And put her folded garments on

A bench some distance from the bed,
Then strut about the room a bit.

All this she did; and Gyges watched.
Was his mind on his duty then?

He shook as he stood by the door.
As the Queen turned her lovely back

He made a noise and then went out.
Alas, he was not quick enough.

The Queen said nothing; she was sly
And thought instead and went to sleep.

Next day she sent for Gyges and
He trembled as behind the door.

She gave him this alternative:
'One of you two goes to the pot.

Either you kill the shameless king
And lie beside me in his bed

And also govern Lydia
Or I will have him murder you.'

The choice was easy: no one dies
Rather than sleep beside a girl.

And the Queen's motive? She believed
(The Lydians are barbarians)

To be seen naked was a shame
Which only death could expiate

Or marriage, as in Gyges' case.
So you see how barbarians are.

Eurydice

If I took your maidenhead
As I well might do,
Softly to Acheron
I would go down.
Parting the rushes there:
'Where are the King and Queen
Of this fell kingdom? Has
Love any part in it?'
Striking the lyre,
Orpheus in every inch.

'If the legend is true
It has some part. Proserpine
Was fetched here from the fields,
April bore her in love.
This reign, so long,
Over the bloodless dead
Began with love.'
And the King with pity:
'You shall have her if you can
And not look back.'
Softly, past the sedge,
I drew back. Eurydice!
Faint words come from you.
When you stretch your hand
It is hardly air you catch,
One voice between us
Hangs and is lost.
Eurydice!
Retracted now. The gates.
Seven days beside the Styx
Orpheus sat, without corn
Wine of any country
No food but tears.
Within the gates of the dead
Eurydice. Weeping,
If there can be tears.
Orpheus goes back to Thrace,
In those hard mountains
Learns to hate all women.
For her, it might be said
But that is false.

In allusion to Propertius, I, iii

When I opened the door she was asleep.
It is thus I imagine the scene, after Propertius.

The torches flickered all over the world
My legs staggered but I went to her bed

And let myself down gently beside her.
Her head was propped lightly upon her hands.

I passed one arm under her body
And with my free hand I arranged her hair

Not disturbing her sleep. She was Ariadne
Desolate upon the coast where Theseus had left her;

Andromeda, no longer chained to the rock,
In her first sleep. Or she was Io,

A milk-white heifer browsing upon her dreams,
I Argus, watching her with my hundred eyes.

I took kisses from her and drew my sword.
Then, through the open window the moon looked in:

It was the white rays opened her eyes.
I expected her to reproach me, and she did:

Why had I not come to her bed before?
I explained that I lived in the underworld

Among shadows. She had been in that forest.
Had we not met, she said, in that place?

Hand in hand we wandered among the tree-trunks
And came into the light at the edge of the forest.

The Rope

Now money is the first of things
And after that the human heart
Which beats the time it can afford.
        What springs
    Of passion, what a smart
        Appearance, Lord!
And are these spiritual things?

They are. And we that are without
Have failed to use the currency
Correctly. For we have allowed
    A doubt
  About the things we see
    To sing aloud
And put our calculations out.

If the external is the hope
We have here, as I think it is,
We should respect it till we die.
    The slope
  Is steep, the precipice
    Is near. And I
Now know that money is the rope.

The Garden of Epicurus

My heart was evil but I did no wrong.
Then I designed a way of doing evil.
Smiling was my first fault. I counted myself pleasant,
Which I am not. And from this there grew
Several keen ways of extruding evil.
My eyes shot glances and I salivated;
My words came like honey and I was just.
Soon I had the rewards of this conduct.
Every endeavour was made to please me.
The mind felt like a sovereign in its own weight.
They were fortunate who knew me. Until no resemblance
Remained to the man who licked the sores of the world
– Admittedly a filthy practice but I think now as wholesome
As anything the successful get up to.
It may be that happiness is a sign of evil.

The Person

What is the person? Is it hope?
If so, there is no I in me.
    Is it a trope
Or paraphrase of deity?
    If so,
I may be what I do not know.

Do not be proud of consciousness
For happiness is in the skin.
    What you possess
Is what another travels in.
    Your light
Is phosphorus in another's night.

It does not matter what you say
For any what or who you are
    Is of a day
Which quite extinguishes your star –
    Not speech
But what your feelers cannot reach.

There is one God we do not know
Stretched on Orion for a cross
    And we below
In several sorts of lesser loss
    Are we
In number not identity.

The Doll

Go this way, that way, or incline
To north or south or east or west,
      The best
Your head can think is that the line
Of its last bearing is its newest choice.

Further to complicate its pride
It can allow some mumbled words
   Like birds
On an indifferent hill-side
To start up with involuntary voice.

And so you think that this is you,
This mere complexion of things seen.
   You mean,
You think, what happens to be true
Without your help and mind enjoys.

Jack-in-the-box with springing heel,
Open your grinning, pasty, jaws.
   The laws
Of optics and of what you feel
May be connected with your ranting noise.

However that may be, your mind
May be a busy market-place,
   Your face
A most important frontage of some kind;
It may be so with people or with toys.

Consider the uncertain state
Of all these tricks and, if you can,
   Be Man,
The fulcrum of size, place and date.
Balance the world and, if you can, rejoice.

Every Reality is a Kind of Sign

The self is the bit that has not yet emerged;
It is therefore completely unknowable.
It is perfect before the discovery of sex.
When sex is known and the children have grown up
What blindness remains to me? And I cannot live without it.
There is only the dark arcanum of religion;
I prowl round the outside and am not let in.
Every reality is a kind of sign.

The Recollection

In darkness I set out,
  O solstice of my year!
Mindful, though I had none,
  Of crowding ancestors.
And yet I grew in fear
  Although in love also.
The dogs yelped in the street;
  I would not run from them.
Terror and love held still
  The balance where I stood.
Terror pulled down the sky
  But love inclined my feet.
My seedling year grew great
  But did not touch its spring
Unless beside the brooks
  I followed to their source
Or under sprouting ferns
  Or the pale cowslip-cups.
My mind had spread until
  It covered up the sky;
No art could make it wince
  Though sleep would hold it fast.
How long this wakeful dream
  Engulfed me, who can say?
The busy heart beat on
  Until I heard it knock
And then my flesh spoke out:
  'Break through the silken sheet
That hangs before the world
  And bellies in the wind.'
Not I, not I for fear
  Or was it also love?
Or recollection of
  A world more beautiful?
And yet at last a rent
  Came in that silken veil
And, neither in nor out
  I struggled for my life.
Where has my life passed since?
  In tatters, thorns and shreds,

Under the briar I creep;
    The puddle is my drink.
The pebbles in the path
    Are my extremist stars
Who treads that Milky Way?
    Some giant, but not I.
I am the broken chalk
    Under his foot, the twig
That lies across his path.
    High summer came and went;
I did not find my God
    Although my body bore
The impress of a cross,
    Faint, almost negligible.
And now the autumn comes
    With pounding strides, and day
Closes her weary eye,
    I find no trace of peace
Nor vigour for the war
    And God looks down upon
One who does not look up.
    The heavens, which held my mind,
Have closed, and left me small.
    Saint Thomas now brings in
My last and shortest day.
    I seek my terminal.
The candle gutters fast.
    Along the corridor
The last foot-fall is lost.
    There is no friend but God;
On him I may presume
    Because He does not come.
O could I have that mind
    I carried in the womb,
Which knew, but could not say,
    This solstice would be birth.

The Critic

The thieving, whoring, lying crowd,
How gentle are they now, how tame
But they are rascals just the same.
        Though cowed
By diligence and duty done
        Not one
Without some title to ill-fame.

And you, my friend? Don't look this way;
The critic is exempt from vice.
What makes my points so fine and nice?
        The day
Is not more moral that I am
        Who damn
And yet explore you like your lice.

The itching crowd go up the hill;
Their bums stick out, they push and sweat
Enough to make the pavements wet
        And fill
The narrow street with gabble, walk
        And talk,
But I am cool for I keep still.

O virtue from the window-seat
Look down upon the human race
And then admire your own fair face.
        You eat
The dinner that your neighbours bake
        And make
Your pretty flesh from their soiled meat.

So, Virtue, join me in my bed.
Pull back the silken coverlet.
We two are certainly well met
        What's said
Is said. Expect no further word.
        A bird
In hand is worth two in the head.

The Alley-Way

I have come to a great blank wall.
There is no escape through either alley-way,
To left or right. Standing on each corner
Are youth and beauty, changed as in a mirror,
Their skirts modishly short. If I were beginning again
I would not eat my heart out for any woman.
Yet that was life. A cloud of unknowing.
Knowledge by comparison is a thin thing,
A smile of evil spread over the face of the world.

I hear a footfall
And turning hope to see someone on the pavement.
The footfall has gone.
If this were a long road it would still be empty
For hope is also an echo.
There is no way in fact out of my dream.

The Withdrawal

Also that you should not withdraw,
As you have now done, or so it seems,
Into the recesses of pain,
Was also a reason why your superficies
Seemed to me as important as your eyes.
Now that Diana has gone, your eyes' Actaeon
It is that my dogs pursue to tear you to bits.

The Spectre

He was born, I should think, under a star
Towed into position by an astronaut,
    Not caught
By the malice of remote constellations, as many are

– Between the jaws of Leo or the pincers of the Crab,
Or pushed along by a bellowing Taurus.
    Sagittarius
Did not riddle him. He did not suffer under the grab

Of Scorpio, was not twinned by Gemini.
Aries did not butt him or Virgo make him promises
    Nor was his
Effigy weighed by Libra. Nor did he

Weep with Aquarius, swim dumbly with the Fish
Or stink excessively with Capricorn.
    He was born
To see out his days with credit and relish.

His birth was antiseptic, though accidental
And after the misconception, the die ran straight.
    No great
Event shattered his uterine life, but all

Went more or less as the clinic would direct.
There was just room for the advice he got
    And not
Enough for anything one did not expect.

His final emergence was of course timely,
His statistics those you will find in the text-books;
    His looks
Neither well nor ill, he was simply a baby

And persisted in that role for the suitable time.
Every age of childhood followed in due order.
    There were
No complications about weaning. His prime

Condition indeed stayed with him till the end
As if he had been a piece for the butcher's block.
          The lack of shock
In his history was just what had been planned.

After the gynaecologists, the paediatricians;
In the end a model for geriatrics.
          In the six-
-ty years between he was treated with entertainments.

I do not want to go so fast, however.
There was I am glad to say paedobaptism
          – An ism
Added to the list not for science but for the air

It gave and in the hope that it would influence
His sexual morals, as you might geld a cat.
          But that
Again is getting a little in advance.

I will not tell you how he played with his excreta
But he knew well enough he had to go through that stage.
          At the age
Psychologists said he should stop, he did. Ah,

He was good as gold. I cannot remember
In what order these vices come, but they do.
          He got through
The lot in exemplary fashion, whatever they were.

His kindergarten was one long game, or they said it was
And he showed no disposition to contradict.
          They did not inflict
Any blow more painful than a Beta minus.

After that he became quite a little man
– A form prefect, and obedient in the scrum.
          His bum
Was occasionally kicked, which gives manners if anything can.

Elementary Christianity and economics,
Some French, a few experiments called science
    In defiance
Of ignorant traditions which preferred the classics.

You cannot found a mind but you can eradicate
Superstition by such means, or so it is said.
    Anyhow it led
To admittance, through the Ivory or Plastic Gate

To one of our superior universities.
His studies were, predictably, in Modern Affairs,
    The bears
And bulls of the market rather than of the mythologies.

He committed fornication, but with discretion;
Spoke fluently and well, but about nothing.
    He would even sing,
Music being part of the embalming lotion.

What eminently learned men cultivated his mind!
It was a treat to see how smooth they made him,
    So trim
About the edges and what emptiness behind!

He was a tabula rasa, but not quite.
There was a faint trace of liberal opinion;
    The Guardian
Was his newspaper, which was of course right.

Need I tell you that he thought for Him Self
About abortion, euthanasia, even religion?
    What fun
To take down a new idea from the shelf!

Naturally he was suitable for the best employments
Where every cultivation is required.
    He was hired
By an advertising agency to write copy, which he enjoyed.

And so began to write for the weeklies
– It was longer you see, and the goods he had to recommend
        In the end
Even less durable, needing imagination as well as critical faculties.

Do not suppose that his personal life
Was neglected among these services to culture.
        The lure
Of experiment had faded at the right time, and he had a wife.

A little more steady with the contraceptives
Than his parents were, his children came when they were called,
        Not appalled
By the prospect of the life which such a father could give.

The tabula was pretty rasa already
But he was determined to rase it further.
        His motives were
Understood and seconded by his wife, so it was easy.

The family lived in accordance with all the graphs
While the children were young. Also when they were old
        For he was bold
And sought freedom with another woman, which is a laugh.

He wrote books, I cannot tell you how many;
They were reviewed, praised, and rapidly sank from sight.
        As was right
His opinions were often heard on the BBC.

Big enough in the mouth for a life peer,
He became one of the chief clowns of our public life,
        His second wife
Clinging on to the outside without a trace of fear.

However, he died, like the rest of us,
A soul in torment, an obituary in *The Times*.
        As he climbs
He finds the universe unexpectedly spacious.

He was last seen passing by Aldebaran
And he had a long journey to go after that.
      God sat
Waiting for him, as you may suppose, with a prepared judgment.

It was the surprise of his life, you might say;
For once he had no opinion to express
      – A less
Cruel deprivation than he supposed, on Judgment Day.

We who remain below, though not for long,
Cannot hope to surpass this man in vacuity
      But we
May prudently join the angels in a song:

      'Existence is
      Not what you say,
      Which does not count
      On Judgment Day;
      It is not even
      What you think,
      Which is but a
      Deceptive link
      Between your God
      And what you are
      – And what that is
      Is far from clear.
        So, Alleluia! loudly raise
        A song of ignorance and praise.'

The Regrets

I

Beware of age.
For I have learned
An old man should
Be kept in chains.
He is a gentle
Psychopath;
The passion that
He had is dead.
His youthful walk
And grey moustache
Conceal a heart
Which cannot feel.
The courtesy
Which he expends
Is poison to
His younger friends.
His virtues are
A kind of shell
To keep him cosy
In his skull.
I tell you mark
This leper well
And send him forward
With a bell.

II

Young men are fools
And now I am old
I am a fool.

III

Lust is the star
Which lit my way
And brought me close
To where you lay
— One wise man with

A pack of lies
Or not enough
To make him wise.
God's blood, they say,
Oozed from the tree.
The serpent sweated
Just like me
But in his more
Enlightened years
The devil was
A gentleman.

The Cave

The human mind is deeper than had been supposed;
It is the same depth as the human body
– That is why I value the soles of your feet
And am only moderately impressed by your eyes.
Your thoughts may be examined at all your entrances.

Yet the very name of thought promises a delineation
Which is not that of any or of the sum of your members.
I am horrified that this ghost inhabits you,
But it is this which brings you into these caverns
I live in. You move towards me across the wet floor.

Can we speak, except in terms of our bodies
And is that language available to us?
Where does speech come from? Is someone addressing us?
Is what we speak what we hear?
Cloud with misunderstanding in my arms.

The Shape

The passions are the shape of man.
I put it on a drawing board.

Show the integument drawn back.
Draw pity round about the heart.

Pity is small and avarice
No bigger, where the nostrils curl

But envy goes from top to toe
And lust runs from the radial point

Into the tip of every limb
And every hair upon the head

And sorrow blackens out the lines
Of every hope; and deep despair

Gathers like bile above the groin
Until it fills the abdomen.

Lucky the shape was sketched before
I drew back the integument.

The Affirmative

The trick of sex, there is no doubt,
First taught the animals to speak.

But Yes is not a word at all;
The first word that they spoke was No.

All conversation still remains
A gloss upon the negative.

For Yes could only hold its tongue;
Its work is in another place.

The Adventurer

When the sun was shining and the back door was open
He went indoors and successively raped seven women.
My own desires are not much different
Since I have given up the desire of understanding
And have not succeeded in ousting my other desires.
He wept and screamed in the dock. So would not I,
But my heart is armoured by intellection;
My heart has been hardened:
On that account I catch my trains with precision
And know how to look after myself, mate.

On the Coast

Thirty years ago I stood here,
Almost naked on the windy beach:
This is the body in which passion has decayed.

This is the clear water that sidled past me,
The white cliff, I can see it for a moment
I have no other authority for drowning.

This is certainly the body I left upon the shore
I found it the other day, crisped against the sea-weed:
This is the house in which I have slumbered these many years.

And now beside the water, walking close to the foam's edge
Before the grey turf, green turf and the brown corn-lands
I am wandering happily as an unidentified image.

But the mind will be applied in far-away London,
Bent over my files, residue of my spirit
The coming and going of thousands: it is a market-place.

I had not imagined anything but a blind future
And that is still with me, still beckoning onwards
Till the voices die and I am at rest.

It does not matter at that point what you do with my bones
These hills can have them or the dustman
So long as Dorset can brood over its grey sea.

Judith

Holofernes had meant to enjoy Judith;
She would have the laugh of him (he said) if he did not.
She sat upon spread skins and ate daintily
While he admired the spectacle for too long.
I put it down to his being a great captain,
Which made the world seem easy to him: while he stared
He grew drunk and then completely insensible.
After that she had only to cut off his head
And took it home folded up in a cloth.
She understood the place of love among
The larger affairs of the world
And was, you may say, a domesticated woman.

Public Places

A boy and a girl with thin bones
Sat opposite me in the railway coach,
Waiting to devour one another like cats.

The girl had white frills under her black skirt
Which slid up her thin black legs above her knees;
She was wearing a black jersey and what dark curls

Fell over her shoulders and peaked and beautiful face!
She leaned against the not less fragile boy
And their eyes were joined more firmly than their fingers.

I do not expect any response from such faces
And therefore they come so vividly before me:
It is so with the casual passers in the street.

Those whom I have known for thirty or for all their years
Have a different kind of impenetrability,
The sadness of shared knowledge

Which, however, is ultimately of so little
That one may walk out into the streets for company,
Images of the lecherous imagination

Being preferred, in the end, by the hard heart,
Though there is Christ even in our sisters
And all knowledge is of the image of God.

In Brewer Street

You had better imagine who you are
As you cross Brewer Street diagonally
If you do not, darkness will fall.

In mind is consequence and sequence,
Importance – ah, my dear, perhaps being –
You cannot creep under that coverlet

Or you could cross the street and re-enter the stones
As if you disappeared between the mortar.
I could not love you without necessity

Nor could my hand touch yours without its ghost.
I do not want it, though I want you extremely.
Neither can meet, unless we consent to be there.

On my Fifty-first Birthday

I

Hare in the head-lights dance on your hind legs
Like a poor cat struggling at a rope's end.
Everything is cruelty for innocence.
If you could mark this escape from death
In your thin mind you would have eaten what I have
And, running from form to form, you would consider
The immeasurable benignity of the destructive God.

II

A great sunlit field full of lambs.
The distant perspectives are of the patched earth
With hedges creeping about. If I were to die now
No need of angels to carry me to paradise.
O Lord my God, simplify my existence.

III

The whole hill-side is roofed with lark-song.
What dangerous declivities may I not descend?
It is dark green where the horses feed.
Blackthorn and gorse open before my eyes.

IV

The gulls come inland, alight on the brown land
And bring their sea-cries to this stillness.
It was waves and the surf running they heard before
And now the lark-song and the respiration of leaves.

Horatius

It is annoying when your sister doesn't appreciate you.
Besides, the sweat of the fighting had been considerable
And Horatius was genuinely tired;
Only in killing could he find more energy
So he put his sword to the throat of the silly girl.
She met him coming with the spoils of the Curiatii upon him
At the Capena gate: the battle had been uncertain –
Two lots of triplets fighting out there, with the hosts
Looking on eagerly as at television
Their eyes following the preliminary javelins like tennis balls
And gasps escaping when they came to blows.
At first two of the Horatii were down
But not before they had wounded the three Curiatii.
Then Horatius had pretended to fly.
The three wounded Curiatii had limped after him
Single file and at considerable distances
And he had turned and done for them one by one.
The last had hardly fought, it was just a killing
So he was quite ready when he met his sister.
Also, her body was a soft one.
The people have no conception of justice
(And he had been so good on the television).
They made him walk under a beam hood-winked
As a sort of bogus expiation of murder
And Numa's successor thought he had better keep quiet.

Adam

I will go and visit the deer
They and the cat being my main accompaniments,
As it happens, in the silence which succeeds work.
The sunlight whitens the top of the chestnuts,
Bare for winter, and the snow
Blazes to gold. The cat is safe in the house.
Out there under the magnificent beeches
The deer have classified themselves according to sex.

Not creatures of man's invention
Still they nuzzle or walk where he has put them.
I, creature of God, am among man's artifacts.
With the beasts I creep into another day.
Nothing commands me to a particular form;
But for my name and address I might be water
Running into a puddle for the cat to lick
Or perhaps stretching its ripples in the sunlight
Among the frosted grass, for the deer to stale.
I acknowledge freely that I am part of the creation
But doubt whether I am a particle for whom salvation was
    intended.
My sympathy is with Adam
Walking in the garden in the cool of the day.
To avoid is best.
ADAM: But that was in fact not exactly my problem.
Like you of course I admitted I was created
– In my case it was self-evident;
God was always about like the breath of my nostrils.
Moreover I was, next him, the lord of the garden
And had given names to the animals one by one
As he presented them to me. It was because none of these
Seemed more than a rustle of the grasses through which they came
That I was presented with Eve. And I was astonished.
There was a new element of correspondence
Not perceptible then in the beasts, though now you see it.
The foolishness of the apron of fig-leaves
Was a first effort to rid myself of that.
When God called there was some confusion.
It was the first time he had spoken so loudly.
I thought he was another kind of Eve,
A more powerful Adam perhaps, like myself.
The conversation that followed was hallucinatory.
It is easy for you to laugh at our evasions.
The future was unsettled.
I decided to walk out of Eden and go to work.
Since then nothing has been clear.
If I see Paradise it is between branches,
A glimpse over the cooking-pot while Cain and Abel
Quarrel over a skin.
It has been very interesting to meet you.
Somewhere between us is the second Adam.

Homo Sapiens is of No Importance

And it may be that we have no nature
That he could have taken upon him.
Plato of course discussed it.
Deborah sitting under a tree
In a time of matriarchy:
Blessed be thou among women,
Blessed be the hand, the hammer,
Blessed the tent-peg as it drove through Sisera,
Blessed the connection between two interiors,
Blessed the wire between the switch and the bulb.
Not for the mind of Jael but for her hand
Not for the hand but for the hammer
Not for the hammer but for the tent-peg
Not for the peg but for Sisera dead
Not for Sisera dead but for his army routed
Not for that but for the momentary ease under a tree
Not for that but for the tree itself
Not for the tree but for the sand blowing by it
If there was any nature it was in that.

Horace

The mind you made, Horace, against all endeavours
Of Time and, as you hoped, in forgetfulness
Of poverty, did it hold
At the last, when the cracks appeared?

Although your father took you to school himself
You must have read what was written on the walls,
Heard the boys' cat-calls and
The immediate tremors must have found you.

Was it you first cultivated the Muses
On the Sabine property where you lived under that other
Builder against time and concealer
Of human blemishes, the divus

Augustus? Were there not others, if you think carefully?
You and Vergil were no doubt the counter-prophets
Who set the finger of death
On the Latin Muse, in triumph.

It is not nothing to outlive the centuries.
I would give something for the secret of your concentration
– I mean yours, not your verses',
Any poet would give his eyes for that –

But to know how you drew apart from the world,
Content to put all your passion into strophes;
How you denied with tight lips
And turned the springs to glass.

A social success, pretending not to notice
The licence which lay at the heart of the orgies;
If the heart has longing in it
It is better never to speak of it.

Is that the secret of your concentration,
Necessary to outlive the centuries?
My living has come too hard;
Teach me therefore you rentier muse.

Bronze, acier, anything harder than that.
Teach me to bury my voice in a dead woodland.
It is better not to be heard
Than to speak for ever.

The Man with a Family

In at the womb and out at the eyes.
There was no pardon for the children he had committed,
Twelve of them sitting round the table eating their porridge.
'How many roses have you broken off my stem
In the illusion that you were doing the gardening?'

In at the womb and out at the mouth.
The first word was fuck but there were a great many after it.
'It is odd that the exercise seeking resemblance
Should end with such great distance between us.'

In at the womb and finally out of the ears
If we may suppose a spiritual substance to seek egress that way.
'I think it may, it does not know whether it is going or coming;
There is a certain confusion which is best expressed that way.'

Orpheus

The inside and the outside of the body;
These are the two minds that I am in.

If I seek to put you in mind of me
I assure you that nothing is further from my mind
Than that you should concern yourself with my exterior.

If on the other hand I put myself in mind of you
It is rather that you put yourself in my mind
And it is as a figure passing, stripped to the skin.

Yet you must be supposed to be also you,
A figure to whom the epidermis is indifferent
Or at best a superficial and tingling dress.

A group of naked figures with Orpheus playing
But succeeding in attracting only the animals
I take to be a representation of the mind.

Lines on the Rector's Return

The Devil has become Rector of this parish
And is having a tremendous success.

Every year the collections go up
As up in the pulpit he denounces Charity.

But the subtlest part of his exposition
Is that in which he removes the grounds for Hope

And the part the Devil seems to admire most himself
Is that in which he twists Faith to his own meaning.

Faith, Hope and Charity, these three:
Look out, here comes Mr Haggerty.

Metamorphoses

I

Actaeon was a foolish hind
To run from what he had not seen.

He was a hunter, and had called
An end to slaughter for that day

And laid his weapons by a well.
Diana knew the man he was

But took her kirtle from her waist.
She gave her arrows to her maids

Then dropped her short and flimsy dress.
There was some muscle on the girl.

I think she knew the hunt was up
But set the hounds upon the man

To show her bitter virgin spite.
There was some blood but not her own.

Actaeon sped, his friends hallo'ed,
The forest rang but not with tears.

His favourite whippet bit his flank:
His friend hallo'ed him to the kill

Which they were sure he would enjoy.
Diana by the fountain still

Shuddered like the water on her flesh
And after that there came the night.

II
– Or else he was a rutting stag
Turned to a man because he saw

Diana bathing at the pool
– As you might turn a foreskin back.

III
Pygmalion was an artful man;
Sculpsit and pinxit were his trade.

He would not have a woman in
The confines of his silky bed;

The ones he knew were troublesome.
Still, he admired the female form

And cut another in that shape
But it was marble, rather hard.

He laid it down upon his bed
And drew a purple coverlet

Across its shapely breasts and legs.
However, it did not respond.

He got it up and gave it clothes
And brought it several sorts of toys.

It did not speak a single word
So in despair he said his prayers.

He did not even dare to say
'This marble' or 'this ivory';

He merely said he'd like a girl
Resembling one he'd made himself.

After his prayers the boy went home
And got back to his kissing game.

To his surprise the girl grew warm;
He slobbered and she slobbered back

– This is that famous mutual flame.
The worst of all was yet to come.

Although he often wished her back
In silent marble, good and cold

The bitch retained her human heat,
The conquest of a stone by art.

May Venus keep me from all hope
And let me turn my love to stone.

IV

O will you take a fluttering swan
Eurotas, on your plashy banks?

Where the dissimulating bird
Fled from a Venus he had coaxed

Into an eagle with a beak.
Eurotas showed beneath her waves

The rippling image of a girl.
She rose to take the frightened bird

And struggled with him to the bank.
It was the bird came out on top.

Its wings concealed the thing it did
But showed the fluttering legs and hands.

The bird became a stable thing:
There are such dangers for a girl.

Europa felt a sighing bull
Beside her, as she gathered flowers.

It was a gentle, milk-white beast
And tried to graze upon her hair.

She patted and embraced its neck;
Its breath grew deeper as she stroked.

At last she climbed upon his back,
One hand upon a stubby horn.

Over his broad and shaggy cloth
The creature felt the gentle limbs

And in a trice he was away.
Europa held the swimming beast;

She looked at the receding shore
And clutched her garments from the wind.

V
When Virgo crosses with the Ram
Expect a rain of falling stars.

A spilling cornucopia
Betokening plenty, but no peace,

A Danae in her open boat.
The eleemosynary shower

That fell, can now get up again
And it is Easter in the world.

The first age was the age of gold;
The age of iron is our own.

VI

The day, the year, the century,
The glacial winter, and the spring

And then the naked summer brings
The rutting stag to the church door.

But first the Phaeton from the crown
Of heavens descends into the waves.

There was no reason in his course
And on his way he burnt the world

And when you visited the shades
Did you see my Eurydice,

Christ, on that terrifying day?
I sit beneath the pulpit for

The bitter, abnegated hour.
I have no notion what you did.

In manus tuas. Afterwards.
Except you walked three days in hell.

Was there numb kindness in the shades?
Who is that nervous figure there

The empty sunlight falls upon
Although there is no light to fall?

Will she resume the upper light?
And when you come to Thomas in

The confines of his doubting room
Was she left in an orange-grove?

There was a garden. Calvary.
And Adam fell where you got up.

But was the resurrected flesh
Less tempted than the flesh of Eve?

The naked figure in the grove
Diana's or the risen Christ's?

Her altar or the flesh we eat?
The world is uncreated by

The death of him that made the world.
By the slain lamb there trots the fawn.

VII
Here are two stories of old men:
The virtuous Boaz is the first.

He lay upon the threshing floor
And dreamed of Ruth, who soon came in

And while in sleep he saw the fields
Where she had stooped to gather corn

She gently lifted, in the dark,
The rug that hid his bony toes.

It was a rather pleasant dream.
Benign and virtuous to himself

He wished he could be warm like Ruth.
And there she was. But he was scared.

He sent her home and merely bit
The aged spit upon his beard

And did it honestly next day.
As he was rich the world approved.

The second story is about
Two men whose desiccated years

Were sheltered in the splendid house
Of Joacim, a juicy lord.

They earned their keep by being just
But saw Susanna every day.

She was a soft and tender bit.
They noticed when she took her bath

And both devised a pleasant plan
To help her with the soap and rinse.

They waited in the garden where
She took it when the sun was hot.

Unhappily it warmed them too
And made them lie to get their way.

Then they were frightened, and resumed
Their great pretence of being just.

Less fortunate than Boaz, they
Could only hope to have her killed

But even this did not come off
And Daniel had them cut in two.

VIII

Which otherwise might have been born.
They carried in a bloody tray

This unripe apple plucked within
The forest of the uterus.

This one at least will not arrive
At ages suitable for tears.

Within this forest everything
Begins. Although I may not say

Eurydice walks with her tears
It is the grove where they began.

It is the grove where I walked out,
Blind as upon my latest days.

I had a kind of folded life.
The butterfly with its wet wings

Has twice the power I had to fly.
And how then to the garden where

The loaded Tree of Knowledge stood?
Deceptively completed man

Beside a woman as complete?
No expectation in his eyes

His member like a falling leaf;
The fronded entrance to Eve's cave

Admitting no posterity.
The shining apples had no life.

Then how could Adam come to find
A tree more naked than himself,

Excoriate of leaves and fruit
And he himself nailed to the boughs?

Some serpent must have let him hope,
Which his glazed body could not do

Without hortation from a flesh
He had forgotten was his own.

Some spasm must have found its end
And broken his tumescent heart.

Eve must have let her children out
From her forced womb, to right and left.

But first, within, the spinning wave
Of sperm had sent its foam-flake out

To meet the southward-seeping egg
And this encounter did not hear

Either the paradisal speech
Exchanged when congress was agreed

Or the reared serpent's good advice
So soft that it became a hiss.

It needed Cain and Abel too,
The brothers Murder and Incite

And Noah with his upturned eyes,
Lifting his skirts out of the wet

And Abraham in fear of God,
Getting his holy cutlass out

The sober, patriarchal life
In which the richest was the best

And now the surgeon with his smile
And sister's deferential cough.

IX

The metamorphosis of all.
Or he was nothing but a child

Magi attended for the star
And shepherds for their singing ears.

Funny how he became a Mass,
To eat his body, when he died,

The first essay of carpentry
Building an ark for the whole world

As you might nail a coffin up.
The golden age began anew;

What had been first became the last.
Declension to the age of iron

Was unimportant after all.
And yet there must remain a doubt.

The giants piling up the sky,
Pelion on Ossa, also rose

And what will rise must also fall.
We know it by experience.

It is the waning of the year.
A death in spring-time is the best.

Stanzas

I

Everything must go to extreme
Though in fact to go there is to go beyond it.
The type of this is the extension of the penis
Which is a thing we all very much have in mind.

II

So long as I can sleep or even pleasurably drowse
Why get up? Since the evidence for existence
Is not the movement of cars and buses in the world
Or even the affectionate figure bending over me,
But awareness of the ice tables stretching by a disconsolate sea
There is no need of any other inhabitant.

III

I like very much to be among derelict people.
If they knew all my achievements they would certainly be
      impressed
It is not that, however, it is the reflection
That if I fell much further I should still be like them
And that their condition is after all tolerable
Since they are sitting on benches blinking at the sun.

IV

Wherever they are they want to be somewhere else.
This is the main utility of the motor-car:
By an incessant change it becomes impossible for them to perceive
That their one serious wish is to be nowhere.

V

Every year blackthorn and daffodil
Are noticed by those who imagine they are renewed
When the year is. But they grow old,
The renewal of hope is vain: it is their grandchildren
Who come laughing along the road, picking the cowslips.

VI

When the old gods went by they became silly ideas.
God therefore be present to me in the flesh.

VII

Ha! ha! the crucifixion of the penis.
A repeated miracle: and it does not end there.

An Essay on God and Man

I know nothing of it. The human race,
The individual, it is fashionable to say.
But what is that, a pronoun?
'Develop the personality
To the fullest extent.' That is a lark
More visible to those who believe their own words
Than to those who want to recall them
The moment they have been uttered
Because they have failed even to trace in the air
Something they had been about to say.
There are, as I see it, creatures with arms and legs
And the variable expression.
Brickbats, temples, words, the sculpsit and pinxit.
There is the night of each mind,
Like a squalid family snoring behind a blanket.
There is something there, you can hardly see it by candle-light.

Love? This monster is supposed to be linked with the person,
But again, I do not know.
It is a fine trick to tie love to the penis
Like the cracked fakirs who put a skewer through it.
'Marriage is for the procreation of children
And the prevention of fornication.'
The former a thing
Which has no need of individual consciousness,
The latter a piece of hygiene,
The mere removal of a possible public nuisance.
'Hallowing the instincts' and that stuff
A post-Darwinian invention in bad prose.
There are, really, only the things you notice,
With, as a matter of faith, those you do not.
But to erect this group of impressions
Into something you call the person
Is a gratuitous verbal trickery
Like many others which keep the world going.
A tree does not talk of developing itself;
If there is something in the way, it grows crooked.
And so may you. A child out of the womb
Has to be nappied, wiped, and educated
But this is something you do to him

As you might wash down your car and tinker with it.
It has nothing to do with the miracle of personality
Which is a subjective disease you first start admiring in yourself
Then pretend we are all growing happily together
As if flowering were not a matter of choking off others.
What you see is what you get.
Your share being different it is certain that you will not
Understand anyone else. What you can observe
Is the accuracy of others' responses, and classify them accordingly.
And if you believe in the Lord God
Jeering over this multitude and controlling their devices
You will not be tempted to anything but the adjustments
Your machine is capable of in its reaction with others.
Lenin remarked
That God was a complex of ideas
Born out of the subjection of man to nature
– And thought he had found him out.
But I cheerfully accept this definition
As corresponding, more than most, to a reality.

The Consequence

I

There is no more to say than No
And Nothing is my farthest end.
A man has pity for his friend
But I am only glad to go.
Now therefore let the handsome crow
Pick out the eyes I would not lend.

II

We feed on death for half our lives
But vomit when we let it in.
The final pallor of the skin
Betokens that the patient thrives.
How earnestly the swimmer dives!
How eager his returning fin!

III

Old age protects itself with hope
And leans to suck the kiss of youth.
How kindly Boaz took to Ruth!
The lion with the antelope.
And what delighted fingers grope
In cradles to forget the truth!

IV

But there is twilight and the rose
And other such ephemera.
The crocus and Proserpina
Distract us to a brief repose.
And I, who have a polished heart,
Harder than any sympathy
But excellent for lechery
Or any sanctimonious part
For ever leave the truth alone;
It crunches time up like a stone
While love, the centre of the mind
Nibbles the flesh from head to feet.
The dusty streets of Sodom find
Two constables upon the beat.

V

Plato, whom reason ate like sex,
Preferred the form before the thing.
But what contentment did that bring?
Whom did that ever unperplex?
Meanwhile incessant number pecks
At form, until the scaffolding
Of all our thoughts is down, to fling
The gates of chaos on our necks.
Judas went out and hanged himself
And so should I, for I am he.
There is no Adam to set free.

VI

The forest of a long intent
Has tracks where I may lose my way
Nor was the place I am today
Intended by the way I went.
The night has only disarray;
It does not see what day mistook.
What was it that the nightmare shook?
Although I heard the drum today
The same occasions day by day
Provide me with identity.
I do what the occasions say
For nothing never is without
The thing it wants, and for its play
A futile gesture is the best.

The new poems from
In the Trojan Ditch

The Discarnation
or, How the Flesh became Word and dwelt among us

I

The individual is the thing
Or it is either me or you.
        I do
Not care which way I sing
        This part
So long as I can somehow start.

There are two ways of looking at
The subject, either from within,
        As in
A scallop, diving bell or hat,
        Or slope
The eyes up through a telescope.

They are two different animals,
It sometimes seems, the man
        Who can
Reflect, and does, the swaying walls
        And he
Who sways himself for all to see.

For to be seen and stir within
The porridge of the consciousness
        Is less
One action than to flash a fin
        And sink
Down to the bottom of the ink.

The seen continuum of act
Of something else, makes that a thing.
        A wing
Or speaking head is doubtless fact
        And far
More so that you can show you are.

But the observer is observed,
You think. He is not. What you see
      Is me
As something linear, straight or curved,
      Which I,
As I, should certainly deny.

Though all the time, to understand,
Men make a certain sort of face
      Or pace
Impatiently, or lift a hand
      To greet
Another pair of travelling feet,

Yet this proves nothing. Every look
Is attribution. What I see
      Can be
So little more than what I took
      Before
As imprints on my mind's clean floor.

From what? What passes there? All ghosts?
Or able spirits like my own?
      The moan
The tree makes touches me, the hosts
      Of eyes
Around me also sympathise.

– And I with them. A comity
Is what we make for comfort's sake
      To break
Our prison, not to be let free
      But bind
Some obligation on our mind.

For our supremest wish, ourself,
Must find its equal, or we die.
      The sky
Is peopled; Ghibelline and Guelf
      Stick out
Of history books like a pig's snout.

And we admit companionship
In people passing in the street.
      The beat
Suggests the heart, likewise the quip
      The mind
Which, multiplied, makes out mankind.

While these unsure companions dance
Before our eyes, we can forget
      The set
They move in is our glance,
      The tears
They shed a humming in our ears.

Also forget that, worst of all,
There is no bottom to our well.
      To tell
What is reflected there, what wall
      Is there
We peer into a breathless air.

But whether in or out, or who
It is that peers, one does not know.
      A flow
Of sorts is there; there are some few
      Dark bits
That float on what are called our wits.

But I is not found there. It is
Not found at all. Descartes
      Was smart
Enough to catch a glimpse of his
      But since
A cogitat has only been a wince.

Conscience perhaps? Or consciousness?
A pool of that is not a man.
      What can
The lizard say? And yet the guess
      Is that
He sees, although perhaps non cogitat.

And the computer reads my cheques
And thinks as well as you or me.
      May be
Our calculus is more complex;
      Its trick
A variant of arithmetic.

But number is concealed in verse
And every preference we show.
      We know
The good from better, bad from worse
      Without
Counting what brought the choice about.

Or do we count but, like machines
Simply not notice what we do?
      Have you,
Choosing a summum bonum, seen
      The hands
Clock up the number of the sands?

The things we notice are a spot
Of light in a dark countryside.
      The wide
Part is unknown but not
      Unten-
anted by animals and men,

Alive and dead. The small part is
What passes for the mind of man
      Or can
Be seen upon its surfaces,
      A glade
In which he dances unafraid.

How came the mind to be that shape?
Or there at all? How first the axe
      Made cracks
In that wide forest, how the nape
      First said
The word that grew into the head:

All that is Logos, and obscure.
The shape is history. A mind
        Will find
The way it has been taught. Past cure,
        It sees
No hope except in its disease.

And when you think you are yourself
It is a kind of learned joke.
        You croak
A dead man's words, take from the shelf
        A book
In which all generations look

And read a line which two or three
Imagine they made their own,
        Though known,
With variants, throughout history.
        A form
Of language is a human norm

And it is made in several styles,
As, 'Dozōō' in the Japanese
        For 'Please'
(Used sometimes in the British Isles)
        Which may
Mean 'Bitte' or else 'S'il vous plaît.'

That is the simplest proof there is
That similar is not the same.
        The name,
Likewise, of Gert or Bert or Liz
        Conceals
Less difference than the subject feels.

And everything we do is form
Of manner, language or physique.
        The meek
And violent equally are norms
        And we
Are less than our mythology.

Yet what we think is less, for sure,
Than what we are, and that is flesh.
        Its fresh
Bloom is the best we know. Its dure
        Descent
The hardest way that we are sent.

It starts in comfort, or at least
It does not know it is a start.
        A part
Unwittingly and, when released,
        It finds
One body has become two minds.

Whether its first thought comes with breath
Depends on what you mean by thought;
        But caught
In air, it feeds on it till death
        And takes
As sauce the ripples the air makes.

Its softness becomes strength, its coos
Turn into words and bite. Its sex
        Will vex
Itself and everything it woos.
        Its eyes
Will see the world and show surprise.

But youth once lost, a lizard skin
Envelops organs with a twist.
        All's missed
That called the appetite within.
        Pretence
At last replaces every sense.

To die is best at last, and yet
The last kick struggles after life.
        The knife
That enters like a prince is met
        By will
Which is the last thing to be still.

II

As I approach my second theme
Decorum stares me in the face.
   No place
For ribaldry or pretty dream
   Which lure
The senile and the immature.

Man is conventional, he lives
According to imagined laws.
   The cause
Is partly in himself who gives
   The rule;
In part they are discovered by the fool.

Confused between discovery
And natural error of the heart,
   By art
He finds he may be free;
   By right
Searches the arrow of his flight.

Two bodies in one mind – the mark
If any, of the lover's knot –
   And not
As something hollowed in the dark,
   But found
As paradise to build around.

And if this cannot be, the flesh,
Which is not dildo or mere meat,
   Will bleat
Outside another mind's thin mesh
   Till cross-
petition makes a general loss.

Or, falling back upon themselves,
Each mind admits the other's fears.
   Then tears
Pour out over eroded shelves
   As of
The dried-up torrent-bed of love.

When they are spent the stones are seen.
There is an end of all soft charm.
        The harm
That lovers do has always been
        The mind,
More calculating then than kind.

And if one mind two bodies touch,
– But not the two of unity –
        The he
Both him and her, and she as much
        Both her
And him, they are not as they were.

No innocence, deliberate love,
Pleasure, but not the blinded hope,
        The slope
But not the precipice above
        The prec-
ipice, high above emptiness.

The body turned to instrument?
As if it could be! But that lie
        Will try
To turn the drift of each intent
        And wear
A face that's slightly more than fair.

And so the flesh betrays the mind
And must be guarded like a jewel,
        So cruel
It is when it is unconfined
        And yet
Imprisoned, it is overset,

Bedevilled, peeved. But bond or free
Are parables of servitude,
        While prude
And lecher both are equally
        Without
The key that lets the body out.

Because the body is the mind
To speak of gaolers is absurd.
         The word
Is friend, the blind leading the blind.
         And so
In tears the man and woman go.

They were not always in one yoke.
They issued out of separate wombs,
         The tombs
Of separate affections, broke
         In fear
Into a separate atmosphere

And lived for years without their sex
Or with so little that the heart
         Was part
Of everything and could annex
         A tree
As well as an identity.

Then doubt and reason grew a twig
On branches formed of love and hate.
         A late
Comer was lust, who is so ig-
         norant
Because it does not hear, and can't.

If lust had raised its roaring voice
Before the mind had formed its ring
         Nothing
Could have withstood it, and no choice
         Been made,
Or else it would have been afraid.

But as it grew, provoked by mind,
By whom it was contained, it caught
         The thought
(Which, nascent, is so near combined
         With flesh)
And so drove on to lust afresh.

The intellectual pursuit
Of all, desire then became.
            The name
Was often changed, although the root
            Remained
And sap in everything complained.

So adolescence turned into
A trap for ingenuity.
            The key
Of everything it tried to do
            Was lust
It would not own unless it must.

So hearts and heads and other parts
Became confused. Analysis
            Which is
So bright, picked out the darts
            Which hurt
And then the youth became alert.

His object then, through thick and thin,
Was much and falsely simplified.
            He cried
For certain patches of bare skin –
            But, kind,
Paid his addresses to the mind.

More wise than he, his elders then
Obstructed all that he essayed
            And made
A ritual with a long amen,
            The which
Denatured quite his primal itch.

But gave him a society,
Anxious and troubled all his life,
            A wife
In whose routine embraces he
            Might find
A body had become a mind.

This practice for paternal love
Employed his economic strength.
          At length
He'd house and crockery to prove
          The plan
Is more important than the man.

Then children came to make complete
His service to the commonwealth.
          By stealth
We have good done to us. We eat
          The food
Others prepared for their own good.

Since every thought must have its act
And not all thought begins inside,
          The wide
Extension of a private fact
          Will give
The failed man an excuse to live.

He fails because there is no man
Except in number and exchange.
          The range
Of one man's mind in no way can
          Invent
A world in which a life is spent.

And there are engines make us go
Without our knowledge. So the mind
          Confined
To what we tell ourselves we know
          Is ill
Accomplished to direct the will

And does not do so. And the heart,
So-called, is only a vague belt
          Of felt
Impressions, so a dimmer part
          Of the
Same instrument of cecity.

But facts and bodies operate
Upon our whims and so we are.
           The jar
Of honey and the sting don't wait
           Till you
Imagine hives, and flowers in dew

Or the digestion or the cure.
The world is ready-made and we
           Who see
And taste and smell are too unsure
           To make
Any resolve but a mistake.

No reason therefore to despise
A little magic in your drink
           Or think
That antiseptic thoughts comprise
           The best
And highest that can be expressed.

Reflect: the first, near-simian men
Put in their rods without a thought.
           They sought
And found, but knew it no more when
           They'd done
Than omne animal post coitum.

The second men observed there was
An act worth taking notice of,
           Though love
Is not imputed to this phase,
           Indeed,
Nor the analogy of seed.

The third men noticed, very sly,
That nine moon cycles brought a birth
           Though earth
And air might have to join the cry.
           But still
They knew the act was not the will.

The fourth man is the Onan-Stopes
(The latter the more technical
            But all
The same in terms of fears and hopes
            – Technique,
However, makes the hope more weak).

Children are born through platitude,
Error or love or anything,
            The spring,
Long winter evenings, or mood
            Or al-
cohol, the same moons bring them all.

And, having come, like stars themselves,
They govern others' destinies
            But ease
No favour in their own behalves
            For love
Comes from around if not above.

So, drawn out by these facts, the man
Who acts the part of father finds
            That minds
Grow in and out of things, and can
            Be grown
Like lichen on from stone to stone.

III
And so with place. A habitat
Is habit in a certain space,
            A face
With thought behind it. It seems like that
            And who
Shall say it has less thought than you?

Places have names because a thought
Lives in them, changing like our own
      And grown
Wily with years, not to be caught,
      So meant
Only by words we don't invent.

Cerne Abbas is a name I like;
Toller Porcorum even more.
      Ebbor
Valley by Priddy has a psych
      -e which
Can be counted to make you twitch.

It is painful that men should die
And be forgotten. Places prove
      That love
Or even hatred will long try
      Not to
Be, and names are to remind you.

If you sit on a barrow and
Play your transistor, still the dead
      Will head
Their way out of the ground, the hand
      Which slew
Your ancestor will be on you.

It does not matter if you don't
Feel it, it is certainly there.
      You dare
Admire yourself because you don't
      And close
Your eyes upon the dead man's toes.

Your ignorance does not seal up
The innumerable petitions.
      The guns
Emplaced upon the coast still plop
      The shell
Into the sea although you are well.

Thomas Tusser still ploughs these hills
Though you may not have heard of him.
                You trim
Your smile to contemporary wills.
                Who said
That you too would not join the dead?

They are living, as well as you;
And their thoughts creep into your bones.
                Rough stones
May have more to say that is true
                Than men
Who do not know how to say Amen.

Labour instead of thought will do
To form the man, for what he makes
                Soon takes
Its part in shaping me and you.
                We are
The subtlest artifacts by far.

The house that grows upon a hill
Remembers like the hill itself.
                The self
Which likes to think it is a will
                Is but
The image of an acre and a hut

And certain kind words are spoken too
Before it knew what they could mean.
                The seen
Enters beside the heard, the true
                Image
Burrows inside the living rage.

That is the man. The furrows eat
His aching brain out as he ploughs.
                To rouse
Him there is the sun. To greet
                His bit-
-ter end there is the mud pit.

Happy if between rise and fall
Some creature greets him for a day
   And clay
Cakes on his boots and a few tall
   Trees rise
Before him to excite surprise.

He is happy indeed if such
As Salisbury spire teach him to expect
   Direct
Fruition outside his own hutch.
   This is
The best of man's artifices.

But number has replaced intent
For most; they are not cattle they
   Betray
The heritage of cattle, bent
   On what
They think they cannot say is not

But no more attentive to what is
Than a sewing machine to cloth,
   And loth
To reject an analysis
   Which tells
At least how to avoid bad smells

And ensures that they die in peace
In well-furnished euthanasia.
   These are
The objectives of our police
   Although
It does not always work out so.

Quiconque meurt, meurt à douleur
– Or so it used once to be said.
   The dead
Do not report on it. There were
   No doubt
Once more who screamed as they went out.

Do not under-rate benefits
Everybody seeks to enjoy
      The boy
Shut away because out of his wits;
      Foetus
Smothered lest it should bother us.

We are the heirs of an emptiness
Of which we are extremely proud;
      The crowd
Soothed as it never was, a less
      Extreme
Nightmare, and a less hopeful dream.

And artifacts less regarded
Than ever before, because made
      For trade
And not for use, and by the dead
      Hand of
Number instead of by our love.

Not even made to be consumed
As is sometimes said. Made so that
      The rat
In the sewer is well groomed;
      The count
Of nothing will continually mount.

Over the hills now there advance
The artifacts, both man and thing,
      A string
Choking the leaders of the dance;
      Their blood
Cannot do their brains any good.

So, departing into Thing
As if the Pied Piper had called them,
      The hem
Of the garment is untouched, to sing
      Is not
Necessary, and that's my lot.

For Patrick Swift

The dishes are untouched
And yet I see them all
Spread out under the moon.

Quiet, which nothing spoils,
Not even appetite,
Hung on the point of wish.

Milk-white, with ruddy fruit
Only the angry heart
Is mean enough to ask.

Ice in the silver night
With the bird voices held
In silver cups, tonight.

No Address

In my leprosy I have lost speech
Which before I had with several.
Now no voices, not even my own.

Pliny, Horace, Cicero, talk to me;
I am a dead language also.
The poetry owners cannot make me out

Nor I them. And the big mouths of learning
Open and close over my thoughts without biting.
Under the shadow of politics I have no teeth.

I am no man, Caesar, to stand by you,
Nor have the whimsical humour of pre-war Oxford
But my unrecognised style was made by sorrow.

Inching towards death, let me go there quickly.
Silently, in the night or in the day-time,
Equally, I would take it like a Roman.

Hod Hill

Ovid, you are too slack. I can see the hill,
Hod Hill in Dorset, where you had your camp –
So I may call it, in sympathy. The natives
Came streaming over the walls. Like birds, you said,
A flight of ill omen, carrying off
Tomorrow's dinner perhaps, even tonight's.
It may be. Your horror was even more,
That walking in the streets there were no Romans.
Even the Greeks were suspect, chatting with savages
In their own language. Over half the houses
Were native-owned. The rough, the treacherous.
Arrows were found in the streets, far from the walls.
No security here. Look back, dear Ovid,
On Rome to fall, but not in your day.

Anacreon

Men have their animosity
And women have what they can give,
Beauty, unless you choose to call
Their presence by another name.
Nothing is new. Anacreon
Said 'crumple swords and put out flames.'

Palaestra and Ampelisca

It was the first foot that came ashore.
The whoremaster with the brilliant eye
Remained on board, the waves ran skeltering in.
Then the ship broke and the whoremaster
Lumbered after the girls. The two ran
With wet garments baffling their slippery bodies.
The girls had been intended for pleasure in Sicily
But things do not work out as men intend.

Haectenus arvorum cultus

Up to now the fields
Have been ploughed and the stars
Sent us home to our cottages
At the end of the day.
There has been the vine,
Even on these hills, and the slow
Growing olive.
Not only the Cotswold shepherd
But I too, with even pace,
Treading where the wind can be heard
Or some horn perhaps. But this is over.
Not even metal ringing
At the smithy, or a voice.
Water sucking the rotting
Piers,
The algae lifted
Tide by tide.
A single gull
Banking, back to the dead sea,
Cries.

The State of the Arts

dedicated to The Lord Goodman

36 poets of the London area
Assembled at 105 Piccadilly.
I hope they did not spoil the carpets,
Hawking and spitting all over the place.
The rent is high, explained the curator,
But we were attracted by the situation.
Have you seen our famous furniture?
I do not know how many pounds per square foot
For the Council Chamber, but then, think of the members,
'Selected for pre-eminence in the Arts'
– A Sunday-paper novelist, and some others.
Into whose hands, Muses, are you fallen?

Presiding over the whole, like a frog,
Mr Wilson's lawyer, 55, unmarried,
Whose career dates from Labour's victory
(See *Who's Who*).

                    Poets, tumble downstairs.
They are marble, and you should be grateful.
There is safety in numbers.

Evening

Sleep has my muscles and a cord my throat.
Faint heart! The rooks at evening repair,
Climbing upon so many steps on air,
To the elm tops; caw, on the balustrade,
Caw from the church-tower, where the dead are laid
Under a passing shadow. I to tea,
Beside the fire in the old house, quietly.

The Salad

To sordid death I go. Time after time
The days escape without fortune of rhyme
Or other incident of better wit.
No mind is manners, none is mine.
I am the epitome of slime,
Church furniture, slum wit, a card
Fallen from the pack. Mix me a salad.

Pickers and Stealers

Pickers and stealers, my false friends,
    You have not served my ends.
No lack of malice on my part
    Holds you back. You lack art.
But here are people to admire:
    The delicate liar,
At home with treason like the cat;
    Softer than that,
The sleight-of-word who does not lie;
    The pleaser. What am I?
The man inclined to larceny
    Who stops at envy.

The Crucifix

I go diminuendo all the time
    Towards a heap of dust or splash of slime.
All good is in the flesh, and what I see
    Answers to this description exactly.
But I must not touch, I must be blind
    To the exact image within my mind,
My ligaments trudge to destruction
    Between high walls. The resurrection
Will hoist me also before the judge
    I do not want to see, and my grudge-
Eaten mind be emptied before him.
    And yet the mind I shall have will be a limb
Of that great flesh of the risen Lord.
    How flesh? and how can it then afford
House-room for discontent? But I here
    Am subject to all want, though my gear
Cannot show any fraction of my needs
    But itch and scratch. It is for this God bleeds.
O crucifix, you are indeed my lust
    You are the examination of my dust.

My mind perjures and twists while you cry
   Silently but so loud you tear the sky.
Wherefore these tears? Shall I rejoice?
   I would do, if I could hear your voice.

Trafalgar Square

There is no remedy but death
And that you need not hanker for
For no obscure oblivion
Waits for your bones, but certain hope
Of coming to a blinding light,
Each part of you without pity
Remembered. No extreme failure
Not matched with desert; honey,
If it is for you at all, laid on your burns.
This is my belief, hardly to be reconciled
With that demure Saviour I apprehend
Somewhere among the shades. But all is mystery,
In pity of my understanding, not
To wrap myself in, here in Trafalgar Square.

Daphne

You cannot start a poem without a word.
   Speak none, for then the silence is absurd.
Even the fishes swim against the tide.
   And do you never want to be outside?
Great God, your prisoner weeps, and so do I.
   Miracles are arranged accordingly.
Ité, ité but you shall not go forth.
   Is it not prison for two pennyworth?
Sleep behind walls. There shall be sleep
   Revelatory as it shall be deep.
Two sides, two pillows. Truth lays its head on one.
   Is there another or shall love have none?

The body, yes. How shall it walk this way?
    Shall it be indiscriminate and pray?
Is love then over all? Are these trees
    Also cared for, oratory breeze?
They are of the flesh of the cross,
    Lignum, the wood he hung on; what he was,
Corpus & sanguis not to be saved alive.
    That so, would it not better be
To be metamorphosed Daphne?

Ovid in Pontus

I am an old man whose death is foreseen,
Bystanders admire my longevity.
I see them eat every word I mean,
Yes, and excrete pity.
Di maris et coeli, what if the air
Is empty enough to receive prayer?
Do I have to pray? Because Pontic cold
Is under my cloak now that I am old?
It is under my skin, fashionable tears.
A suitable place to die, or to make amends;
Failure makes enemies as success friends.

Ambition

Ambition is what fools remember;
Excise then from my mind the same,
The fruit whittled, the bough cast.

No mind now seek through darkness
What mine has sought, and slewed away,
In youth love, in age content.

In the Trojan Ditch

I *Troilus and Cressida*

There is a mountain
Left forgotten
Under the uneasy eye of Dulcimer
I betray you? I, I, I?

Wizened with wisdom
The peat hair shagged over his brow
Armour is bright.
You to attempt me? Or who?

Basnet, basons of thunder, sword out
Elephantine in the extreme day
Night
For such encounters I say.
Helen
Troy down upon your altars.

Thus say all sages and I too
Vergil, necromancer, renounce Troy.
Aeneas sailing away, Dido is lost
To find one, Palinurus, your loss.

Sage Cressid, stain on your bed
The eye-glass in Pandar's eye
Uncle, how go maidenheads?

Dawn broke on the city, that day
Arches and battlements, the same
Light coming through them, the same.

II *Helen*

The horse looks over the wall
Ulysses like a pack of monkeys
Is it the face or the arse?
Crude sufferers, a tail
Is worth a face.
It is the mind

Dallying through all the strings
From feet to toes
To hands to fingers all
To head
Curled in a smile part custom and part taste.
The walls
Are high
What is within
On flock beds, altars. Houses all
Contain the kernel of the savage world.
Go home Penelope
And Pelops line
Drawn through the centre, O.

III *Athene*

Excoriate
Exaggerated, near dead
Racked, ripped
Uncovered, dismembered
The ribs
Cracked in a nut-cracker, the head
Opened with a tin-opener
The tongue
Extended like a flash tie
One eye
Turned upwards while
The other plays on a curved toe-nail.
This is my mercenary self
Also my best
Elegant, denuded, damned
Correctest
Extrapolation of fancy going inwards.
Outwards indeed
There is the epidermis, yours and yours
Form, measure, feet
Athene
Like a rock.

Van Diemen's Land

I
Down
In the drink it
Might be called, for no
Reason but the best

There are no bearings down here
Nor instruments, the
Nauseous epidermes of mermaids do not
Through the transmarine darkness
Show any light.

It is hell and ham-bones, gnaw-
ing the specific meat,
In retreat
From all the world, like a squid
Into the sand,
Law
Sub-burrowed by a conjunctive and
It is no more than that and
The conjunction is not firm it
Waits
To establish nothing is
Variable as wind, flitting
Between cliff pillars of if and when,
Itself less and more uncertain.

What the sea
Dictates it answers
Amiss, or comes softly home
To the west windows, home
But does not enter. No
Voice could. There are daughters also
Of sea-urchins and the moved weeds
Who exceed, they say, in all beauty
But the crabs walk by them indifferent.
I have kept
Several seasons without endeavour
And slept.

II

I do not see it
As others do
Nor shall anyone see
What indignity
Is to be suffered by love
Which alone
In the Crucifixion
Scarifies the bone.
A pauper walking to Henstridge
In a white coat,
Four tallies for feathers
And this I hope.
How many miles to Martock?
King-estrich toun
No mind for this kind
But the wind for seven.
This also be it said:
Van Diemen's Land,
Shackles upon the feet
And hand.
No answer from the exception
To any rule.
Each man his children
And a fool.

III

The mind's
An elusive fish
In a deep pond.
Satan are you there?

Swimmingly.

Aller Church

The art, the artifex, and I.
    Let the wind blow softly.
Currents of air over the plain.
    When shall I see England again?
The mouse creeps in the sedge. The fire runs
    Over the stubble against the sun.
This world is not yours. Walk here
    Under the half edge of Sedgemoor.

Envy

Be prudent, comrade, as the wind
Which does not let itself be seen.
    My spleen
Exacerbates your skill. Admire
I must, and cannot quieten desire.

When every promise has been thinned
To nothing, there is still this bourne,
    White scorn
Between my enemies and one
Who would gladly have lied as they have done.

True-lips, and a tumescent tongue
Let no man call virtue. They are
    A bar
To my extravagance, a trip-wire
To my feet, in any courtship.

The bed lies empty, the great dung
Heap unshifted, because if any will
    Or skill
Is required, I am not the man.
Envy kiss-my-arse, only you can.

Summer Green

The voluntary world is far from me
Therefore I came here, where the woods fall down
Pell-mell into the fields. The timber lies
Broken and does not care, the spread leaves hold
Like fingers, air and let it run away.

Good Friday

Christ, on Good Friday,
   I sit and mope.
      Hope
Is out of place, today.
Penance is not my way.

I, who hope little,
   Contrairy, find
      Mind
Today say that it will
Rather than sit still,

Rather than hear thud
   The bumping cross,
      Loss
Echo here, garden mud
Turn up here as blood.

Teach me to repent.
   I will not, I.
      Die
I will, for easement
Only, my will is bent.

Make straight my will, it
   May be if not
      Rotting
In me as mine, fit
Matter for a vain wit.

Nothing is mine, let
   Me know this now.
      How
Why and what, are set
Like dishes before me, not to eat yet.

The Usk

Christ is the language which we speak to God
And also God, so that we speak in truth;
He in us, we in him, speaking
To one another, to him, the City of God.

I

Such a fool as I am you had better ignore
Tongue twist, malevolent, fat mouthed
I have no language but that other one
His the Devil's, no mouse I, creeping out of the cheese
With a peaked cap scanning the distance
Looking for truth.
Words when I have them, come out, the Devil
Encouraging, grinning from the other side of the street
And my tears
Streaming, a blubbered face, when I am not laughing
Where in all this
Is calm, measure,
Exactness
The Lord's peace?

II

Nothing is in my own voice because I have not
Any. Nothing in my own name
Here inscribed on water, nothing but flow
A ripple, outwards. Standing beside the Usk
You flow like truth, river, I will get in

Over me, through me perhaps, river let me be crystalline
As I shall not be, shivering upon the bank.
A swan passed. So is it, the surface, sometimes
Benign like a mirror, but not I passing, the bird.

III

Under the bridge, meet reward, the water
Falling in cascades or worse, you devil, for truthfulness
Is no part of the illusion, the clear sky
Is not yours, the water
Falling not yours
Only the sheep
Munching at the river brim
Perhaps

IV

What I had hoped for, the clear line
Tremulous like water but
Clear also to the stones underneath
Has not come that way, for my truth
Was not public enough, nor perhaps true.
Holy Father, Almighty God
Stop me before I speak

                        – *per Christum.*

V

Lies on my tongue. Get up and bolt the door
For I am coming not to be believed
The messenger of anything I say.
So I am come, stand in the cold tonight
The servant of the grain upon my tongue,
Beware, I am the man, and let me in.

VI

So speech is treasured, for the things it gives
Which I can not have, for I speak too plain
Yet not so plain as to be understood
It is confusion and a madman's tongue.
Where drops the reason, there is no one by.
Torture my mind: and so swim through the night
As envy cannot touch you, or myself
Sleep comes, and let her, warm at my side, like death.
The Holy Spirit and the Holy One
Of Israel be my guide. So among tombs
Truth may be sought, and found, if we rejoice
With Ham and Shem and Japhet in the dark
The ark rolls onward over a wide sea.
Come sleep, come lightning, comes the dove at last.

Saint Anthony

There were no chances and changes about a life
That was, after all, given over to resisting devils.
There were no events after that but
Many imaginary temptations.
A happy life this: beneficent, for
He protected sage martyrs against himself
Fly-blown and fly-proof, a concentration of follies
– Who had started with twenty years in remote Egypt
Of suave girls, silk wrappings, and fast cars.

Mortalia

In the leisurely days which precede my death
There is nothing I shall not regret. Dorset my hills
You have the shapes I have missed, the smile
Of contentment that was never mine.
Nothing but tears is hidden under your soil.

Seeming

What the imagination could only imagine
Is, ah how different from the thing done
Which is only a done thing, fine
To the spectator perhaps, but not to me.

It is somebody else's imagination.
Beauty, are you so?
My heart craves for you. Eaten out, hollow
What is this space for then, and how lived in?

Hollow heart also, you have nothing to live for.
It could not be me, for I am nothing at all.
Are you there, certainty, behind that beauty?
Are you there, or what?

Morpheus

Naked people
Stepping, under mackintoshes
Through the dim city

The elect, the dead
The indifferent, head on
Into the underground. Morpheus.

What underneath? Proserpine dances
Exactly with legs, arms curled
About her head like a duster

There are green fields, below
Memory cannot reach, trees discover
Or old tales render probable.

It was a snake, some say
Bit at her ankle. So
I would myself.

It was thorn
Entangled her. I
Could wind about her.

It was the wind
Caught and advanced her flying
Hair. It was tears distresses

Of my hope and finding
Destroyed, unkindly, what hope there was.
That was my failure.

So against the crowd, perfect
I stand like a lamp-post, they flow past me
Stoney eyes, mine or theirs.

In the Great World

In the great world where beauty is
A rarity, ambition is
As common as the dust we eat.
And who, I ask myself, are you?
You are the child against the wall
The fierce nun's ruler did not hit.
You are the younger sister, strong
Because the house took care of you.
You are the virgin with a smile
And beauty as your best excuse,
The tatty girl protected by
The aura of the well-to-do;
The office wonder who performed
The gagne-pain of a city lout –
What is so wonderful in this?
The mind is what the eye can see;
The only freedom is to give.

In Spring-time

Another time, this way the primrose,
I lost my way before my age was full
In a deep valley. And the cleft said nothing
But perhaps, I am limestone, grey
Lichen upon me, grey.

No voice. Came summer yet no voice. Came once
The lark, the plover and the hare in March.
Almost the wind is speech.

What turns I took and then the cock-crow came
Not once but many times.

Sumptuary Laws

Still with the hope of being understood,
Of understanding myself
Or understanding someone else,
I engaged in restless action.
It was no good.
First because
It had no issue, secondly because
If it could have had, I would no longer care.
The problems of age are semblant, one thing
Like another, no thing identical,
The things having been seen, the passions
Expended in better times by a better man.
So outwardly and above
We turn, gracious and empty
The old hypocrites, counting the stars,
Loving the children, counting them like money.
Thanking what stars we have that the wrong turnings
Have all been taken, a life of comfort
Assured, as it may be, to the last deception
I could call this life respectable but
I must call it mine, which is worse.

Somerton Moor

I

You are unusual, but the touch
Of innocence may sear a mind.
I know who say so, for I am
The prisoner of a loving ghost

O death, come quickly, for the fiend
Crosses the marshes with my tears.

II

Under the peat, dark mystery of earth,
Fire of the hearth, enchanter of my heart
The smoke that rises is a sacrifice
The peat moves over in its sodden sleep

And I, who should have touched her with my wand
Let her evade beneath the burning turf
And now through smoke and bitterness I speak
Words she would recognise and no one else
And she can no more hear than oyster-ears.

III

Last speech. Accustomed as I am to speech
And she to silence, excellence is hard
For nothing that is facile can be heard
And nothing hard can be endured for long.
So sleep. Pass out between the willow-boughs
Out of my dream into the cool of death.
There, where the resurrection that you hope,
Though tardy, comes at last
The instrument I carry is untuned.

Ha! Vieillesse

Good-bye then love, good-bye holiness
In which at one time I put my trust
One of you disappointed me and one I could not attain
I begin to hobble as I grow old.

In insula Avalonia

I

Huge bodies driven on the shore by sleep
The mountain-woman rocks might fall upon
And in the cavity the heaped-up man.

Sleep on the island like a witty zone
Seas break about it, frolicking like youth
But in the mists are eyes, not dancers, found.

Hurt is the shepherd on the inland hill
He has a cot, a staff and certain sheep
Stones are his bed, his tables and his bread.

This is not where the sirens were, I think
But somewhere, over there, the next approach
Behind that other island in the mist.

That was the song, beyond the linnet-call
At the cliff's edge, below the plunging gull
The fish it found, the enemy or Christ.

II

Counting up all the ways I have been a fool,
In the long night, although the convent clock
Winds several hours around Medusa's locks,

Geryon and Chrysaor are with me now
– Sure there was bad blood in that family –
And yet the worst of all was done by love.

The fool: but not the bow and naked babe
But top-coat murderers with sullen looks
And yet Medusa was a temple harlot.

Under the river-bank a seeping wind
Ripples the bubbles from a passing fish
No colder memory than gloomy Dis.

Look, for you must, upon the fine appearance,
The creature had it and is formless dead.
Now come no nearer than to straws in glass.

III

Dark wind, dark wind that makes the river black
– Two swans upon it are serpent's eyes –
Wind through the meadows as you twist your heart.

Twisted are trees, especially this oak
Which stands with all its leaves throughout the year;
There is no Autumn for its golden boughs

But Winter always and the lowering sky
That hangs its blanket lower than the earth
Which we are under in this Advent-tide.

Not even ghosts. The banks are desolate
With shallow snow between the matted grass
Home of the dead but there is no one here.

What is a church-bell in this empty time?
The geese come honking in a careless skein
Sliding between the mort plain and the sky.

What augury? Or is there any such?
They pass over the oak and leave me there
Not even choosing, by the serpent's head.

IV

O there are summer riders
On the plain
in file or two by two

It is a dream

For Winter, one by one, is wringing us
The withers, one, and scrotum-tight the other

Yet I am here
Looking down on the plain, my elbow on
The sill

From which I night by night and day by day
Watch
for the moon pours swimmingly

Upon this field, this stream
That feeds my sleep.

Be night
Be young
The morning half begun
Palls on the waiting mind and makes it scream

O Minnich, Minnich

Who is the lady there by Arthur's lake?
None is. A willow and a tuft of grass
But over bones it broods, as over mine
Somewhere
Except
nowhere

Bind up your temples and begone from here
No need to answer. What is there to fear?

Only the wind that soughs, and soughs, and soughs.
Some say it does, and others contradict
Some say sleep strengthens, others that it kills

This music comes
                    from Wendover I think
Where meaning is at least, there, sure, am I.

V

Out in the sunlight there I am afraid
For dark depends upon the nascent mind
The light, the envy and the world at large

A field for flood, and fish and such-like deer
The willows standing in between the pools
Great siege this morning, in the morning-time

The water rustles like a turning page
Write then who will, but write upon the stream
Which passes nonchalantly through the hedge

No word of mine will ever reach the sea
For mine and words are clean contrary things
Stop here for envy, go there for your love

For love of persons are the passing geese
Swans on the flood, the dopping water-fowl
The cloud that cumbers while the sky is blue.

Awful at nights, the mind is blue today
Enlarged without a purpose like a lake
For purpose pricks the bubble of our thoughts.

Climb back to sleep, the savage in that mine
Picks with his teeth and leaves his skull to dry
O skull and cross-bones on the earthen floor

My earth, my water, my redundant trees
Breaking the surface like a stitch in skin.
No word but weather, let me be like that.

VI

A ruminant in darkness. So am I
Between the skin and half a hope of hell
Tell me till morning where the savage stops.

His eyes beside the fire. The burning peat
Is quiet, quiet, quiet till it shrieks
Not what the hammer was but what it says

The eyes on Thursday and the mind that waits
For sabbaths of intent but does no thing
Not seeking, waiting for a peaceful end

What wind is in the trees? What water laps
Extravagantly round the seeping hedge?
A house on sticks, where several yearned before

The skin, the furze, the movement into sleep
The watery lids beside the river bank
Mirrors of emptiness, O what way in?

VII

A mine of mind, descend who can that way
As down a staircase to the inner ring
Where figures are at liberty, and play

A plain of ghosts, among the rest a girl
(And none had touched her, though the serpent's teeth
Met in her heel below the flying skirt)

She gathered flowers, exacting from their grace
An outward parallel for grace of skin,
Petals for fingers, petals for arms and legs.

This transient surface is the thing I seek
No more, perhaps, than scale upon the eyes
Do not walk with her, winds are blown that way.

A storm of leaves and all may disappear
And yet below the circle of my mind
Playing in spring-time there is Proserpine.

But I am rather Cerberus than Dis
Neither receive nor yet pursue this child
Nor am I Orpheus who could bring her back.

I stand and roar and only shake my chain
The river passes and gives others sleep
I am the jaws nothing will pass between.

VIII

The mind beyond the reach of human time
Mine or another's, let me now perceive
Time has turned sour upon the earth for me

A little earth, walking upon the earth
A molehill, Mother, on your credent slopes
But moving, time against me, everywhere

This is the lump out of which I was made
The hands, the feet, the brain no less is mud
What does not crumble must remain in shape

The shape of man, but moles are better off
Boring the hill-side like a nit in cheese
They asked for blindness, that is what they have

But I for light, for sleep, for anything
Moving my hands across the surfaced world
Exacerbate in darkness, though alive

I never came from any natural thing
To take this shape which is not mine at all
Yet I am I am I and nothing more

If any took this shape I took this shape
Yet taking what I did not ask to have
And being nothing till I took this shape

The shape of shafts of light and falling suns
Meteors incarcerate in balls of mud
A cracked example of a better kind

Admit you came because you could not know
Walk in the garden as you did one day
And if you cannot flatter, answer back.

IX

Some seek examples in the world of sense
They slide across the retina like dreams
Yet are objective in the world of deeps

Which swimmers may attempt, that move all ways
Across the current, from the pebbly floor
Up to the surface where the morning breaks

If any capture what the water-weed
Holds brightly like a bubble on its stem
Or what may disappear in lengthening dark

Volumes of sleep will turn the swimmer's arm
His leg will gently bump the feathered rock
Gulls cry above, sleep has no place for them

A call, a cry, a murder in the street
Is sign of others lonely as yourself
The Lord have mercy, others may as well.

X

I do not know and cannot know indeed
And do not want a word to tell me so
A sentence is construction more than I.

I feel, I vomit. I am left to earth
To trample and be trampled, in my turn
But always rotting from the day I came

Thy kingdom come. And could I pray indeed
I would be höhnisch and destroy the world
This is not what is meant and nor am I.

So let my silence fasten on a rock
Be lichen, that is plenty, for my mind
And not be where I was. Where is he? Gone

The empty space is better than himself
But best of all when, certain winters past,
No one says: There he was, I knew him well.

*Dialogue of the Soul and God,
or of Psyche with Cupid*

I
Love, hear me come
I rustle up the stairs and am with God
Come over me
You winged ecstatic stranger in my bed

I come
Psyche lie in the dawn
And do not turn your head
I may be Christ

I lie
Covered in flowers
Nature's fair canopy, and dream
So must it be

I wing
Across an azure main, far out
The sea is mine
White gulls

Though I lie still, I fly
With you, against the cloud
It cannot be
Yet I am you I know

Ah, take no candle dear
To spoil your dream
I am the edge of things
And will be gone

Will you not love
The resting limbs in bed?
Not I, my dear, the wind
The kami-kaze I.

II
Lord Wind
I am your patience so I am not I

If you were you
I would dissolve
So not in peace

I, I
The entropy of every beast
Sigh out your wind

Dissolve
Be less than nothing now
I hawk

You kestrel on the wing
What wind
Can hold you now?

My police
Is in my eye

My current flows away
Less than the wind

Hawk not

Not I

Descending

I

I rise upon the wind

I, I?

III
No mind has spoken yet

Nor will
You catch-cheat, catch-care face
You foot

I foot
Wandering upon the ground

You badger-track, you walk

Split eye
Half looking up, half down
What shall I do?

Do nothing more, but sleep
Geschwind

IV
This is the end
Of all I ever made

You make?
The makeless maker is the make of you

Down eyes

Down head
And do you feel my foot across the nape?

My hair
Mops up your feet as Mary Magdalen's did

Slut, I am there.

In Arles

The bitterness is covered but not buried
A little light earth, that is all
The centuries will not discover, nor the footfall
Be light upon me.

Lying there, in the light, unable to speak
No penny upon my lips
To send me thither to the Tartarus of Time.
Have mercy, Lord.

My eyes open, with eyelids pulled apart
I stand here before time
Have mercy goddesses, standing in the long avenues.
Death is in your keeping.

The bright eye, let me never be parted from it.
I hear the drum now
I hear the whistle, there are pipes in this shrubbery
And the owl is near.

Pallas Athene, my dear
Look kindly upon my plain endeavours.
Light spins over the Camargue.
Evening is here.

Christ of the mass-priests, farewell, yet in the shadows
These have my tears
A crucifixion, a crucifixion, and the dogs howl
Nearer than death.

My tears, and my Saviour, this stone
The candle to light upon him
Eyes in the dark, the hidden light
And Pallas Athene is gone.

Yet she stands there at the entrance, smiling
The horses thunder by
– Is that money with which I cross her palm? –
I will come directly.

Martigues

I
Myrtle, roses and thyme
And the rose laurel:
I too have something that I wish to forget
There, where the woodland path
Passes into the concrete
And my tears are for a master.
At the gate I picked a leaf of laurel and said:
Dante
Wore these pointed leaves.
Here, in the bitter south,
A madman, between gaolers.
Whisper it to the myrtles we may, crushing the past
In our tingling fingers,
Or picking the thyme
But the rose laurel

It is all I have, the bitten past,
Not all I came to.
Speeches were made and names taken, the heart
Burst out of his side.
No love like the unspoken
Ferocity, the bitter tears, a battle
Standing instead with brimming eyes
Looking out over the *étang*
The poverty of a few fish
And a garden of roses.

I too have something that I wish to forget.
Myrtle and roses, the same.
Controversy among apes is no custom
And my limbs fell hard
Against the rail of the scuttled ship. You may cup your eyeballs
For ordinary uses now.
My faith
Sprang into the air with indignation.

II

At the corner of the streets
The fishermen stand in groups
With brown faces: they have them from the Moors
And the wind blowing across the *étang*.

In the garden
Pierre, or perhaps Adam.
I shake him by the hand, brown also,
A fisherman's face, gardener's rather.
Help us with the language of saints.
Adam spoke
Softly, and in the old *patois*,
Knowing no other.
Myrtle, roses and thyme
And the rose laurel
Never to be let go.
I took him by the hand
Old friend
Whom I have never seen
Your ghost is my beginning, I have tears
For what is here forgotten
And in the winter of my age my hand
Cut the air with scimitars.

III

Roses and thyme
But leave the myrtle, leave the myrtle here
Roses and thyme
Fed on a garden where I made my home
And southward facing over the *étang*.

In Somerset I crumble up the soil
And linger on a terrace looking south
So minds have ears no voices
They have eyes
Which look upon the land and do no harm
But avarice is cupid in this game.
Yet love came after all, olive and rush,
The tart wine held under the cupping hand.
One taste of death. Good-night to all this lake.
The olives in the garden after all
Eat up the man and put him under ground
How should he turn his hand?

IV

Pallas Athene, wisdom in all this,
Mistress of olives and the curling prow
Let not your lids drop on this falling earth.
Set enmities at rest or let there be
Sufficient enmity to stir up love
And bring the sword before you bring smooth tongues,
Harsh enmities are best
And Judas put his silver in the ground.

V

Night falls, perhaps, upon my wide *étang*,
Joseph of Arimethea riding home.
The Saintes Maries
Await another pilgrim at this time
But now must sleep. And did he sleep or wake
Who walked upon this terrace in his dream?
The Saintes Maries put out their lights at last
And Joseph's ship touches a barren stone.

VI

He took a flower
And gave it in a morning without hope.
Hand down the rose
Hand down the myrtle, stuff the air with thyme.

There in the garden where it all began
Seek nothing for yourself. Seek nothing more
Than time will offer to dishonesty
And patience and the like. Silence at last
And Abraham's voice seeps through the air.
David is King. And then the dragons come
The thud of horses over the Camargue,
But silence first. The rose,
Myrtle crushed in the hand
And the rose laurel.

Anchises

Saint-Rémy

I should have descended, perhaps
The hill
On a May morning
Ma bello is it I can please you?
That can never be.
You have pleased, you have pleased, all the long living
Not a tear from me, I wipe it, in telling
Et les aieuls, grandfathers, grandmothers,
Down the street, in procession.

Tears
Are not always there for the danger of having them
Sometimes they pour out
In pleasure over the thin cascade
Down the steps, from the sacred source
There is no pleasure like that of descending
Hand in hand, plucking the rosemary
Plucking the thyme.

Over this effete cavern the sun

Sets
Down the hillside, walking
Rosemary, this time
At the foot of the cavern where the nymphs stood
I did not understand her, not I
The steps descend
There in an underworld, in that water

Black

I intend no evil, come a little nearer, plunge
The water is extremely salt, I did not
Expect this effect
Nor can understand it now.

Once below the stream, what pleasure
What shall be seen
Awash

I came back to the same shore
Wrapt in mist
Here I laid up my boat. It was
Centuries ago, the black prow
Still there in the sand
And the ghosts walking to and fro, my friends

Perhaps

However that may be there is no other
I would find myself beside
The light over these arenas is dead

It was a nice dream
But I do not know its meaning entirely
No truth that is understood is entire
For wondering I go
Into the crypt where St Martha
Obscured herself from me
Won't you lie under the apple tree
With Our Lady of the Pommiers?
No news is best news from those quarters
And yet silence
Cannot tell all there is to tell nor
Knowledge
Be without silence.

Frigolet

Thyme, and cicadas in the grass
The white light of idleness.
Empty as a shin-bone, a hare
Or a bird from anywhere

Alyscamps

Old man of Alyscamps
Aren't they dead enough for you?
You, with your palsied pleasures,
Seeking marrow-bones among the dead?

Cotignac

River, deep as death, deeper, Avernus,
Red water of ox-hide, ox-blood, clouded,
Drawn across these caverns like a taut sheet,
What is down there, under the cliff edge,
Deeper than hell? Village
Lost to all time, under the sick archway,
The lost steps lead there, the life
Stirs like a movement of moss.

If I were to awake in that underworld, whom should I see?
Not Nestor, not Paris,
Not any heroic shadow, long putrescent,
Blown into dust: no woman
Caught my wandering eye last summer
Or any summer gone. The friends of shadows,
The commonplace merchants of ambition,
These are the ones, bragging in the market-place
So vain is all philosophy
My teeth were set on edge by such merchants
Half a caravan back: and when they came
To the high street where the palms set the form
It was eating and drinking who must,
Who laughed loudest, who spat,
While I stood by discreetly.
Worn hours! bitter heart! petty mind below all
No kiss of sun can cure, autumn eyes
Seeking rather between shadows the hurt.

There are gigantic shadows upon the cliff-face
I have seen them scowl and lour over the village.
All villages have them: they are the governors
Living among themselves without passions
Touching our parts. I had lived among them as evil
No man knew better their vain twists,
Admired what he hated most
Or so fell to dreaming of impossibles
Which are only eaten ambition
Knives in the heart, or pure reason.

A handful of almonds, a few grapes
All that the fine fingers could pick
Out of the residue of the world
Was not enough for this termagant.
The fine surface of bodies touched
By the sun and rendered potable
Was not enough for the eye-palimpsest;
The half-eaten moaner must moan.
What cages for tigers, whips for scorpions or other
Replicas of effete damnation
Had been prepared, must find a place
Within the cataclysm of each mind.
Mine was none of the stablest, I felt,
Looking over the impeccable scene,
The cicada chipping the hillside.

Sillans-la-Cascade

Water falling over these rocks
Like tears
Not for myself, but for another.
Lovely hair, cascading over a brow
Troubled now. I saw her in sleep
So touching and so betrayed.
There is no enemy but the hater.
Once passed, once gone
There is no meeting but in Acheron
Where the full-fledged ghosts wait underneath

And the rock falls
Sisyphus.

What mind from under the dragon's tooth
Sprang in these places, tightened
Between rocks, fastening with chains
The innocent contender, the wise owl
Hoots from the barn.
It is morning under a steel sky,
The horses running;
A splinter of bones and a crucifixion
Against the sky.

Do not ask why I came to this place
To find
What I am better without,
Old memories, sudden as images
On the castle wall,
Armour and hard words.

This is the hour when my bones too
Are ground to powder;
The marrow snivels on to the path
And I am nowhere,
In the pool
Where the cascade falls and Acheron
Opens its gates.
I saw nothing of that in my book
But the mind
Returns to it and it does not leave me.

Entrecasteaux

Entrecasteaux has hatreds
As other cities have loves
So had I but the teeth of the Sibyl

The juniper is bitter and the holm-oak is persistent
The juniper is masked and the holm-oak is hooded
Spring comes down the mountain

The juniper is abundant and the pine bobs before it
Atys your tree upon Mother Ida

Entrecasteaux has hatreds
As other cities have loves
So had I but the teeth of the Sibyl

Spring comes down the mountain to the narrow ravine
Twist your waters, avenging river

Entrecasteaux has houses
With rooms for intrigue and murder
But above all for persistent voices.

The Quantocks

Sheep under the beeches: the old dykes
Reflective over centuries, the sheep
Stationary over escaped time.
My nails are ground by biting,
There is no remembrance
Does not taste like aloes.

The Clouds

Nothing, nothing came out of the dark evening.
First the river came, it was not in that.
Then I noticed the sun, falling over the hay-fields,
Behind mist – or cloud was it? – an obscurity –
Plunge westwards.

Fell evening dragon, Tarasque,
Coming out of yourself, Phoenix,
Self-burning corn, smoke under your thatches:
No mean day must follow.

The nightingales are asleep.

Gardening

What night, corrupt, as this must be, with dreams
Gathers around this age and finds me now
Here in this garden, not in Eden, no
Another garden and another time

But there is neither slope nor sun can make
Amends for what I missed under your hands.
Old fool. Reproaches I could buy for nothing
In any market-place. How can I turn
This ageing sorrow to a biting wind
To catch me like the tangles of your hair

Gone and imagined? How can I turn
This burrow in the crumbling earth to peace?
Like a worm under stone. Or like a beetle
Making away and does not understand
Its movements, passions, parts.

Seed-time

Pinpoint seed or seedling I cannot tell which
So deep I look past the petalled leaves
Which once swayed for me as all
So deep
There can be no exchanges or crossed winds
Recognition is one-sided, I am invisible
Or should be, husk of myself.

So a bonfire burns and one looks into it
Fallen ash, green houses
Sticks
Charred till they whiten and the winking lights
Move round the bole.

There could be no meeting again on this earth
In any furrow or perhaps anywhere
Seed-time is a tear-drop carrying the eye
Into the interior of the womb, where hope lies
Crouched for its disappointment.

The Evidence

If you had hopes once they have turned to reason
If you had reason it has turned to evidence:
The evidence is against you.

Philo the Magician

They are going mad in there. His head was sloping
As he ran down the corridor
Square lights flashing, aluminium
A tinkle

There was murder done

The running man
Signified myself
But I, crossing cunningly from another direction
Collided with a grinning face, which is not mine ordinarily
But of which the yellow skull could be mine

'For thine is the kingdom'
Pulsated, I expect an orgasm
In the ugly night
Of the power and the glory
They passed like spectres beside my ear
Singing, pulsating
I do not want this dream and I do not want
Any

Who came, in this dream?
It was Philo the Almighty
Magician
Yet the face I saw?

It was like the nightingale
I remember now, in summer.

Divine Poems

1

Work without hope is the best recipe
For a harmless life, if any life can be harmless
That is born of woman and goes back into the slot.
There was one, harmless, who came that way

2

A broken spirit, a contrite heart
Are acceptable, taken together
But the native spirit that I have broken
Does not go with contrition.

3

I can no more be contrite, God
Than I can understand your magnificence
A creeper here, a boaster there
My conscience is under the tarmac.

4

Abjection is also a vice
For there is nothing which could be abject
In nothing, which is what I am
Stamped with the maker's image.

Eastville Park

I sat on a bench in Eastville Park
It was Monday the 28th of October
I am your old intentions she said
And all your old intentions are over.

She stood beside me, I did not see her
Her shadow fell on Eastville Park
Not precise or shapely but spreading outwards
On the tatty grass of Eastville Park.

A swan might buckle its yellow beak
With the black of its eye and the black of its mouth
In a shepherd's crook, or the elms impend
Nothing of this could be said aloud.

I did not then sit on a bench
I was a shadow under a tree
I was a leaf the wind carried
Around the edge of the football game.

No need for any return for I find
Myself where I left myself – in the lurch
There are no trams but I remember them
Wherever I went I came here first.

Marcus Aurelius

I do not want to pour out my heart any more
Like a nightingale bursting or a tap dripping:
Father no more verses on me, Marcus Aurelius
I will be an emperor and think like you.

Quiet, dignified, stretched out under a clothes line
The garden of my soul is open for inspection
As the gardener left it, chaque cheveu à sa place
And if you do not believe me you can comb through my papers
    yourself.

Of course you may not agree with: No hurt because the lips are
    tight.
The psychologists have been too much for you, but that rascal
    Freud
Did nothing but devise his own superficial entanglements
For his readers to trip over, while he smiled.

Old devil of Vienna, moving among the porcelain,
You were the beetle under the ruins of an empire
And where the Habsburgs had protruded their lips
You pinched your nostrils.

If I were a plain man I would do the same,
Dexterous, money-making, conforming to another pattern
Than the one I seek which will cover me entirely:
I hope to be an emperor under my own mausoleum.

Drowning

'With well-made songs, maintains th'alacrity
Of his free mind': or, as in my case, stutters
Eats out his heart at will, maintains friends
In expectation of loving, but does not love:
Twists words
Till they should have meaning, but they have none,
Kisses the earth, muddies his lips, and all this

Does not amount to a paid song, a footfall
Under the Almighty's feet, or a cool hand
Placed where I would place it, on the bare side
Of my shelled mistress, Anadyomene
Rising out of the sea in which I shall drown.

One Evening

There are also bland days; they supervene
On fury and defeat
Open my side, see where the heart is

A smooth skin, traces of cool stone
But marvellous to the hand
What is there, Tertullian?

In my mind the roots quiver
Where will you touch, O root?
Mark this, the land set out.

But my mind is eaten by a strange fish
Chub or tench, stationary in the water
Only the lips moving.

It is

It is extraordinary how old age
Creeps on one
First it is not believed, even noticed
Then one notices symptoms but says nothing:
At the last nothing is what one says.

Perhaps

Perhaps something was said
But now the man is dead
I cannot hear him now
I cannot hear him now
I cannot hear him now

Perhaps he spoke, but if he did
Nobody heard what he said
I cannot hear him now
I cannot hear him now
I cannot hear him now

Do not pretend to listen
It is of no importance
I cannot hear him now
I cannot hear him now
I cannot hear him now

The House

They went into the wall and became no one,
The best person to be, if you ask me
But their retreat could be painful to the bystanders
Who had seen them there and then again they were not,
Only the house with the clock ticking and the meals at regular
    intervals.
There are worse things than becoming a house.

The Garden

Am I not fortunate in my garden?
When I awake in it the trees bow
Sensibly. There is a church tower in the distance,
There are two, underneath the maze of leaves

And at my back bells, over the stone wall
Fall tumbling on my head. Fortunate men
Love home, are not often abroad, sleep
Rather than wake and when they wake, rejoice.

Antres

Shade, shadow less than nothing within my dream,
Less than myself in that you have receded
Within this shell, yet more
In that you have gone further and fared worse, and also because
I pursue you still, and am unpursued
While it is I who am open to every persuasion

Yet within myself
There is no such thing as you are, I miss you
There are caverns you go through like an echoing voice
I am not even an echo
Yet all this is me, for it is not you

I cannot catch at my antres, or you wandering
Nothing therefore
And it is no use representing that as blackness,
Placing sentries, touching upon the walls
Though they drip moistly, suggesting downfall.

Nothing is not pepper or salt, or any taste
Cinnamon, ginger
It does not water the palate nor arrose the smell
Can it imagine, holding within itself
The recession of anybody?

The Corridor

1

Nothing is what I have done
Where I have been
These long years

No such thing
As metaphysical
Escape
There is a safe
Kind of body begins
With the toe
Continuing through
The bones of the foot:
Must I go
Through every damned bone,
Filament, ligament?

2

Yes, a figure like a light at the end of a corridor
Justice heard her voice
And with attention
Scored
Marks on the brightness
The inexpugnable wall

It was Atalanta ran down
Either foot equal, the hands
Flying like butterflies

3

It is not where I want to go
But I have no choice
Past the buildings, along the straight road
My thoughts with me, I do not want to take them

I plod on
The internal way is best, I am concentrated.
Down on my head a lead weight

Under my feet
The pavement
Rising so hard that my feet are splayed.
Smiling from the side-walk is inappropriate
My intent is serious
A small liar
Heading for an immutable destiny
In whatever disguises
I change my suit several times as I walk

There are dragons at some of the cross-roads
Hedged by privet
Dusty and dull and the long red-brick avenue
Will they reach me in time?
There is hardly a fear, I am so protected
The collar of my rain-coat turned up
The walls of the street and of my eyes so firmly blinded.

You could be lost before day break, if it will
Where are the snares
With which you were threatened?
Where are the entanglements
To trammel your feet and make the way less easy?
The very simplicity is deceptive
It is achieved by the rejection of voice
Touch, smell, taste
No music or shape, that is the best way
Say some

A morass of feet
Mine moving the least certainly among them
There is no way to go on
Which foot is mine?
I can no longer tell, I go all ways
At least there is mire, I am in it, there are others
Is this a walk or a rout?

Where are they going? How many feet have they got?
Where is the rest of them, baulking giants
Without any theory to account for them?

I have my theory, which is just this
From here I set out to there I go.

4

If I opened my eyes, what should I see
Any of this?
A crucifixion, with the blood dripping upon me

Or hands down
Picking a flower
Or exacerbating a butterfly
Taking the wings off a beetle?

Glory to God, three figures
Graces perhaps

5

There is no news Homer among the
Rushes, useless to pry, looking
Here and there in case anywhere there should be
Satyrs, leprechauns there is no news
Homer there is no news. I once saw
Homer advancing and peeping into a dustbin

6

I wanted a way out
From this
Neither can I think
Of any
Except

The paradigm
Of the extended body
Lying in furze
Under the sedge
Or twisted
Under effete grasses, dead also

Surely it stirs
Its moment has not yet come

Yet it will
When

Headlong

Out of the earth
Rising like a jaguar springing

Yet it is not like that
Smooth
Foiled

7

What night
Are you bound for?
Is there any?

I cannot answer that question, I am
Not the man who answers

Who are you then?

Not the man who answers
Not? Not
Not for any man
I am not the man who answers any questions.

Do you ask?

I do not ask
I am not the man who asks

Not? Not

I am not the man who asks

Who are you then?
Not the man
Not the man
Not
Not
Not

8

There is a thread I cannot follow it

There is a way
There is no other
Through darkness

Walk then
Long
Through the corridor

That is not a light then, though it is supposed to be
A lake rather
A guttering candle lights up the surface of it

Black light

I have gone through the door

9

I understand oceans, which do not change
In volume and composition, or not very much
Yet the surface changes, following the day's weather
The depth marches up, the superficial element
Bobs underneath more or less

Movement of sea, volume of water
Moving up from the depths, while the surfaces
Fall, losing themselves
Fathoms
Below, but do not sleep there, turning silently
While the great fish swim through them
– There is no seaweed
Below a certain depth, but –
In palaces
Darkness
The outcome of which
Cannot be guessed.
If there were an encounter
Could it be otherwise than of shadows?

10

The darkening shades are the way I go
How could it be otherwise? I come from lugubrious waters
The hunt and prayer of our hearts

11

Dreams are of no value
They move intangibly
Not turning the wheels
Not moving the limbs
Causing no embrace

12

I walk splendidly, and indirectly
Looking where I am not going
Blowing against closed doors, looking into the open ones.
Monsieur est distrait? He is plain distracted
Old hat askew, travelling boots
Travelling nowhere, or the toes pointed
In the direction opposite to movement, or 30°
Or 37°, or 2.5° or some odd
Measure of distraction from reality.
Behind his spectacles the eyes
Entertain improbable speculations
Rolling, rolling
With little half-movements, aspersions
On this or that aspect of reality.
Why will your feet not take the floor
Those large hands
Close over something not the edge of a mirror?
Dreams are of little value
Old hat, perforated head,
Stuffed with dreams
If that were all

But the direction of movement, the skid and skad
Drawing a circle where there should be a square.
The way it is worth going
Is not an easy one, for intellectual persons
Such as I, nauseous perhaps
To the more intelligent.

Out from under the body politic
Walking in twilight, one after another
Yet a conversation
Hurts, it is a string tied round the body

13

Hanging on a tree in the Garden of Eden
Thirteen days and thirteen nights
Give me some drink: hand me a loaf of bread
Down from the tree, I come and get it myself

There are saws and maxims enough

Before I can sing
Anything that I will
There must first be the elision
Of the individual mind,
Closed like a crack of the earth
The earth itself
Is what I now sing, wish to

14

The backward road
Must be under the marshes
Glutinous, harsh
Darker than ever, resistant
Darker than ever, I would go that way but I cannot

It must be darkness, whether forward or backwards
The light has left me
There is not even a marsh taper, a flicker
A deception one moment believed, though the next doubted
There is not even the taste of death if I go forward
For death is endless
Tasteless, it is infinite
The great cloak
Waiting to be put on
And when I walk in it
I should struggle like a caught thing wanting to use the flesh

Convinced for all eternity that I have it
Torn and feathered like a spent bird
Neither believing
Against my unbelief, nor holding solidly
While these tatters, my flesh
Blow away like salt to the edges of the universe
Death is the only costume I put on
It does not disguise me now, it is my own
Sleep I hoped for
Pre-monitor of the resurrection, mother of language
Leaves me now
Yet there is nothing it leaves
Sleep is for flesh
Such as I used to imagine
Not stretched like mine to the edge of the universe
Compacted marvels
There could be speech with, which, where I now am, is not.
It is not silence, which I have also known, for that is the cessation
Of rustling. Where I am now
There are no leaves to stir or cease from stirring

Avert my eyes, I am no longer required
Where the dragons walk, there is certainty
Where the angels
Fling up their trumpets, there is mediocrity
Where peace is
There I would go forward, and not be I
The Incarnation
Came suddenly
In another place, and I no longer stand there

I am on the edge, beyond the touch of reason
As of the flesh
If a word takes me, it is in its flight
From another mouth
It cannot be my ear
Hears

15

The indisputable master of all this,
Old age
Assays no more the gold under his hand
The ways you did not follow matter more
Than those you did
That is why eyes look past
The things you love to those you did not love
The hand is cupped
To catch the silence as it falls between
The chatter that you did not want to hear:
The man who would be off is dead already.

The Lizard

Plant thrift and do not marry
Samphire and throw yourself over a cliff.

Anchises

This is my proper sightlessness,
The invisible pack hunting the visible air.
There are those who exist, but it is not I.
Existent are: bodies, although their existence is
Not proven; tremors
Through the vast air expecting some other thing
Not known, or hopeless; or else hoped for and lost.
One could devise invisibility,
Walking by it as if it were not obligatory
As it is with me, *moi qui n'existe pas*
NON SUM, therefore NON COGITO, although there are shapes
Upon a mind I sometimes take to be mine.
This is not much to show for sixty years
Here by the Latin gate, or where the Baltic
Spreads its white arms over the barren sand.

Do not number me on this seashore
Where the effete light from the north
Floods over the ice-cap. I came from Troy
It was not after she had ended, but before.

Over the Wall

Berlin, May 1975
To C.J. Fox

I

He will go over the tell the king
Or whoever is top dog in that country
How there is feasting here, the wastes are empty
The nine governors sleeping

Not a prophetic sleep, with the lids opening
Upon passion, dreaming of conflict
But the eyes turned inwards so that the whites
Gaze upon the world, and the heart ticks steadily
To the combustion of a strange engine
Not in the heart, more like a bee
Buzzing in the neighbourhood. Lost heart, lost head
There is no reflection under the cool brain
Which thinks only of last night's dominoes,
Glibly at least. Over the wall,
Knives drawn, teeth drawn back,
Swallowing the rattle they make in case the night
Should interpret their wishes.
Here in the west, far west, slumber
While death collects his paces.

I am not warlike but, once the frontiers are falling
Each man must put on his belt, it has been done before
And the whimpering must stop, Death being the kingdom
Of this world.

II

I have seen the doomed city, it was not my own
Love has no city like this, with barred hatreds
All bitterness, all shames. I do not think there is any
Feast to be eaten or long shawls
Trailed in the dust before the fanatic mob
Only quiet people live here, eating their sandwiches
Under the lilac while the boats go by,
Interminable imitation of reality
Which is not to be had, and should the frost fall
Should the eagle turn its head
The city of too many desperate adventures
I have seen them all, or so it seems, the Uhlans . . .
And now from the steppes
It is as if the Sarmatian horsemen came back,
Yet they do not stir, or make themselves visible . . .
One street I remember
There is no majesty in its lost endeavours
Speak to me no more, I have heard only
The marching men.
Sleep comes to those who deserve
Funerals under the chipped archways.

III

I do not think this is the end of the story
There are battalions enough behind the wall.
The tall policeman bent over me like the priest
Of an evil religion, as if I were the elements
And he the emissary who was empowered to transform me.
That was not the same
Dream-ridden solitude I had known before
Where a flame climbed the walls there was no one by.

IV

I know only aspen, beech, oak
But here on these wastes the turtle
Sang among the sands, sitting upon a pine-tree
No man has meditated this regress
Yet the afternoon sun falls upon faces
Less tame than tigers.

Langport

The elder tree grows by the rhine
White elder, red elder
The elder tree grows by the rhine
Black elder, oh!
I walked this way in a shower of rain
Nothing is dry when I walk here again
Tears drenched my eyes oh!
Ham-stone fritters and gables of play
The sun is out with the moon today
Ten fine muskets out in a line
Nine of them twisted down in the rhine
Ten twisted elbows there in the rhine
Ten wrenched shoulders there in the rhine
Ten humped bodies down in the rhine
Red elder oh! black elder oh! white elder!

An Elm withered by the Dutch Elm Disease

A score of rooks on a withered tree
What news from Barbary?
A score of rooks on a withered tree
Tartary hordes oh!
Look, is that a man in the hedge?
Is that a rifle? Who are the others?
They cannot all have come down from the hill.
Or did they? And why? Will they scare the rooks?
They come too quietly. Why do they stand?
They have advanced to the edge of the land
They are walking now: and the heron will rise
And the rooks will clamour against the skies.
There will be shots, but the bastinado
Is not intended to beat up the partridge.
Trees wither oh! elms wither oh!
Trees wither!

The Noyade

This is not a satire, nor indeed an invention of any kind. The Fifth Edition of the Dictionnaire de l'Académie Française, *published in 1813, has a supplement containing the new words which had come into use since the Revolution, with new senses for some old words.*

The vocabulary of the Revolution, it seems,
Was much the same as the one we use at present,
   Which shows that in liberating the human spirit
   The *grands ancêtres* provided amusement for centuries.

Administration centrale is one of these,
As also the *administrations intermédiaires*
   With the *administrateurs* and the *adjoints*
   Engaged in the new administrative employments.

A also contains the useful word *amendement*
In the sense of a 'modification proposed to a draft
   Of a law or decree to render it more precise';
   Why else should anyone propose an amendment?

There is also *anglomane* and *anglomanie*,
Which sounds odd now, but England was then the exemplar
   Of an imagined liberty which attracted the writers
   Who, then as now, wrote faster than they understood.

Aristocrate – it was nothing to do with aristocracy;
But 'the name given to the partisans of the old régime'
   – A kind of lying which has been improved on since:
   Think a moment and you will remember our words.

In A I might also mention *arrestation*,
'The act of arresting a person', much practised by citizens
   Who regarded the appellation 'subject' as odious
   And declined to pronounce it, in their political chatter.

B was for *barrières* 'placed upon the frontiers,
With offices designed for the collection of taxes'
   Though one knows that, in fact, the barriers had other uses:
   There was no more going abroad without a passport.

Bureau central, bureaucratic, bureaucratique
Place, function and qualification are now universal;
  It was, after all, for mankind in its generality
  That the Revolution was made, not for those who inhabited

A mere particular village, town, city or country.
C: and observe the history of *carmagnole*,
  'The name at first of a dance, and then a shirt,
  Afterwards of the soldiers who wore that uniform':

Finally – because a soldier is only a soldier
When he is used by somebody, *carmagnole* achieved a new dignity
  As 'the designation of a certain kind of report
  Treasured in the bosom of the National Assembly'.

I say nothing of *centimètre* and *centralisation*,
Citoyen, civisme – 'the zeal which inspires the citizen' –
  Or *carte de sûreté* – something for paid-up members –
  Or *club, conscrit*, or *conscription militaire*.

O Liberation! those were inventive days.
Contre-révolution – but better have nothing to do with it.
  Démocrate, démocratie – 'is employed at present
  In the sense of attachment to the popular cause'.

Département, for an administrative area
Bearing no relation to the place people live in;
  Déporter, 'a revival of the old Roman banishment'
  You were lucky if you got out: *détention*, imprisonment.

I pass over E – though it covers new kinds of *écoles* –
To arrive at F, and the *fonctionnaire public*;
  Fournée, once the word for a batch of loaves,
  Becomes a cartload of people condemned to the guillotine.

G is for *garnisaire*, 'a man put in garrison
With taxpayers who have got behind with their taxes';
  Grand-juge-militaire, 'in each arrondissement';
  Also for *guillotine*, 'perfected by a doctor

To cut off heads by a mechanical operation'.
Homme de loi – H – is the name given to the *légiste*
  'Instructed in the most modern jurisprudence'.
  Indemnité, 'the pay of members of parliament'.

I pass over K, for *kilolitres* of blood,
To get to L, for hanging on lamp-posts or *lanternes*
  – Which explains how *liberté* acquired its new meaning
  Of 'doing whatever does no harm to others'.

M, the *majorité*, still of major importance;
Maison d'arrêt, a place of arrest or *détention*;
  Masse, 'collectively, all together, especially
  To go *en masse*, with the crowd, as in an assembly'.

Neutralisation – of treaties, so 'only provisional'
– Unlike the fate of those who suffered in *noyades*,
  Which is pushing a boatload of unpopular people
  To the middle of a river, after making suitable plug-holes.

O, *organiser*, in the sense of 'organising
All the interior movements of any body';
  Passer à l'ordre du jour, as in an assembly,
  To avoid the discussion of anything too awkward.

P is the *Panthéon français*, designed for the cinders
Of those who are favourable to the Revolution;
  Permanence, in the sense that a public assembly
  May be *en permanence*, and never stop talking.

Préhension, for the seizing of any commodity
Which has been made the subject of price regulation;
  And *propagande, propagandiste*, a body or person
  Charged to promote the most acceptable principles.

Q – a *Quiétiste*, used to designate persons
Who do not join in the fun of the Revolution;
  And a *question préalable* is simply the Question
  Of whether a Question had better not be discussed.

For R we have *radiation*, the rubbing out
Of the names of people you are advised to think no more of;
　Réfractaire, for those who have proved refractory
　And therefore must be excluded from their functions.

Réquisition, 'not only used of commodities
But of young men who are needed for military service'.
　S for *septembrisade*, a general massacre,
　And the verb *septembriser* – 'she was septembred'.

Souverain – 'the universal collection of citizens'
– Except the *suspects*, suspected of being indifferent;
　Which brings us to T and to Terror,
　Terroriste, terrorisme, in the end thought slightly excessive.

Travailler is working, but not in the sense of producing
Anything more substantial than disaffection
　'In favour of a faction'; and T is also *tyrannicide*
　– Only be careful that you name the right tyrant.

The alphabet is exhausted with U and V;
Urgence, 'the pressing need for a resolution',
　– A *résolution urgente*, there are no others.
　V, *vandalisme*, 'destroying the arts and sciences'.

V has a final fling with *vocifération*,
'A clamorous way of proceeding in assemblies';
　And *visites deomicilaires* – you can guess who visits.
　The man they are looking for might have written this.

Swimming the Horses
To Pippa and David

Swimming the horses at Appleby in Westmorland
– Or Cumbria as they now call it, God damn their eyes.
The rest of the verses *desunt*: they were meant to say
Damn all politicians and bureaucrats
Who cannot make fires with uncertain materials.

They imagine that their voices will be heard above
The ripple of rivers and the song of cuckoos –
Which they will not be, or not for long
If they continue with their inordinate charges
To feed reputatious mouths, or none at all
And think that generations of mud-eaters
Can be stamped out to serve a committee slicker
– As they can indeed, but eaten by a dust
That will soon settle over the whole of England.
Those who kick their ancestors in the teeth
Prosper for a time, but in adversity,
Which soon comes, there is a change.

Drought

The sun has risen over the parched plain
Where the water was, gold drops
Fall, thicker than hay-seeds through the light
Golden the floor on which the light pours
Golden the sky beyond the dark hills.
The Golden Age has come back, with metallic hand
To touch the drought, and spring is senile.

The Spider

Carry, tarantula, into your house in the shade
This iota of meaning: that man's dream
Fled as I twanged the wire and let him go
It is with me he would have disappeared.

The End

I shall never hear the angelic choir
Sing, as it assuredly does, I shall walk in hell
Among tinkers and tailors and other riff-raff.
Another damnation for imagining myself among those
Whose fornications came as easy as winking
And whose pilferings of other people
Were a social bounty which did not stop at themselves.
I knew early what there was to be known about me
Only lacked courage, fortitude, *élan*
And so descended into a consuming whirlpool
Round and round, here I am at the last gurgle.

Virtue

Virtue instead of failure, a fine choice,
Virtue is its own damnation. I, who see man
In his external shape, acting and bowing,
Take no account of his inner movements
Which are lies only, must admit
Myself virtuous although my heart is a sink
Where ambition swills round with lost lust
And even the last words are spoken with envy.

Sunshine and Rain

Each day is so brief, a tiny spasm
Of light between dark. It is falling now
Having shone brightly between darks.
How is it? Once the days were long
Nights were unseen, unless in a flash of terror.
But all is night now, where I move
What I taste smells of dark. To my lips I take
A mushroom falling to powder, an orange agaric
Unnatural as nature has now become
Shining there in the dark, between sunshine and rain.

The Weather

The weather is most noticeable, for what else
Should I notice, I who have become wropped
In my own silence, no word saying anything
Although I speak it? Others' words come gently,
Like breezes, they are of uncertain origin
They come round a bush with surprise, through the willows,
A heron carries them. If there were any speech
It would be of roses, blackberries trailing
Over the effete comfrey. Spoiled is the world
Spoiled, autumn says, and so say I.
Neat words then, better than none at all,
Talking of nothing while night falls.

The Inscription

It says that my work is done. Why do I wait
Here on this threshold?

Are there any more words to say? I do not think so.
Those I had did not reach the things I had.
Now on this threshold where I wait for death
To invite me in, I cannot remember my needs.
There are no beggars now, it is absurd for an old man
To stand suppliant even before his memories.
Why imagine what you cannot encompass?
It was not my need, I have none
But the supposed voice of the incorrigible Adam
Who knew Lilith in deep sterility and begot on Eve
Pro-figures of his departed desires
On which the world was built. It bursts out
In thunder and lightning in the following of Adam
And still lours over the horizon. I am not flesh
More than in his dream, the following of Adam
Enacting perilously before my eyes
What I have a part in, though I stand from it
Distant, above two hundred paces, a spectator,

Seeing what I am not and cannot touch,
Being what I want and cannot be.
O gateway! Downwards, I pour myself a libation
Dis manibus.

It is a rich country and I am in it. Every rat
Peeps from his cellar, every cat extends
His flattened body under the hoisted fur.
Leave me alone in this street. The houses topple

It broke through. It was not death that it came to.
Death is the surrounding country. In this city
Other manners prevail.

                              Who are they, my comrades?
Alive or dead, whatever I am myself.

This city I revisited on a day
The ghosts were paler, I had seen them all before
But less perfect, their eyes less direct. It was evening
Before, with the dusk hiding them, now it was morning.
Each face shone in its light, waxy, corrected,
Hair parted more than normally straight.
What eyes were those? The eyes of the dead or the living?
Did they see? If so, was it me they saw?
Why look past me as if I were not there?
Were they looking at anything? Could they see one another?
It is a strange city which has no citizens
And yet it seemed that these did not belong
I saw no couple clutching, heard no timbre
Of affection in any voice. There were no words,
At least they had not the intonation of language.
There are three numbers which, if I can remember them
Seemed significant. There was a prize Almighty
Sitting at the end of the street like a statue of Baal,
Hooting through the wind-pipes. Perhaps this was the one
Behind whom struggle the still sensible dead
Like a basket of serpents. Down the street came marching
Four-square, evocative, echoing, like armed soldiers
The damned dreamers exercised without sexes.
Huzzas from the windows, but the spectators listless.

I stopped by the bridge and watched the procession pass
They walked into the air or out of the gate:
I was for a darker dream. Under the river
Into which he fell, through the surface, black sinews
Closing over his head.

                        Not formed
Nothing but darkness, the hell
Of a lack of expectancy, the river
Itself gone, not even an underground flow,
Nothing from a to b, no a or b,
No confinement or even location.

Ulysses

Ulysses in your boat
In the curved waters where the eddies are
As the stream turns

                        an old dressing-gown
Swirling in the water
                        round and round
Where is Sackcloth?
                        drowned drowned drowned.
Out from the river-mouth
                        into the sea
Ulysses, traveller, glides on top

Out on the incalculable sea, new stories
Ringing in his ears, he has made them up,
Towards the Pillars
Standing at the edge of the desolate sea
Or so they think
Edges beyond edges

What fell
Over the bridge, into the river, is here before them
A ghost
Laughing in the mists beyond the Pillars of Hercules

(I have no desire to continue this)
Beyond the Pillars

I want to know which way they went
Which way they were delivered
One pole toppled over, the sky
Full of stars, showering the boat fore.
Aft, like a wake, the bubbles receded
That sky dying out

Having departed from Circe
In a small boat with a few educated companions
Who understood that subtraction
And did not want mercy, they were too advanced for it

Peace now, under the wind
Under the keel the barnacle
Considers

Baffled like a ghost tied to the mast, unwillingly
I went from Circe
Torn by the wind, fastened by recollection
Over the peak
Of one wave falling into the trough of another
I had come over vast times as well as waters
Africa on one side, Spain on the other
I do not remember when I drifted through
Into the Atlantic drain

It does not matter how the dice fell, here on shipboard
She runs south homing on the mountain of purgatory.
It is the whirlpool. The wind came from the mountain
Like a whiplash. The boat gurgled and fell

A curl of smoke
Rose from the conical mountain against a blue
Paler than light.

Sea-fall

Amiable world
Why have you been so little to my liking?

No touch is best
No horror

                    Against the world
I had taken arms, and lost. They were not the arms
Of charity, than which there are no others
Prevail. I stumbled, walked and stumbled
And now I am sorry for what I did not do

Now it I am the enemy of myself
It is because love failed, my own.
Temper the wind to the giants, the performers
Have more need perhaps. Yet I
Am only need. It is myself
Which I have denied, and should, yet
Without whom, what am I? Nothing.

Tolerate nothing, it is extravagant
To hope. So the wind changes
Nor' nor' east, nor' nor' west.
Gone
Over the headland the gull
Drifts

Wind, water, cliff, the last sight of
Land.

The Turn-down

1

It is idiotic to pretend to
Any particular knowledge of anything
As, the making of soup, writing of poems,
Things which succeed sometimes, and sometimes not.
Any certainty in the matter of future
Or even past events, is an imbecility
– Not exactly that, for the imbecile moment
Is that of retraction from a single hypothesis
In order to take up position with another,
Or that of the return journey which will probably hit
Not the setting-out point but another mark,
A mad pendulum swaying, not to and fro
But this way and that, sideways, all ways.
There is no position which can be called Is,
The best names, therefore, are those which assert nothing,
Not, as abstractions do, comport a theory.
So the names of objects, stone, tree-trunk, branch,
Sky if you will, cloud, go far enough.

2

Action is not always murder, though murder
Is the fruit of action, the sequelae
In more or less, of the once decided
Apposition of cheek to wind or resolution to independence,
A dangerous, however small, movement of the mind
Towards the non-acceptance of what is acceptable.
No resolution is best, it is not needed
Where the balance is perfect, the rays fall
Equally.

3

I did not have what I wanted, when I wanted it
And now what I want is to want nothing more,
A form of death, but not a super-abundance.
Holà there servants, bring me a pot of nothing,
Extinction is in the cup, and I will drain it.

4

No further from, or to, is the plain decision
Of the do-nothing, say-nothing, waiting for everything
– The last thing that is likely to appear, if you ask me
But even you would be wiser than to do that.

5

Nothing to look back on, for everything has succeeded
A *miracle*, with the exception of myself.
That is to say each thing has been played out
To its bitterest end, nothing is left unfinished
To be regretted, continued or re-commenced.

The Well

Grave speech, but it is not my will
Not my words, as I speak them ordinarily
The speech that I wanted is not the speech that I have

Who spoke it? I
Waited by the side of a well
Not for any master, not for a frog to jump
It was mere distraction. The good names,
When they come, come softly. Charity
Is not in my heart, nor love
Even of spiders. There is no miraculous intrusion
No sound of voices, only the pen automatically
Doing what the body tells it, the silent one
Who never spoke by any issue of consciousness
Nor can plan its actions

There are many lives but only one dream
To which does the body belong? The many lives
I alone have lived, and do live, simultaneously
Not living but acting, being them without consciousness.
Can a voice come from that? Or from the dream,
Somatic perhaps, which the iron touches now

There are more kings than emperors, we
Are numerous enough, who are neither. The twitching hand,
Twitching mind may be subject, yes
Where it is to be read and
Silence becomes shapes.

Simois

Well I remember that dark night in Troy
To whom was the moon friendly?

The Simois flows
Into the green

It is another world, thin
As paper
Cattle
Painted upon it, horses
Raising themselves

I want only to die
No other
Stands over against me now

Caught in the same vice
Screwed
Under the same press

One turn more
Of the great wooden handle and the thread
Bites deeper

Subject not object
And therefore bodiless
As leaf, crown, cattle are

Damned leaf
Hanging on the last tree in hell
My only love.

The Fire-bird

1

O darling Lesbia
What word can I write for you?
This is not a poem
It is not the digested
Matter of a thousand days
But the growth of one
Rising like a miraculous
Plant and bearing its leaves
Unsteadily in the air

And then your voice
And those hands
Fingers between my own
That brow
Bent half upon me, but half away
O other half
Come to me. Be me
In replacement of this
Tatterdemalion
Shadow I am.

2

So long matured
This wish
Born before you, with you and after you
And now here
This miraculous presence
Cannot be counted in days
There are no hours

Because I imagined you
Before you came
Yet did not imagine your hair
Your eyes
Did not imagine how you would be, or why
Where you would come from
Only
That you might

It is an extraordinary fortune
Which has brought you at last
I do not thank you
Only take you

3

It happened before time
Which is old already
Though not in you

It happened before touch
Look, or imagination
There were no eyes in it

But now that the eyes play
On what was not imagined
Could not be
Was not

4

What will be the answer?
You must say.
You are not allowed
To hinder or prevent
What was settled before
You had any reason
Settled when I was
In spite of your years
Which are none

5

Useless to run
Where you are, I am
Useless to stay still
You will melt in my arms

6

There must be no turning back
This is the way, we must go there
It will not be easy, all things are difficult, but
Confusion if we do not go

So I have clarified my mind, do you likewise
You are intellectually precise, it is your duty
Precision does not end with two words it is
The continuing victory of its own effort
– Not so much effort –
Has to be lived out, like poetry, to the end of the line
Not chosen exactly, delivered and not prohibited
That is all you can say
It is this precision
Leads to your bed, or to my rejection

7

But do not be in love oh not in love
That is what we cannot help it is not our doing
It is the choice which determines the love, there is only a choice
Of whether this must be, but not of me

8

I am burning to death and you let me
Fire-bird, for you are burning in my flame

Troia

So in the morning light she came to him
Light-footed

But Troy the common grave of Europe and Asia
Troia (nefas)

The Sibyl's cave
Aeneas standing there
and it was only a descent

ad inferos
Speaking any words
wildly
Hair streaming: Aeneas founding a city
among the dead
Troy speaking again
only through the mouths of the dead
the city pardoned
the libation poured out and the ox-hides spread

I noticed this peculiarity in Troy
That the soldiers, looking out over the walls
Were sightless, they had long been dead
and a Roman capital
Stood in the desert, half broken.

The Dew

Ros, ros
roris, the dew
'raus, heraus
Speaking no words, retreating
with a gun pointing at him

the frame of the door

backwards

But Ow!
a hand seized his hand
behind his back
'Down on your face
Eat the dust, eat the dust
Sir
Down on your face!'

A jackboot on your neck
a boot advances
also from the front
to push your skull in

These were the habits among which I was brought up
And I fear not altered.

Cato

How can I climb the Mount of Purgatory?
Cato, are you there?
– Looking so virtuous while your dream associates,
Dante and Virgil, cough behind their hands.

I who have never seen the last evening
– No more had Dante then – slip in behind
It is not for me to intrude upon the company
No supreme lady called me; if I go upwards
It will be stumbling, by myself, unobserved.
I should avoid all company on the way
And fall flat on my face if I saw Paradise,
Over the loose screes till I hit the earth
Head-first. There is so little content in this idea
Of a progression towards beatitude.
Beatitude is here or not at all
'The kingdom of heaven is at hand', or under the counter
For special purchasers who have enough money,
Coin of Caesarea. I wanted three things,
Lechery, success, never at any time virtue
But a faint approbation that makes life tolerable
As long as one lives in the city of weak smiles.
I have run counter to every device
That could bring happiness as I suppose it
Which is quite contrary to the way I have it.
O my dear absent one, oh my dear absence
When shall I be absent from myself?
Absence is mourning; absence is also love;
That presence may be love is all I pray.
I wait here and hope it may be morning.

The Question

Questi non vide mai l'ultima sera

1

No praise for anything but love
The body rhymes with helpless times
No praise for anything but love.

How often, Sibyl, have I wept
To touch the body as I would
How often, Sibyl, have I wept

My mind is now the only space
In which your body is at ease
My mind is now the only space

My word is now the only hand
That touches you, that touches you
My word is now the only hand

Your lips are now the only lips
To speak the words that I would speak
And I am not the man to hear

2

No speech in summer. Now the light
Falls upon apple-flower and blue-bell
You are not here. No more am I.

The water rushing past my ears
I stood there. You had gone away.
Now you were here. Now gone away

You waved across the standing car
Useless to turn the mind away
It homes upon you like a bolt.

3

What I felt when your post-card came.
I had retracted every wish
For every wish I had is vain.

Turn mind, like Whittington. I turn, I spin
Nowhere is London. Like a heap of sticks
I burn and crackle till I fall to ash.

4

One word would be enough. Better, a kiss
And best a night of love with my fell hand
Racing your belly while I kept your eyes.

Harsh senile dreams. I spit them from my mind
And have no peace until I stamp you out.
Or ever? Not because of you, my dear

Nor anyone. Because a bitter mind
At sixty years can have no peace at all

5

So turn to God. The old immutable
Accessible great mountain of my soul.
Here on the lower slopes I will remain.

No mind can master me. I pick no flower
But kick and scuff the pebbles in the stream.

Est in conspectu Tenedos

I

The day goes slowly, it is the first day
After the fall of Troy. I walk upon the beaches,
A ghost among ghosts, but the most shadowy I
O Tenedos O the thin island
Hiding the ships. They need not hide from me

I am the least figure upon the shore,
Which the wind does not notice, the water refract, or the sands
     count
As one of their number. I was a warrior,
Yes, in Troy
Before all reason was lost.
Where did Helen come from? Where is she now?
All reason is lost and so is she.
I was only a parcel of her reason
Now of her loss
Ghosts
Cannot be companionable; parts, shreds,
All that I am, ghost of a part of a part

II

Desolate shore, dark night
I have lost so much that I am not now myself
That lost it, I am the broken wind
The lost eagle flying, the dawn
Rising over Tenedos

III

Not any more I, that is the last thing
Rise or fall, sunrise or sunset
It is all one. The moon is not friendly
No, nor the sun
Nor darkness, nor
Even the bands of maidens bringing offerings
Pouring libations, buried
Among the ineluctable dead.

IV

Dead, ineluctable, certain
The fate of all men.

Exactions

The Desert

1

This is the only place that I inhabit:
The desert.
No drop of water: no palm trees: nothing.
No gourd, no cactus: sand
Heaped on all sides like mountainous seas
To drown in.
Luckily I cannot see myself, I am alone
No mirror, glass, plastic left by an Arab
Nothing
I cannot say it too often
Nothing.
The sand itself would diminish if I said yes.
No rascally Bedouin,
Praying mantis, or nice people
– A mirage of them, occasionally.
But they are not there, any more than I,
For all my vocables, eyes, 'I's,
Other impedimenta of the desert
– Khaki shirt, shorts, chapli,
Mess-tin, for nothing to eat;
Water-bottle, nothing in it.
It is an amusing end, because desired.

2

Alone
But to say 'alone' would be to give validity
To a set of perceptions which are nothing at all
– A set as these words are
Set down
Meaninglessly on paper, by nobody.
There were friends, they have faded into the distance;
With my disintegration the vision becomes blurred,
Rather, disintegrated, each bit
For all I know
Tied to a separate nothing, not I.
Enough of laughter, which echoes like a tin eccentric
Round the edge of the desert:

Tears would be ridiculous
If I could shed them,
Eyes shed them, one
Then another again, weeping
For different things, not joined.

Shatter the retina so that the eyes are many
– Hailstones, now, it can be sand for all I care.
The damned unrepairable, I sit
Like a vehicle sanded up, the desert
Is frequent with images.
Could night come, that would effect a change,
But the sun blazes:
'I am all you have to fear, extreme, hot, searing
But the end is dust, and soon.'

The Mirabel Sea

As I was walking by the mirabel sea
Down-a-down, the mirabel sea
There came a monster walking to me
Hey down

I wept intransitively, there was no-one
Who could be the object of my tears
Down-a-down, by the mirabel sea
Hey down

There were tears tears tears but they were only the salt sea
Down-a-down, the salt sea
Only a tear and no eye to weep it
Ho down

Exactly as I said, she said it was, he said
But say as they all say it is still the same
Hey down, by the mirabel sea
Murder is laughing but that is not exactly

Down, by the mirabel sea

Au Clair de la Lune

The less
        we mean
The more
        we say

The less we mean the more we say:
Put together like that, marvellous.

I see no point in meaning,
Nor any;
Reason is deluded, old hag.
No need to talk of the affective, Love:
The machine itself is enough.

There is no entry into any city
There is nothing but fornication,
Parties picked, packed and
Repeated.
No bloody nonsense about the king of hosts:
No arsing around with the dialectical process.
There is nothing up against the wall
But the prick stopped in the plaster

This is the end of everything, of everything, of everything
This is the end of everything
On Christmas Day in the morning.

So I came through that territory
With camels, at least I had the hump,
Down several deserts where there were wind-breaks
– Sliding on the dunes patched with light:
They fell under my feet like truculent reality,
Would not be still, offer foot-hold to foot-fall, feet
Sank, ankles sand, the knees
Found the sand flowing about them.

Motion stopped, except the hands waving
Hip hip hooray.
They are gone at last,
Under

Starting from nothing, returning
To the same place or no-place;
Passing *outre* only to pass beyond nothing
Into nothing
– A spacious place, I expect
Too big for you:
Where salvation was expected, hardly by me
But arranged in order for those who expected it:
A pile of rocks heaped, gigantic pebbles,
Weathered at least by some trick of the centuries.

A great bowl of sand. I alone am the moon-figure
Walking there.
Is there no hovel for fornication?
The palace of luxury which is alone worth finding?
An old hermit, sitting at the door – it is myself –
And inside,
Her limbs stretched on a bed, rationality
– Smooth as lard.

Place

We have only to live and see what happens
– Nothing perhaps; for it may be that history,
As Mairet remarked, is coming to an end
And we shall wander around without meaning.
That is what most of us would like, and it is death
However it puts on the masks and opinions of life.
If we live here, it is indeed here that we live.
We cannot afford to scoff at the *pays natal*,
Unless our minds are to be born without content;
Nor at the acres in which we spend our childhood,
Unless the things we see are of no account,
Do not fill our minds, are nothing but generalities.
What do we see? Faces on a television screen
Which are more vivid that tnose we pass in the street.
So we live no-where, but somewhere there is a *place*
Where life is lived, a kingdom of the blest,
Perhaps, in which the programmes are prepared.

Reason

Reason had a pair of shoes
But quickly wore them out;
The uppers still looked very well
But, underneath, was doubt.

Of course, that let the water in,
And then it let in stones:
They skinned her feet, the flesh was thin,
And soon, she walked on bones.

Why not? But now, the trouble is
The joints are working loose.
At what point will the girl admit
You can be too abstruse?

The Zodiac

And so we need divide the year;
Also, the human character.
Aries at first, Aries the Ram
Whose neighbour in the sphere I am:
Taurus who, lowing for Europa,
Must be content with grass for supper;
The other neighbour being Gemini,
Though two might be thought two too many.
Cancer crabs everyone in sight
And therefore has the shortest night,
While Leo tries to be benign
In spite of his ferocious sign.
Virgo, we all know, cannot last
Even until the summer's past;
Her Libra seeks to equalize
With equal balances of lies,
Though Scorpio would bite the tail
Of any too ambitious male
And Sagittarius shoots arrows
At aeroplanes, and brings down sparrows.
Capricorn is a goat, and cannot

Conduct himself as if he were not;
Aquarius with watery eye
Does nothing else but cry, cry, cry;
Pisces, however, swims in tears
Till harmless Aries re-appears.

Why quarter and divide in three?
Too much brilliant astronomy:
The heavens would not stay still, and grew
Quickly to circle out of true,
Till all the scholars, from their book,
Knew that the sky must be mistook.
Then came a learned supposition
That the erroneous position
Taken by the wandering stars
Must reflect on the characters,
Not of astronomers and pedants
But all the new-born innocents
Who had not yet twisted their minds
Into the pattern of mankind.
In case the constellations faltered,
Science would see that they were altered:
So anything you care to hope
Is enlarged in your horoscope;
Whatever makes you shake with terror
Is grimmer in the written error.

If Aries only were a ram
And Gemini, twins in a pram,
Taurus among the cows, and Cancer
Not so much favoured as the lobster;
If Leo kept his woolly head
Inside his cage, and Virgo's bed
Were no more visited than most;
If Libra weighed up pounds of tea
And Scorpio died of DDT,
Who'd be afraid of Sagittarius
Or find no life-belt in Aquarius?
If Capricorn were only goat,
The fear of butts would be remote,
And indeed, but for scholarship,
Pisces might end as fish and chips.

The Pool

1

All options close: a devious life
Flows no more beyond this point.
Devious and plentiful stream, you come to a stop
Here, in this meadow, I am incredulous
– Instead of river, a pool, no bigger than nothing,
As if the source must end as it begins.
Does it go underground, does it go at all?
Liquid and deep and still, that seems to be all.
So deep, that it has transparency
Like a cube of glass. I could get through easily:
Yet not, for a million reflections this way and that
Warn against any movement, better stand pat.
If I moved, I should go topsy-turvy,
More like a hall of mirrors. While I waited
On the bank, looking at the interior,
It sometimes seemed farther and sometimes nearer.
Seen through a telescope: if so, through which end?
Stutter foot, slur speech, you slide, my friend.

2

I held the meaning of life in my hands
For a while: then I abandoned it.
Why? There were several reasons: first,
The life it was the meaning of was not mine.
Then it was a mistake I made about God.
I simply imagined that there was somebody there
And, having imagined it, strove to be polite to him.
But egotism is all I have to say,
God, the lot! He and I are much of a muchness;
More than that, he is the principle of identity
Which I should certainly find hard enough without him.
The imagination ends: the self disintegrates.
Good-bye to a bad self, and the good god with him,
Who was rather better, because imaginary.
Flies and whiskers growing out of a dead cunt.

3

Somebody else's egotism, the prime motive
In most rational action, if it is rational
To curl and twist and do as others command:
The egotism of self, which is also God's,
Noticeably has a more urbane look,
Twisting others, perhaps, which should be pleasant;
Or finding excuses for non-intervention
In quarrels which are too silly for speech.
So I pray to myself: O God,
Allow me to be extraneous to myself,
Using the word YOU to MY SELF
– Playing with one's own genitals, it might be said.

4

All that has now gone, because
For many years I imagined another YOU;
Not so ingenuous as to push for the Magna Mater,
Or Diana come down from the sky to admire Endymion:
No! but a principle of heterogeneity,
Masked by desire which, being my own,
I put myself behind. Snap!
God and myself are one.

5

Hope was my primary theological virtue,
But this I never succeeded in placing anywhere
Except on the surface of a female body:
Tactile corpus, visible also, the image
Ever before the mind, in Christian torture.
The torture was mine, the body itself was blind
– Reversing the evidence of the crucifix,
Where the body was tortured and the onlooker, benign.

6

I will act my senile part as the Furies desire,
Having discovered too late what I knew already:
Nothing is new, nothing miraculous;
The tree grows and flowers in order to fall.

7

In order to fall, in order to fall:
Only my life is without deflection,
The *declinatio* which created the world
And might create me now, were any permitted.

I have been the fool of myself long enough,
Mocking, impeding, now in permanent discourse,
And now it appears there is not one fool, but two.

8

The only fact that matters is the fact
Of the matter which happens to be the matter today.
How the blow falls, why nothing is anything,
Everything nothing, remain secrets from me.

9

Pass down, pass down the explanation;
Credit it if you can, if not, pretend to:
Guide yourself on a banister of air
As if your fingers were touching something solid.

10

Damn all extravagant moralities,
The Muses say, the Muses say:
Let horror have a holiday,
And be content to please.

11

I should say nothing but the mouth will open.
Although the last man on the last shore
– I say, but the whole thing is a pack of lies –
Etc., etc. But why finish the sentence?

12

I end the year in discouragement.
There can be no more years: a rubble of time
Only, to be pushed before one in the stead
Of winter, spring, summer and autumn, which mark
The evading hours for those who are in life.
It is a cold tunnel I go through, the other end,
Which was dreams, not even an hallucination.

The door on the outside world has shut for ever.
It is not night, for night implies day;
It is not prison, for prison implies escape.
There is none.
The world, which was made in six days,
Has contracted. A week, a minute, an hour,
Are short enough to comprise it.
The pinhead light
Has gone out:
Nothing more here, for hope or for consolation.

And yet not despair,
Which also implies hope, and I have none:
Equally held, because blackness
Knows no points, up or down;
Because nothing
Has no weight, has no self to be conscious of,
Neither exists in itself nor by any reference.

Reference would be too much, the long and short of it,
Which has neither long nor short, nor any enigma,
Nothing to solve, no question to ask.

Differently

If I had done differently I should have done well;
Differently is better, it could not have been worse.
I cannot stand, looking, as into a fire,
Into the past. There is only the charred wood.

A Baby asleep in a Passing Car

Sleep your way into the world,
Baby pressed against the glass.
The car moves on, nothing that passes
Does not enter your dream;
Sorrows and mechanical penetrations
Will not escape you. Your mind
Opens like a rose on smiles,
But is nothing, it must wither, change, fall
Before the ripened hip holds – too compactly –
The little you could learn.

Where?

Where am I? Far behind myself
Comes the thud of what I say;
What I have said, in the early morning
Seems like unextricated dreams.
Not here! Not here! the amiable man
Lying in bed with the morning paper,
Or surly old devil who bites your head off:
Shadows and shells, you could say no more,
They are no more me than my words.

Licence to speak

Since I am out of my mind
I must be in my body;
There is nowhere else to be:
No fruit and all rind.

What is identity?
The heart of others,
It there, is there rather as
Mine is in me.

A clock may tick but not know
The time, and so
The evidential senses throw
Dust in our eyes, and through.

Even hounds give tongue.
Is that not speaking but saying,
Not saying but exercising
The larynx and the lungs?

Why should my mouth not open?
Something or other must wag;
There is movement, and the gag
Is no tighter than before.

Whiplash

A
  trace
      of
        God
          in
            an
              inanimate
                body
                  is
                  like
                    a
                      whiplash
                      on a
                slumbering
              surface
            the
          pulp
        of
      the
        brain
          say

It
is
not
as
if
the
excoriated
shape
represents
a
unity
even
chained
couples
of
skeletons
may
be
so
regarded

chairlegs
populous
cities
or
the
leaf
the
sparrow
carries
in
her
mouth

her
eye
or
the
bull-dozer's
grab
and
shovel

                              so
                          the
                    pirouette
              turns
              or
          the
weather-cock
          crows
              like
                  live

                      loses
                          his
                              head
                          to
                          the
              mechanical
                      slicer

                              It
                              is
                              an
                                  option
                          which
                      to
              choose
          except
              the
                  flash
                      is
                          not
                          in
                      the
                  flesh
              it
          is
              the
                  whiplash
                          falling

                    the
                crack
                    of
                        the
                whip
            over
excrescences

Style

Although a person is a style
– Whether a woman or a man –
I am past style.

I am not speaking of writing now,
Fads or labours, or anything
To do with how

Anything is done, if that means
Deliberately, but even helplessness,
Which is in between

How and what and more like what.
A quiddity is amusing, but
It does not take me in.

Ham Hill

Nothing means much now,
I am stone;
Cool, golden, not cold,
The temperature of the air-flow.

You might have spoken to me
Or across, it would not matter;
Sat on me, or not regarded
My location or entity;

Not seen me entirely
Or expressly said, A stone;
There is no occasion
For such familiarity.

It is enough to be here,
Not too much, enough;
The equal of love;
That is why I am here.

New World

New world, I see you dazzle,
Like the sun on a door-knocker
In a straight street inhabited
By people I do not know.

Moon-rise

It is the evening brought me here,
Or I the evening.
So I, which is the writing finger,
The hand placed on the sill, the night
Coming up from beyond Kingsbury:

Another foot, or hand, perhaps,
Perhaps a train, passing along
Down the line by the signal-box;
Or that rising star which may be
The next one to come out of the west.
Which way? has no meaning because
The moon rises, as we say.

Nightingale, you sing no more;
The tree you sat on is not there;
The night you sang has also gone:
And I alone remember you,
Or am the nightingale tonight.

Night of the day, because succeeding;
Or of the night, because pleading;
Or of the Lamb of God because
Bleeding.
Useless to ask any question of
This night or any:
Answer as lightly as you ask.

The Garden of the Hesperides

If I knew what to say, I would say it;
But as I do not, I send it,
This:
When there was time and place, I lost it;
Now there is not, I regret it:
That.

＊ ＊

Faithful, ingenious, I mean to say, witty,
She-Jesuit, you are the writing on the wall

Or I am the wall and you are the writing;
Would I understand, if I knew my letters?

Will you teach me? What if I am ignorant?
Beyond teaching, savage? A kind of faithfulness

I read, although there is none, of the understanding,
In which the writing has erased the wall.

Or suppose you are the wall and I am the writing;
On your witty surface the lines are erased.

What did they say? Mene, Tekel, Upharsin,
Three names for doom. There is one word for pleasure.

* * *

O, 'I' and 'you' are two conceptions
Neither of which is justified;
Neither 'you' by 'I', nor it cannot be,
'I' by 'you' exactly.

One could imagine talking;
We know better than that.
What is said is what is what,
And that is in doubt.

We could imagine looking
At a world not there;
Eating perhaps or drinking
In the thin air.

Conversation is not
Where there is not I.
Who spoke? Who draws breath?
Not I.

* * * *

However, something has happened. The thin air
Is certainly thinner and finer than before:
I can see things. It is not that there is light
Anywhere in particular, unless it is every night
Has its moon, every day its sun,
Equal everywhere. Trees tower and streams run.
Everywhere lights. Animals come out
In broad daylight fearless, minnow and trout
Agitate in a water clear as air.
What is the meaning of this? The meaning is where
The objects are, it does not bother me.
All of us are disproven, but gently.

* * * * *

Not yet said, because unsayable,
Not yet read, and unsayable,
Star enclosed in a vocable.

Absurdity, when to be absurd
Is more than the fortune of being heard.
What is there that is less than a word?

* * * * * *

My object is to say, there may be you,
Equal in nothingness, as in all else:
Therefore the water shines, therefore the dew
Hangs on the grass as big as melons.
What mind is in all this? Not less a mind
Than any pulp within whatever rind.

Apples and oranges is what we are,
And you especially, though side by side
We hung, across the glade seemed far
To me, which was because of pride,
A defect in the garden of the Hesperides
Where all the apples have to do is please.

* * * * * * *

You is transferable, the angels say
To you and you and you, a fragrant light
Falling past every soul by day and night.
Whether this may be so, I know no way
Of proving, beyond the happiness of today.

.

A Sleep

They melt to one another in their sleep,
The day being bold and obstreperous,
The waking night either fitful and deep
To the point at which it becomes cavernous
Or alive with forms, movements and blind eyes
Moving among them without surprise.

But sleep brings what the day did not bring,
And remote cots are as it were side by side;
The engines of wrath are silent. The range
Passes over the mountains, the running tide
Manages each wave to distraction
And all differences are only one.

Wake from it? Wake from what? Wake from death.
But not from this sleep which is also life,
Eternally here, the Atman of each breath:
There is no Christmas or Eastertide
More hushed with the eternal night than sleep.
Roll over and the pillow is your dream.

The Herb-garden

When a stream ran across my path,
I stopped, dazzled, though the sparkle was at my feet;
The blind head moving forward, Gulliver
Walking toweringly over the little people.

Not that smaller in size meant, in any way, lesser;
It was merely that I could not see them, my eyes
Crunched on them as if they had been pebbles,
And I blundering without understanding.

Large is inept: how my loping arms fall,
The hands not prehensile, perpendicular
Before an inclined trunk. The legs do the damage,
Like the will of God without rhyme or reason.

Epithalamia are dreamed in this atmosphere
Which towers like a blue fastness over my head.
My head is full of rumours, but the perceptions
Dry like lavender within my skull.

Herb-garden, dream, scent of rosemary,
Scent of thyme, the deep error of sage,
Fennel that falls like a fountain, rue that says nothing,
Blue leaves, in a garden of green.

The Surfaces

And so with the natural surfaces,
Like comfrey gone to waste, there is no loss,
Only the passage of time. And the singing mind,
Like a telegraph wire in the waste, recording time:
Intervals, sounds, rustling, there is no peace
Where the wind is, and no identity
Clapping with herb or tree, or the wild waste
Of skin and shrub-land, which are only perspectives
On time

No heart to be eaten out, a womb to be caught
Sometimes as it were casually, for a new flower.

The South

The louring south says: I am in the blue
End of endeavour, the scowl and lour;
If I say dawn, it is morning

If I say night, it comes, but there is cloud
Under my eyebrows for thoughts, from which come
Uncertainties, inventions. It is this

Mood which constrains me now, nor will I say
What may be, or when.

Della la Rivière sont

Beyond the river there are
Three girls, all charming;
Beyond the river they are:
Then jump up and are away.

I lost, sitting here,
I lost, sitting here,
A cap, it was my friend's:
A cap, it was my friend's.

'And you have it' –
'And you're a liar' –
'Who has it then?' –
'We do not know.'

Beyond the river there are
Three girls, all charming;
Beyond the river they are:
Then jump up and are away.

A Visitor

Put on your coat
And go home.
Nothing is said;
Nowhere to go.

Take off your shoes,
Stretch out;
Somebody's leg;
Nothing is said.

Somebody's foot,
Somebody's toe:
Maybe at last;
Nothing is said.

Go home.
Go where?
Nothing is said
In the thin air.

The Red Admiral

The wings tremble, it is the red admiral
Ecstatically against the garden wall;
September is his enjoyment, but he does not know it,
Name it, or refer to it at all.

The old light fades upon the old stones;
The day is old: how is there such light
From grey clouds? It is the autumnal equinox,
And we shall all have shrunk before daylight.

A woman, a horse and a walnut-tree: old voices
Out of recessed time, in the cracks,
It may be, where the plaster has crumbled:
But the butterfly hugs the blue lias.

The mystery is only the close of day,
Remembered love, which is also present:
Layer upon layer, old times, the fish turning
Once more in the pond, and the absent.

All could not be at once without memory
Crowding out what cannot be remembered;
Better to have none, best of all when
The evening sunlight has ended.

Its fingers lighter than spiders, the red admiral
Considers, as I do, with little movement;
With little of anything that is meant:
But let the meaning go, movement is all.

The Last Day

Answerable is the last day and every day
Is the last: it is by love the day waits,
No day without, a day without anybody
Not being a day.

The Morning

I do not know what the mist signifies
When it comes, not swirling,
Gathering itself like briony under my window

The trees stand out of it,
Wading, you might say,
Have their dark tresses trailing in the water
Which began the world.

For Passing the Time

For passing the time it is a very good thing
To say, Oh, how are the vegetables growing?
How are the artichokes? Are the leeks coming on?
Will there be decent parsnips when the time comes?

I expect so: nature does not deny her abundance
To those who are patient and don't expect too much;
The leaves wither, and the leaves sprout again;
It is unchangeable as change can be.

Down by the river there are events
In every season; and the river flows
In all seasons, sometimes more, sometimes less:
It is hallowed time which passes along its banks.

But for me how can the time be hallowed?
I seek no remedy in it; there can be none.
The scent of rosemary is pungent in the nostrils:
Break the lavender stem, and recorded time.

Three Emblems

1

Cloud passes cloud like mind on mind
– All mine, if I am any body.

2

The hellebore with dark green leaves
And pale green flower with toothy smile.

3

A spot of crimson fire in the west
Under the cloud of evening.

The Cobblestone

1

O green, green, eating out my eyes,
A yellow-livered green in a wet light;
Daffodil-light falls on the wall
As I sit here, not pleased with anything.

2

Why tell the truth? None but a fool
Would make a habit of it.
One sometimes must, but as a rule
A lie will bring more profit.

Of course. And the best lie of all
Is the great lie of virtue,
Smooth as an egg. Tell that one well,
The world will not desert you.

3

It is not happiness which remains with one,
But it is a visitor which comes sometimes;
It is the pleasure that I do not have
Which makes the dream in which I pass my days.

4

Blue flowers everywhere: blue of forget-me-not,
Borage, blue-bells all over the garden
– Blue is the word, but the flowers are different.
So am I, caught between Tuesday and Wednesday
– The name the same, but the world my odour,
My sight, my hearing, touch, my taste,
A world gone, changed between Tuesday and Wednesday.

5

Her mother lost her and she lost the spring.
O Proserpine, why should I speak of you?

6

Being a thing and not a person,
There is no occasion now for boasting,
For any sentiment, for any feeling;
No reason to seek for any pleasure
Other than what comes without memory,
Without intent or any attempt at retention.
I lie in the gutter there is
Sunlight and dust on top of me, but nothing there,
The old cobblestone which still defines the sunlight.

Narcissus

corpus putat esse, quod umbra est

If I could only find a little stream
Which leapt out of the ground over black pebbles
And wore a hat of light on every ripple,
I should not care for the imaginary
Problems of I and Me, or Who and Why.
This corner of the world would be my mind;
What it saw I would say, if it were cloud,
Blue sky or even wind told by an eddy:
But what I would not see is this body,
Aged, severe, and, written on it, REFUSE.
If that came back into my little stream
It might be I should wake shrieking from my dream.
To what? Ah, what is there for us to wake to?
When pain is past, that is our hope or pleasure.
But nail that nothing now, keep me in vain
Beside the water, not seeing any shadow,
Only translucence, only the pebbles and earth,
A weed swaying, a fish, but nothing human
Or bearing any resemblance to man or woman,
Nothing compels our nature to this shape
For a stone will resemble the friends we make.
The mind is not peculiarly under skin
But might lie loose upon a high mountain.
A corner of a cloud would do for mind,
The bright border perhaps, with the moon behind,
The wind, recognized by its wandering billow
Scattering to surf as the moon comes and goes.
I thought I was a man because I was taught so.

Circe

Now we must try to be interiorly
What we are exteriorly: grey and civil.
Yet if we are approached by one of those creatures
Still holding sway in the world, the young, the beautiful,
Changes take place: it is the transmogrification
Effected by *la Sirena* on the high seas.
It is hard indeed to believe that it is she who is changed
As I approach her. Yet this is what Dante affirms:
Cosi le colorava, as love desires.
The duty therefore of geriatric manners
Is incumbent, not only on the exterior,
Which manages such things *tant mal que bien*,
But on the internal market-place
Where the reflection is born and love moves.
That is a vulgarity; what imposes itself
Is total surrender to the reigning world;
Quartz crystals become oneself, seeing all ways,
Seen of none, escaped among the hexagons.

Leaves

Leaves are plentiful on the ground, under the feet,
There cannot be too many, they lie below;
They rot, they blow about before they are rotted.
Were they ever affixed to trees? I do not know.

The great connection is from the leaf to the root,
From branch, from tendril, to the low place
Below the burial ground, below the hope of the foot,
The hand stretched out, or the hidden face.

On all occasions, or most, remember this:
Then turn on yourself like a small whirlwind of leaves.

The Prospect

This is the nature of life: on the inner side, nothing.
It is the outer attracts me, hermits and shells.
Rose to a rose, expired with ripples.

                                    In the pond
Ripples and water-lily, the fingered weed,
The fish darting or staying, under a leaf.
It is not enough for life, it is not enough.
Ah, what pretence when the white cloud blows over!
And do not cattle frame the meadow better
Than any trees? And only a figure walking,
Given, *donnée*, sealed on the green surface
Like wax on parchment, where the meaning is?

The Goldfish

Everything that is beautiful must be taken away
As that goldfish was. Shining, and plated with gold,
Its mouth trembling, its eye stony with solicitude
– I gasped when I saw it; it was my own cry.

The Resurrection

'He seeks to see it all again
In the resurrection.'
And yet it is not so, the sap
Is missing for the hope, perhaps.
The young man puts his hand around
A virgin waist, and in a bound
Is ten feet tall, and full of hope
In his own, not another's, growth.
A small life will creep out, to give
Him his instruction not to live.
Good-bye to hope when that is born.

The Skull and Cross-bones

The boy is strenuous, and possesses
   His limbs in hopes and promises;
The young man, when he pauses, seeks to lie
   So that the needle threads the eye.
It is one world, one flesh, and not his own.
   The true meaning of 'spirit' is 'alone',
So that is what he is, but so is she,
   And out of world and flesh, confusedly,
Come other spirits, like hunters from a wood,
   One after one, a group, they look.
Nature has wrinkled her brow; his own is clouded
   And the word that issues is said aloud.

It is in this way that the world is peopled.
   What savagery! We are better asleep,
Dreaming of wizards and the extreme edges
   Of the unmagical circle, and the wet sedges
Beyond which is the kingdom of the dead.
   Where does it lead to, when all is said?
Having gone round the world to no purpose,
   The old man sits and broods on the whole circus.
He has visited the female body, and the Spice islands,
   Now he sits here in silence
Except for the croaking of his own body,
   Here a discomfort, there he is uneasy.
Nothing to call out for, the world is flat.
   There is an end of him, when you get to that.

The River

O river who wind away from view
I speak to you more confidently than to
Most of the people who live in sight of your banks.

Your sinuosities are better than a brain pan
Dry as a scoured saucepan, or a frying-pan
Left on the fire till all its thoughts are smoke,

More likely to take in and remember
Or to turn deftly into something interesting
Whatever words come floating down from me.

Autumn Poems

En rond, nous sommes en rond
Ainsi, nous danserons.

I

The plunging year, the bright year. Through the clouds
Comes sunlight, sunlight, making iron-grey
The under-belly of the cloud it comes from.
Golden the dull leaves September wants to turn,
But dust is everywhere, not free, but plastered
Thinly over road, pavements, even bark
Branches and leaves, and the old iron buildings,
Ochre walls, fall. Not so, and yet it seems so.
Dust is the country way and dust the rhyme
Which equals everything in this sad time.

II

Broken-backed willow, elder and the sharp tree
Which is loaded with berries presently,
Heap upon heap, hawthorn, while the rose-hip
Beside her offers me her paler lip.

III

The world which was not mine, should I have wanted it?
By eating deceived, as Adam was,
I tell myself, but I do not believe it:
Belief is difficult after sixty years.

IV

Once there was bitterness which had regret in it
Or even hope, now there is none of these:
The bitterness itself is muted,
Not by satisfaction, which is not
But by etiolation, defoliation, the leaves
Growing whiter and thinner, and no wind through them.

Once I found sleep, it was
In the hollow of anybody else's hand
As the world sleeps in God's; now there is waking:
Not to receive the world, as some do,
But to watch, as the old, suspiciously.

I am looking for contentment out of nothing
For new things are made out of what is new
And I have none except this: the birds' song,
The rain, the evening sky, the grass on the lawn.

V

I am a tree: mark how the leaves grow
Sparsely now; here a bunch, there,
At the end of this thin twig, another
And the bark hardening, thickening. I am allowed
No respite from the wind, the long
Thorn trunk and branches stretching like a swan's neck
In torment. And the hiss
My own malice makes of this wind
Gentle enough, in itself: I can imagine myself
As this tree but what consciousness
Should go with it – that,
Screeching neck, I am blind to.

The Whale

Think nothing of the whale: you may be sure
He thinks nothing of you, and since the grand cetacean
'Conversing chiefly in the northern seas'
Makes no mention of you in his conversation

Except for an expletive when you come near him
– An expletive which is not hard to explain
In view of the charming way in which you accost him –
Why should you exercise your brains about him?

After all, he has the more sizeable body
And who are you to threaten his majority
By exhibiting more brains than he has himself?
It is against the supremacy of his thoughtlessness.

Jonah went into the belly of the whale
And prayed when he got there. Is it a mark of enlightenment,
Perhaps to swallow the whale and then assert
That empty seas are an improvement on creation?

Across the Winter

1

Quiet. It is winter and the frost
Stretches away into the mist;
A circle of dark closes in
Under the predicated stars.
How, under them, can you be content
With the light, the fire and the Christmas tree?
Or the gesticulating screen
There by the bottles in the corner?
What spirits move? What memory
Stirs in the human race today?
What in me, for I cannot find
In my drunk and incapable mind
Any entrance. There must be one.

Exit you mean? No, a way in
From this disorderly side of a hill
Which does not matter to me at all.
To what? To what? We must first get in
In order to know. But whether we go
Into the hill or into the blue,
Opening it like a money-box,
Is not a matter I can determine.
A dream is an entrance. It would be better,
Perhaps, to spell out every letter
Of the rational alphabet,
Tekel, Upharsin, on the wall.
Or not. But with enough reason
We may go in and turn about
The chambers of the past. It is this
Monstrous alternative to living
I now attempt. On the underside,
There also, where the inverted life
Has its beginning and its end.
Useless to talk of freedom in
The corridors of an old castle;
Gaolers lurk at every corner,
Clanking their keys. Grill after grill
Goes down, a chiaroscuro of
What may, possibly, be love.
But first, it is a memory.
Stapleton Church, which is not fine,
Or only so because it is mine
To skirt and go down to Black Rocks
– Better to go there over Snowdon,
Dangerous because well-known,
With roar of waters from a barrel
Of drains, a gap from one to the other;
A stony track, a shallow river,
A cave for crawling and for terror.
Eastville Park! Down through you
I came to this Elysium
– Which I call it in irony,
In old man's language, because no freedom
Was without terror or was mine.
I walked, yes, and climbed the daring
Slippery places under the alders.

A dog would frighten me, a fall
Threaten me, an eye – my own –
Fear to look. Where the brown
Eddies smoothed themselves was calmer,
Yet there was no safety, nor I either
For if I was alone
Trees might descend on me, the whole bank fall;
If there were enemies they would know all.

There was also, below Stapleton Church,
That entrance to a superior world
– I mean, just, higher up, but hills are green,
Distant and open. To get there between
High walls of pennant grit, with bridges over,
A lane for a dog to shit in, or a lover
To press a squealing girl against a wall.
This kindness also was terror, like the demented
Ill-spoken louts, with faces screwed or gaping,
Roaring, if they said anything, rather than speaking,
Who looked down from the walls and seemed to jeer
As I passed by, also a pilgrim there.

What of the further path, the falling tower,
The lake, Stoke Park and all defences down?
When will you ever be where you want to be,
My treason-top? There is a long track,
Passing the dangerous gates, of white chalk
– It seems in this moment's memory,
But is not – winding away – it does not –
Under a sky extravagantly hot,
For here the journey is long.

2

In this holy season there is remembrance
Here also for me; my enemies rise up
– But not here, for all is in the past –
Only the dark season of Christ brings them
Here to my door, with the snow.
But it is a summer's morning when I go
Along by the fishing stream, through the meadow
Which brings me to the edge of the plunging pool

In the quarry, from whose appalling ledges
The green water looks like a kingdom.
Is that a newt there, dragon-like?
Or, further, where the reliable stepping-stones
Cross the river, shallow but
Alive with brown bubbles, and the froth
Of unknown causes, interlaced with twigs,
A leaf fallen, or a stray blossom,
Minnows, perhaps, may wink.
I, far in mid-stream, the bank
Holding, like watchers over me, great trees.
No enemies there: but on the way back,
The boy with the stone, the big girl
Looking curiously at me: 'What is it?'

But this deep season, in which remembrance
Is not mine, takes me rather,
All that is gone. The mind that hovers
Over me like a hawk, is mine:
Its prey, and yet itself distinct,
Finite in looking, infinite being looked at.

Against the pavement where my feet had chattered
Thousands of miles, here I am, here is she,
Two distances, distance beyond distance.
Yet Shoe Lane is sharper where I stooped
On the hill-side, surely my purgatory,
To buckle my mistress's shoe, eight years old,
And that dark look of love so pitiful,
Or so it seemed. All love is infinite,
And now there is only memory,
Axbridge and Bleadon Hill and bleak Shute Shelve
Where I encountered her beside a well,
Ate my burnt porridge, slept under the wind
And flapping canvas, hold that love for me.
I am, she sang, the inescapable siren
Who sings to mariners on the high seas
Until they fail, and the green sea goes over them.

3

But Uncle George and Auntie Ju
Find place in my memory too
– The Lodge, The Conifers and all
There is beyond the garden wall.
How dusty the road was, I came,
How silent the precincts of Ham Lane:
And how extraordinary, when I was there,
The apple-tree in the always vernal air.
How strange the summer-house, with rotten sticks
Holding it uncertainly, with the planks
Sloping to make a dangerous floor,
And the grass tousled round about and deep,
An occasion for looking, rather than sleep.
How far the Lodge, where Uncle George
Leaned on his spade, looking over the garden
Which edged upon mysterious territory,
The Big House, with its lawns and walks and swing:
That is where the nightingales sing
In retrospect, that did not do at the time
– Uncle George, watchful, saying little, a smile
Was his language, gleaming more than his shirt-sleeves
Always rolled up. He limped when he moved.
It was he that my Aunt Julia loved,
Her face hollowed a little, but always sweet,
Full lips, eyes in hesitation
There in the stone kitchen, neat and small,
Aunt Julia dominant over all,
Sweet in each corner, with her lumpish daughters.

There should be a ballad for Auntie Kate
Who lived at Hambrook, the address, Myrtle Cottage,
Stumpier friend and confidante of Miss Good.
The two kept a shop, there it is,
With small panel windows, it was called the store;
The grain in the bins ran in the hands like money.
Beside it, under the archway, was the yard
And, opening out of that, the coffin-maker's:
Carpenter, joiner, priest of the great saw-pit,
With wooden ladder that ran out of it,
Up to the loft, where there was work to do
But what exactly it was, nobody knew.

There should be a choral for Aunt Anne
Who had been a beauty and whose face glowed still
With the pleasure she had given and could give.
Neat as a Prayer Book, no aunt could be smarter,
And she was trenchant even in her chatter.

Aunt Bessie queened it in an old farmhouse
She was not queen of; none of them was queen
And yet not one of them but might have been
And all of them had had untidy loves,
Perhaps.

4

The dark season runs into sunshine
In which nothing more is illuminated,
The paradise of snow that the cold holds.
Do not turn that into imagination.
It is better to see the peace the New Year brings,
The sky blue as it need be, sunlit branches
Motionless on the beech, waiting for green.
Spring will come, and after it the summer
Extending across the moors like a bow drawn,
Waiting to shoot its arrows into autumn,
The line of hills which always promise winter
And beyond that.

An Afternoon

After the harsh weather the first day of spring:
Even, on the river, someone in a canoe
– And, in the soil, the worms turning.

The pushing buds look up enquiringly:
'Shall we push?' as they do, like children who enquire
Only to be told nature may have its way.

I am past nature and may not have mine
Which is the way of all flesh, and so peculiarly
That of the generality of men

And so peculiarly not mine, but this
World's which, this February afternoon
Looks at me like a May morning.

Remembering the Dead

Down the basement steps, by the hall table,
A ghost stands. It is I who write this.
Flagged ochre, black and red, the floor is cool.
But where are the white mice upon the table?
Pink noses trembling, pink eyes uncertain
Or empty. When the cat came, winner take all,
Clapping her paw down like a pound in money,
The mice fled. Or did one stop from fright?

There was a tortoise in a box of hay,
Wintering in the lavatory at the back.
Dead or alive? How know when spring came?
Its flaccid legs hung from the superb shell,
Its head small, eyes sunk deep, but how
Be sure that it was not death? But it was death.
The large blue-bottle settling on it said yes.

The hutch in the garden where the white rabbit
Lived behind wire netting. How did she die?
I never knew, for she was taken away
– Betty, my best, my love, for she had suffered,
Biting her hind left paw till the bones showed.

And Marjorie? I never saw her dead.
'No' I said 'No' and still I would not know.
She lay there quiet and beautiful they said,
Her natural colour, she who had never had it
But I would not see whom I had loved.

Almost I crept in quietly by myself
On Sunday morning early but I dared not
– For I dared see her, although I did not,
But not with others who would bring my tears.

The Commonplace

A commonplace is good for nothing now,
Yet that is how the world goes, all the same:
Nothing is what you had when you set out,
And nothing you will have when you go home.

The Grandfather Clock

If I had not stood where that clock stood,
On the stairs, stood opposite it rather
Until I imagined I stood where it stood;

If I had not imagined its horsemen
Riding, but riding darkly under the varnish,
I should not have told time as I told time

– Endless, circular like that rodeo:
But now time is small, there is properly none,
It moves to fast as I move more slowly

That I shall surely catch my coat in it.

The Forest

1

It was because of the hope
Which was to be deceived
That the body tautened,
Breasts stood up, belly became friendly
And the patch of hair
Stood still like a forest
Till the body spun round it
Like a wheel on an axle.

Because of a dream
Too long nourished
A kiss on the lips at
The heart of the forest

2

Now that the road is lost
No heart in the forest now
Cowslip or kingcup or
Bracken pale and curled
It is a road gone
Night will come over it.
Trees down, like your hair
Their dripping boughs.

The Plant

A man is like a plant, he has to grow
And then to die. Not always in one place,
Yet he is rooted. What does the stem encase?
Nothing that did not come from the root or the air,
Which is full of voices; nothing which does not go
To the shrivelled heap and the Lord have mercy on it.

In Flood

A word for everybody, myself nobody,
Hardly a ripple over the wide mere:
There is winter sunshine over the water,
The spirits everywhere, myself here.

Do you know it? It is Arthur's territory
– Agravaine, Mordred, Guinevere and Igraine –
Do you hear them? Or see them in the distant sparkle?
Likely not, but they are there all the same.

And I who am here, actually and statistically,
Have a wide absence as I look at the sea,
– Waters which 'wap and wan', Malory said –
And the battle-pile of those he accounted dead.

Yet his word breathes still upon the ripple
Which is innumerable but, more like a leaf
Curled in autumn and blown through the winter,
I on this hillside take my last of life:

Only glad that when I go to join them
I shall be speechless, no one will ask my name,
Yet among the named dead I shall be gathered,
Speaking to no man, not spoken to, but in place.

The Matter

There is not Nothing if not I
For 'I' is only emptiness.
And what comes flooding in? The Time,
The Place: the Matter, nothing less.

The Dark

Dark, will you not come? Great veil,
Hide the plains and the woods. Lock out
My extension in you and do not fail
Of any blade or twig, O perfect cloud.

Burrington Combe

Not what I think but any land beside
Hidden from human speech, is where I go
As that dark leaf of thyme pushes its way
Into the empty world, and so speak I

Blackdown and Burrington and the deep combe
Which was my land, is also what shall be
Arraigned by time. I make my way only
Backwards, where I may look indulgently

And yet the indulgent land, where silence is
Is not my friend nor ever was before
The great ferns held terror as well as love
Who was lost on the heather-covered moor?

If I could climb out of this bitter combe
Into a lucid world, nothing there said
Could equal now the silence of your grief
Or the exchanges of the recorded dead

The word stands still upon the frozen lip
The eye is glazed that should have danced with love
For such days as are uneaten by the years
A nod, a commonplace will be enough.

* *

O Light, I do not want you
The years have taken away
Whatever there was lovely
In the day

The land stretches to doomsday
The rivers to the sea
And nothing done and nothing said
Matters to me

The age laughed in its hollow skull
And strove to be polite
But how can the dazzling fingers equal
The shepherd with his pipe?

Travel across the lips you bones
And do not stop for me
If there is nothing but death in the whistle
It will do for me.

* * *

So I address the musing mind
Which has no mind to speak
Which can hear nothing, see nothing
And has no heart to break.

The key of the kitchen is frenzy
And the cook stands by the door
Pobble-de-hope fair stranger
What is the ladle for?

A fortune for your porridge
The hope of a transitive verb
Is only to find its object
But the best word here is, Starve.

* * * *

But this is where I came
And where I wish to be
Burrington Combe, half in the dark
Half in the light of the moon

Ellick Farm you are buried
Deep in your greenery
And there is nothing miraculous left
Under the sky.

* * * * *

Cry up the pastures of the moon
They stretch from here to nowhere else;
A weed grows on a mossy bank
Its roots go down and down and down.

Down to the dark the dark the dark
Forget the light it is ending soon;
A cloud scuds over the face of the grass-land
Down-a-down and a hurrying moon.

I stood exactly over the valley
Looking down on the changing light.
What vixen cries in the hollow?
What owl passes the barn tonight?

I am not caught in the falling thunder
I am not pierced by the spits of rain;
Six foot long and six foot under
Never to speak on earth again.

Yet the mind hovers like a falcon
A bird of daylight and of dreams
Over the meadows and over the willows
But only hears the barn-owl scream.

* * * * * *

I came to speak to her
It was no good
No sign in the bushes
Or in the wood.

No sign on her lips
When I found her
There was nothing nothing nothing
But the chill around her.

The willows, she did not see
Or the ditch
Her eyes stared as if the day
Were black as pitch.

Me it may be she saw
As I were any thing
Stoned and stoned and stony
Not living.

And scarcely I am
Or I would not stay here
Walking, talking, proferring
And cannot break her fear.

* * * * * * *

If night falls, there is nothing more
If night falls, there is nothing more
If night falls, there is nothing more

And it does fall, it is falling now
The light is less already, see how it goes
Smaller, smaller, smaller, the circle of light;
But the scent of the rose

The scent of the wallflower, the night-scented stock
The scent of thyme, never off my hands
Except when rue chases it, or fennel, or sage
– Whose hands? –

Except when the bonfire that I have tended
Leaves me with nothing but its acrid air
In my clothes, in my finger-nails
In my hair.

Wherever I sit, as night falls
A last blackbird, perhaps, such things are
The moving night, and I awaiting it
And the first star.

It should be enough, but it is not
When night falls, it will take away
All I wanted and all that I did not
With the last day.

Patience, it is all that is required
Night is patience itself, when it falls
Not even memory disturbs its dream
Loser takes all.

* * * * * * * *

When I walk out there will be nothing missing
That I can see;
The pond will be there with its fish,
The rosemary

Spreading itself over the garden
As if still aided by my hand;
The mulberry-tree I planted, and the cherry,
The old apple-trees and

The plums stretching up against the wall
Over which the church-tower still looks;
Starlings and swallows, the swans flying over,
And always the rooks.

And that distance into which I shall have vanished
Will still be there;
It was always dear to me, is now
In the thickening air.

No distance was ever like this one
The flat land with its willows, and the great sky
With the river reflecting its uncertainty
But no more I.

Nobody hears what we say

Nobody hears what we say
– Nobody, nobody;
The echo has gone away
– Body.

Echo, echo come back!
Echo will not.
Live in a land of lack
– Or not.

Wherever nowhere is
Is the place for you;
Stay if you will, go if you wish,
Do!

**

No, no, it is only no.
All the songs they sing;
     Ring
Ring the bells till they go.

Go, but go they will not,
Nor will I stay;
     Today,
Today ended in what?

In incompletion,
In hunger want and dearth;
     Earth
Wheels in her street of stars.

***

O mercy, Saviour!
No eye can see
Where she goes, whom she robs
Or what the end will be.

England rides on her back,
Born and born and born
Till this last extremity
Of Christ's morning.

Now ring the bells backwards,
Muffle them, peal
Betrayed betrayed betrayed betrayed!
Drive home the nail.

For The Queen's Jubilee

What use in following
So many queens and kings,
Elizabeth of our spring,
Elizabeth of autumn now?

What use, unless you see
Music and poetry
Standing to your honour,
As we do now?

A coronation robe
May run in holes;
The Koh-in-Noor be sold
To pay the grocer:

But there were Muses once
– Muses, what do I say?
In the language of today,
Things which affront:

The severe line the draughtsman traces
Whether anyone likes it or not;
The clearly expressed thought
Which takes the smile off people's faces:

These are the Muses, it is these
Which call for no man's protection;
These it is which will be free
Against any venal objection:

It is these, too, which can save
Your reign in memory;
Your sceptre, your sway
Still live, for poetry.

Miscellaneous poems since
Exactions

The Time of Year

She asks me how I do
It does not matter how
Well and ill are all the same
Now.

I live beyond touching
Beyond friendship now
Do not ask oh do not ask
It does not matter how.

The night has gone from me
And the day is going
Oh the world oh the world turns
And I on it.

Who, I? Or the world itself
Turning, turning
Between the moon and the clouds
Its head spinning.

What price the cul-de-sac
Where you must certainly go?
Patience is getting in
– And the rest you know.

Know it as unknowing
No-way-to-go, unknown.
The fields whisper to harvest
– You go home.

Death, though I cannot go there
Is a neighbouring land
Stretched before my window
But not touched by my hand.

The willows are brown now
It is the time of year
– Look again, look again, orange!
So have no fear.

The Badger's Trail

animula, vagula, blandula,
hospes comesque corporis

Direct across the moor
The badger's trail ran from far distant fields
To where the wood hung like a wrinkled brow
And is one now. For in a hollow I
Consider conscience, what it is, and how.

So much for winter. But when summer comes,
As it must come, over my bones perhaps,
There will be laughing there between the trees
And, where the blue sky pours itself out for us,
Not a thought in the mind or in the blue.

Wind, winter, summer, all are over now
And nothing waits for nothing, at a point
Poised midway in the blue, or on the eye.
– Now goes, animula, animalcule,
Pure is not, is, or suspect, written on
The glass, the phial of the blue universe
Which shatters into darkness. *Hospes, comes.*

Sequelae

*

I have turned aside from God because he blinds me
Although I know that nothing is without him
And I am nothing as I turn away:
Nothing is what I am, therefore I turn.

* *

Heart, nothing came
Out of the blue
Or the deep disturbance
Of the yellow clouds

Or the water-lily
Splayed in the pond
With the goldfish passing
Under and beyond.

A notion of directness
As out of the sun
Arrow arrow arrow
It is the hours that run.

* * *

The present master of this empty house
Is ego with it plastered on his face
Mountains of self for breakfast, empty cups,
No-one in place.

* * * *

The mind that gathers round its death
Is short of wind and short of breath;
The wind does not blow any more
The breath is what was drawn before.

The blood ran round which now must crawl
The fingers stroked which now must maul;
The age of perjury is come
So speak, my perfect, to the dumb.

* * * * *

What we are is hard to say
I have often thought of it, still do:
At one time it was enough to say, body
But that will not do.

A complex of tangled messages
Half given, half meant
A sleeping fire burning behind that
That is what is meant.

Yet that is not exactly it either
A gracious smile
Brings all flashing back to the surface
As you smile.

* * * * * *

If life is bitter
Let it glitter
If it is awkward
Let it go forward
If it is blank

* * * * * * *

A moral saw is not worth an I see

* * * * * * * *

If any man is in this room
Let him speak up: he can't be seen.
The book-shelves hide him, or the books;
He looks like nothing because he looks.
His head has gone inside a volume
And he is no more than a margin,
The print is elsewhere, as they say
You cannot see him in the grey
Light from the window, but beware
He is not thinner than thin air
And may return, he may, he may
Yet he has vanished for today.

* * * * * * * * *

I have seen the mallard fly out of the rhine,
The snipe skip round the willow and then away;
Nothing to be touched, O the creation my friend
And the dawn will rise upon a cold field.

A Stray

Oh it is pale, is pale, this afternoon
Like that blue flower, strayed in my garden
Chive or marsh-plant perhaps or some pale bloom
Straggled out of the night

Paleness is light
Defect of darkness, mother-of-pearl, pearl
In a dark ocean heaving all around.

O turn away
Wind, from me

Turn away light
Fail into watery light
And underline the hills
Till they come to night.

The Spring

Observe what's happening in the world
Is all that I can recommend
To anyone that's leaving it
– Not either bad or either good
Only desirable or not
For that, consult the animal.

And so into the ground, the earth
From which the fox looks, for he knows
By the direction of the wind
What is his fortune in the world.
And so is yours, will be the day
Of any resurrection.

Christ speaks so softly that the breeze
At lightest, is more loud than he
I speak of him because I must
Yet cannot see him anywhere
Or feel him, touch his risen flesh
Or hear his whispers in my heart.

The world goes by and I with it
Or altogether no-one there
Its promises are not enough
– Fulfilled they are, for they said, Grow,
I grew, Be old, I was, and now
They promise death and I must die.

Yet still I watch the social world
With fur and feather, skin and bone
I see the twists of many hearts
And watch the bodies crumple too.
The young live on, in jeopardy
Being the only way to live.

Although I cannot be a cloud
I watch it, and the sky the same
And now I gather human life
Into my eye but not my heart
The recessed point from which at last
I shall make one remaining spring.

No garden

No garden to walk in
Nothing to say
The moon at full now
As if it were day

Nobody to meet there
On the wide scene
The world empty of creatures
And myself unseen

Empty world, empty world
What use in calling?
Is, was and has been
Are the names of all.

The Dog-rose

The dog-rose, flower of England, now is rare.
Let petals fall where they will and strew
The ground where some may find them but not I:
I am the absent one, yet the world lives
Within my mind as if I were the gardener.

In the Silence

*

The spoken word of God is God's own word
Hark, how it echoes! I hear nothing now
The age of crucifixion past, the resurrection
Shows up for what it is and all of us
Sit around waiting like the workhouse poor.

* *

Silence the word, for silence is the word
Without which speaking is impossible
And who said nothing never is or was:
The night is coming, utter nothing then.

* * *

To watch, to wait and know that nothing comes
Watching is waiting, what is watched is here
Seen from my window like the flagrant sheep
Who munch, head down, into the feeding grass.

* * * *

The dimensions of all sorrow are negligible:
Joy is invincible, but unattainable
Because it is only for what is there
And therefore cannot be longed for, in its nature.

* * * * *

You are left on earth, standing, on the bare earth,
No mind that does not come to you from the outside:
So lift your eyes you cannot, they are lifted;
Praise you cannot, the whole stream runs together.

The Hedgehog

The garden is mysterious at night
And scented! and scented! in the night of stars.
The hedgehog snuffles somewhere among leaves,
Just by the arch-way. So it is with time
– Mute night and then a voice that says nothing,
Busying itself, complaining and insisting:
When this has end, silence will come again.

The Forest of Dean

in memory of Francis Webb (1913-1975)

The forest is immutable they say:
There by the pond it seems so, for one day
– Great oaks, dark water, that is what I see
And yet the blood dries underneath the tree.
Are you there, Francis? Were you ever there?
A heavy body thinner now than air
As oaks determine in a smaller thing
Than acorns, dust or wind, as fish can bring
Their images to nothing when they sink
And there is no more than a thought to think.
That least of things! A trace that is no more
Than a lost ripple on a watery floor.
So you, now nothing, may be called to mind
But not to conversation with your kind.
In the great kitchen where you last fell down
There was you gasping, but no other sound
– The kitchen clock perhaps, or your wife's cry,
But it was you alone who had to die.
Now one earth covers you and her, in turn
I stood beside your grave-sides, not to mourn
But, *Salve atque vale*! and now here,
Where you were young, there is no place for tears.

The May-Boy

*This is a term, picked up locally, for a stray potato – I
suppose originally for a child born under a hedge.*

Poor scattered bastard, straggling out of the row
And out of kind, green where the earth is brown!
As for tomorrow, beyond meditation,
Under the haulms plump the insistent tubers
Which nature had intended, but not I
– Willing to take over the garden tomorrow
And fruit remorselessly when I die.

Black Rocks

And those Black Rocks which overhung the stream
Remain still sturdily within my dream.
Black Rocks in summer! when the river rides
By them like muddy sea on shallow tides,
Yet lively where the ripples hump and blink.
Dark-surfaced stone had dried like Indian ink
But trees were darker where they stretched across
Like staring cranes, and to its certain loss
The mind crept out on branches without hold.

I can explain those mornings, fishing net
Firm in my grasp, but I have nothing yet,
An empty jam-jar swinging from a string,
The home to breakfast and that other thing
More dreaded than a stranger and more cruel,
The over-shadow of a day at school.
Where, when I come, and once within the gate,
No use of language, hardly am I here
Except to register the scale of fear
– An exile from the world of flesh and bone,
The prisoner of minds and walls of stone.

Two Capitals

'Sieg Heil! Sieg Heil!' It came then like a roar
Across Berlin in nineteen thirty-four.
Herr Bargel, Dr Mohrhoff and young Schmid
Answered its echo like a natural need.
By the old Reichstag torches lit the sky
As the brown-shirted Fackelzug went by.
The heart of Germany! But not my heart;
I stood with thousands but I stood apart.
What peace for England? That is all I knew,
The awful menace of a dream come true.
And France? Months later, there was I, as one

At table, rue du cardinal Lemoine,
At breakfast, lunch and dinner: René Chave,
Febrile as autumn, nineteen and a half;
Old Monsieur Duchemin, discoursing reason;
Madame, who bought the vegetables in season
And clacked over the price of artichokes;
Jacques who irrupted with his silly jokes;
Hélène who once let slip an awful word;
The Madame Picart who was so refined,
Contrasting English Sport with the French Mind;
Henri her studious son, who chose the latter;
Kreitmann, who had his own thoughts on the matter
As on most others. What do I make of it,
Forty-five years later, in Somerset?

Winter has come and I welcome it
Despite grey cloud which hammers down its lid
Upon the flat world, flat as it, and still.
Oh, it is cold, but not with that cold will
Which laid itself over the multitude
That hurried, clouded, gathered or just stood
Below me in the Schäferkampsallee.
There it was cold, there there was steel to glint
If in no more than in a massive hint
As the leaves fell, had fallen. Yet again
Can I not feel it in the icy rain
Threatening to fall over gabbling Europe?
I am too well instructed to have hope
Yet softly, do not speak. Only prepare
To walk out naked in the bitter air
Trusting what is not to be trusted, love.

The Robin

O morsel of mortality, dead robin,
You my familiar I have known hopping
About my spade, not caring for me:
But I care for you, uneasily,
Not out of kindness, except as of a kind
With all that brings mortality to mind.
You hop and die, objective to the end;
I am subjective so you are my friend.

Athelney

The apple trees are dulled in the red sun,
The fruit unpolished and the day is done.
This is where Alfred crept by on his marsh,
Wet straggling country still, but now the harsh
Road runs on blue and dark beside his ghost.
Headlamps begin to count the sodden posts
And catch a nosing heifer here and there.
The squawking ducks are home, and the wet air
Settles more heavily as the night comes.
'A bit of fire-stuff, like': a voice close by
And a dead branch is dragged to Athelney.

The Friend

If I had believed the afternoon
Capable of extension – not to end soon
In red and orange sky behind grey cloud –
I should have left the garden and walked out
Over the river and across the moor
Further than I had ever been before
Or any man can go more than once.
Instead I went down to where a bunch
Of hawthorn berries hung, still unconsumed.

In the dark mansion there are many rooms;
Voles know some beside me, and water rats
Who seek as I do something that will distract
From the objective, unimagined end
Which knows nothing at all of death the friend.

A Reflection

The floods are back, that should have gone last month.
O watery world, images in you now
Of trees and cattle multiply nature
– One world to touch, another world to see
And I am on the outside of them both.

Pocket-size Poems

1

Rain falls and falls. There can be sleep.
Would you play, lightning? Orange keeps
The western sky where the sun was.
The garden yields up a wet rose.

2

One-Tree Hill is what I see;
It is a hill that has one tree
– A good name for it, therefore, I
Have no such plain identity.

3

The last reproach of all is age,
There is no answer to its rage.
It looks across the mountain-side
And points to where the heroes died

And gibes with its uncivil tongue:
'There is the cross where one was hung
Who managed all at thirty-three.'
What is the use of that to me?

4

Feet and inches measure man
Better than a metre can.

5

A hawk before my window hangs
Like a puppet on a string
Come down and get your man.

6

A missel-thrush on a walnut-tree:
What has it to say to me?
Sing on, sing on, I say to it.
It answers, Tiraloo, twit, twit.

7

A robin flies into my room.
'Prisoner!' he shouts, and so I am.

8

When I thought what I would do
Fifty years ago, I knew
There must be something I'd do well,
What it was I could not tell;
I had not done it, that was clear.
Nor have I now. How can there be
Ignorance enough left to me
For hope to feed on, when there isn't
Enough delusion for ambition?

The Mistletoe

Rather than speak, I would crawl under a leaf.
Here is the mistletoe growing mysteriously
In the middle of the old apple tree.
What hand put it there? The hand of God?
Lantern of leaves in the lighter leaves of the apple
Continuing in the dark branches of winter,
You hang there luminously, as of a certainty.

Mark how the stem passes into the bark,
The branch, its lithe green of another world
Into the tatty and encrusted bark
And, hang from hang, reaches out into our world
As if the crusted groin were a great womb
From which the parturition was never achieved
But teemed on, monstrous.

This way I can go into the night:
Not returning, for I did not come from there,
Not issuing from, nor can I now
But joining in its blind issue, joining
From the nothing I am into that something,
To be absurd, lost, unmercifully
To turn and twist with growth, and become solid.
Green, that is what I will be,
Smooth, solid, a leaf, a congeries
Of leaves
As if from mere inside to become outside,
Losing the outward look and becoming outward.

Would it be re-creation? Whose hands
Would mould me if so I became?
Would God be re-created, an empty world
Fill with his presence like a cluster of leaves?
How, if my voice were silent, and if green
Had become all I was, and smooth green
Not by me perceived, but hanging?

Arcane world no more, I am myself
What I saw in less happier days.
And how to be secret from oneself
As the living are? Their gentle
Hands and voices stretch into the world
Indicating unknown sources.

Birds of augury, the garden is full of them,
Crashing through the green tree to eat the plums,
Or one pauses musically by the pond,
A single blackbird,
Tinkling the tiles as it hops;
Or, where the cat lies, the bees
Burrow or so it seems in the tall fennel
– These too are augurs but,
So they say, have to be told.

The harvest of this or that is the best emblem
As leeks, carrots in season, coriander
And sweet-smelling things making delusion
Of consciousness two-fold:
And the mistletoe
Works towards its luminosity
But blindly.

The Rose

She looks towards the south
As all such roses do,
So, away from the house
And away from you.

She looks after the rose
Far, and far away
And all is in decline,
Even the day.

Nightshade

Enchanter's nightshade is
Of all flowers the least;
I saw her poisoned sister
Gleam from the hedge.

Wild wood-bine, cover her,
Sloe, move away!
And yet it is she
Remains in memory.

Teazles

Teazles in the swamp
With the convolvulus
Climbing among them, the willows
Backing them up.

So plenty, although it is poor
And in decay!
Harsh world, where all is
And nothing stays!

Thistles to lamb's wool
And the nettles fade:
No need to be here
When spring comes again.

At the Window

It is as if there were mountains:
Low hills only, and stars
With cloud lounging along the horizon
In the evening hours

– Miracles none too willing to be performed
Or night will fall
And with it, what? The expectation of morning;
Nothing is final.

Come winter, comes the spring
Comes light, comes dark
Come havoc, comes also peace
Or some other part.

The part lasts, but not for long, the whole
Perhaps for longer
The elements dancing, we among them
But beyond knowledge.

Is knows – is, was and will be
Knows, has known, and perhaps will
When even the quiet has gone, with the tumult
Yet all is still.

I do not think that anyone
Can know the things I have to know
And yet I know them as everybody
That ever was, knew

There being no exception to any rule
Least of all I,
Measured but not by me, irreversible
Until I die

Which issue is not for my knowing
Not for me at all
The remote structure takes me, I am part of it
And that is all.

So, when the last evening, which may be this,
Tumbles over the horizon, good for me
And no harm for anyone, only I not included
When they say 'we'.

A considerable universe
Will send its flares
Across the evening sky
For any that are there.

Not it is morning
And all the lights ride
Menacing new beginnings
From the other side.

More of the same? More of like?
Fresh wonders at least, be sure:
They never cease, my mother said.
And so ends the year.

Frost

A single fisherman in the icy water
And the river red with the sun;
He lifts his rod to the bank, winding, and packs
Then clumsily runs

Along the bank, his breath like a kettle's
In the frosty air.
I pass on the hard mud of the drove:
No-one else there.

The fields are winter now, the mallard fly
Thoughtfully, nowhere to land in the hard pools:
So am I thoughtful, less thinking than looking.
Words are for fools.

Therefore I write this, to show that I am with them
With an empty mind
– And a loose tongue, the indispensable appurtenance
Of human kind.

A Purgatory

Old people, hammering
Across the table
Their mutual disagreements
As they are able.

One says: 'Lay them out there,
The bulbs.' The other
Objects – nothing else to object to
And there must be bother.

Seventy creeps on to eighty;
Half-blind eyes
Round the kitchen table, shielded from the north wind
And the open skies.

Stepping heavenward over the rubble
Of enough years, battles, importance;
The meaning has gone, the quarrel remains
Till the last cornice.

In the West Country

The rooks rise, the pee-wits rise
Mud on the ground, cloud in the skies
Enough space for all those wings
Caw said it, the pee-wits signalled
Pouring over the empty skies.

I am alone within the circle
Of low hills, I know its ways
Somerton Moor, slight hills, great girdle
Green floor and most open days
None walks here without intention
Even I, when here, have mine
But the floors of all the oceans
Have no depths more submarine
Here we are under the heavens

As under waters, birds are fish
The sky changes, a shadow passes
As it were a passing ship.
No place for anything, the extreme
End of the world, whether depths or shore
A finger of sea merely a lane
Whether from after or to before
Time falters but March will come
And break the pee-wits into pairs
With slow flight and mournful cries
And spring the sun-shine in the air.

So it is with Engellond.
Whose bones rest here? Who was found
Lying there beside King Arthur?
Whose bones followed after
Everywhere through the land?
Not a thing one can understand
Name nor yet enumerate.
Yet we are with it and the great
Ancestors lie with the small
Not disturbing us at all
And cannot forget them, or if we do
It is not because they ask us to:
Even Brutus who came from Troy
And landed at Totnes, so they say,
Fought with giants, like that of Cerne
Who held the island in those times.
So it was. That much is firm.
Whether the whole British race
Sprang from him, may be doubted.
But at Ozleworth I dare say lie
Some of them and you will find
My ancestors among the rest.
Elias Wyrloc not least
For he lived before Polydore
Somewhere there on the Severn shore
Though he was an outrageous Saxon
– The best stock, when all's said and done.
How do I trace myself from that?
It does not matter, it can't be done.
Yet that man who climbs Rat Hill

Is my brother, I know him still:
And that woman is half my mother
Who passed Pig Hill with a basket of eggs
Three hundred years ago, if you will
Or four hundred, it does not matter.
All gone now? It is perhaps
And nothing can make it more than that.

Who was it, from Ilminster
Spire, as he calls it – it is a tower –
Found the English people missing?
But they are there about their business
As in other places, Birmingham
Say or Hull or Immingham
– I mention such unlikely places
For I have seen as many faces
Of my compatriots, perhaps more:
More, certainly, rich and poor.
A soldier who had lost a thumb
And came to visit where the trams
Screeched to a halt, 1918;
A queue outside the chapel hall
Waiting not for jobs but the dole;
A thumb without a soldier, found
Later, upon Irish ground.

By Mina Road I crossed the Frome
Hic, illic, I knew it had come
Past beeches near Oldbury Court.
The Fleet runs underground, the Lea
Has no swans now. I know what ought
To be, what is and that they are
The same. I love the squalor
Of the long cut which used the air
From Warwick Road to the Horsefair,
I walked along it to save the fare.
I am at home in Stapleton Road.
You cannot frighten me with cities
Or exact a fallacious pity
From me, for I know them all,
The posh people, the smaller, the small.
I know the gentle boy whose mother

Was gaoled for stealing from the workhouse.
There were bare feet in Freeland Buildings
And Berkeley Street. And I knew Pooch,
Beaten, precarious,
Son of a drunk in the old style.
The well-to-do had only a smile
A plant in the front room, and fear
Of less before the end of the year.
These horrors are not horrors to me
But only a picture of what must be.

What was has this advantage
That it is truer than what is
For that is gone in a moment
And the future never comes.
Irremediably old, as old is
I could do worse than look at water
The floods shining between the willows.
Unnoticeable time has gone
The inconsiderate hours have run:
I stand like time still.
Nothing but folly in the will
And amor vincit omnia.
Myself whom time devours
Heard love once, louder than any
What seemed an end was a beginning,
Now ending, as life does. All
That has passed this way is magical
No wonder therefore if the light
Falls upon England tonight
Extenuating what is ill.
Others may hope but not I
Yet what may be tried
Crossing the stream
To drop a pebble in.

Sleep

The nights are horrible: I lie awake
Caged in a body that is in decay
As are all human things. Night, you are empty
And I am full of ingratitude.

Sometimes I rise and watch the great moon
Inquisitively at the study window:
The clouds fly over it with a laugh;
Perhaps the moon herself is sardonic.

And yet sometimes she has a troubled face
But if I pity her I pity me;
Neither is in need of such attention:
I have only to wait for the last day.

But what comes indeed is day at last,
A new morning, ordinary like the others,
Nothing intimidating, the smallest hopes
Serve to plaster over the wound of night.

And yet enough remains for me to say:
Sleep is my home, sleep is where I belong.
It is not night but this exultation
Awaits me at the last but, oh, how long?

The Holy Family

Rattling away in utter outwardness,
The family that looks like an advertisement,
Suitcases shining like a bandsman's leopard-skin,
Go on their holidays where others went.

The children smile like products in a super-market,
Mean-eyed and hearty as they wave their toys.
Stand by the car! Lash on the plastic boat!
Never was such a family for noise.

The television screen looks on their doings
As they look on the television screen;
Only a little flicker on their faces
Shows that they see in order to be seen.

Which is which? What is what? There is no who,
The who has been extinguished in a hoot;
They are whooping noises even when their mouths
Stay open but the sound has been turned down.

Sweet children of unnature! Here they come,
Filling the world with cans, while every sleight
Of voice or countenance imitates death
Death before life! should be their only cry.

But their lips move to the obscene orders
Not of things seen but of the things they say
Of which they have no inkling: they are said
Only as they are seen, with the mind away.

See us! See us! We who are imitated
From far examples, which in turn are spliced
Into other and yet other far examples,
A rope of circumstance and nothing besides.

If they come from God, it is by a long route,
Through lenses which deform and desecrate.
Look at their box of toys and you will see
A grinning face, for HANGMAN is their game.

The Evasion

The life I lived was sombre and obscure
Or so it seemed, or so life always is;
The outward symptoms were ordinary,
Those of a commonplace which fails to please.

Whom? Me? Or was it I failed to please others?
As certainly I did, yet I have had
Friends and enough at all times of my life
To say the only true friend is God.

As loving, perhaps. But I have never loved
Him, or found him at the end of time:
In the world, maybe, as a remote voice
Almost heard, never quite, like a half rhyme

Or half seen like smoke on distant fields,
It might be mist, it might be rain falling.
The splendour of the sun was not my *métier*.
There might have been those who had a calling.

I am the wanderer of old stories
Or that one now making across the moor:
Old time is my time now, I am at home
With my incertitude for evermore.

'Come home to bounty' is a plausible
Request to make to those who are in need.
I look for nothing but what I find
And find nothing unless I seek indeed

As I do, can, will not. I go my way
Against expectation or surprise.
The moment that I turn is when I turn
Into the landscape and the landscape dies.

Vauvenargues

Luc de Clapier, marquis de Vauvenargues
(Fifteen kilometres from Aix-en-Provence;
I know the defile and I know Aix,
However much the latter may have grown
And the former been fouled by picture-postcards)
Found no resting-place on this earth.
Although he is supposed to have loved glory,

Such a fool, probably, he was not:
Only set out from home, in poor health,
To conquer what he must in the world.
He left behind him so grim an example,
His father who, after all, did the right thing
– No-one could say he did not, for he stayed
While people died in the streets of Aix
And all the other magistrates had fled:
The plague, 1720, when the boy
Was five years old and could not leave his mother
Waiting for news of death in Vauvenargues:
Seven thousand five hundred and thirty-four dead
But not one of them her husband Joseph.
Good non-news or bad? We do not know,
But she waited for it perhaps a year,
Until August, 1721.
They say the boy did not learn much Latin
But got drunk on Plutarch – perhaps Amyot?
How many years of barracks after that,
Inspecting guards, collecting up the drunks,
Trailing his pike in the muddy streets,
Garrisoned at Besançon, Arras, Reims?
There were campaigns, though nothing much perhaps
Historians would really care about,
Still, after all, he went from Metz to Prague
With Belle-Isle in 1741
Retreating in 1742.
It was then that, in camp beside a river
Beside which the rain put out the fires,
He learned that happiness was to be found
Creeping into the shelter of a hut
Where he could not hear the water any more.
So much service goes to a single maxim:
'CCXXIII. The contemplator,
Cushily lying in a room with carpets,
Invective' – that is the verb he uses –
'The soldier who passes the nights of winter
By the side of a river, watching in silence,
Under arms for the safety of the *patrie*.'

Anglicans

She was down on her knees before the grate
In the cold rectory, crossing a few sticks
To make a little flame look like a fire.
How long her fingers, long and slim her arms!

Then suddenly she sat back on her hams
And gazed, interrogating, serious,
Up at the heavy marble mantelpiece
Yet had no question for it, I felt sure.

But all her straight back and her jutting face,
With so fine nose and chin, and so fine lips
Must have been asking something – not of me
Who sat there as a stranger in the house.

How had her thirty summers for they were
Still summers with a touch of early spring
Come to this house to be obedient
To all the rector's nearly seventy winters?

He stood there now above her, slight and grey,
With bones as fine as glass and silver hair,
A scholar in direct line, as it seemed
From himself more than fifty years before.

Father and daughter they might well have been,
But they were man and wife, and still surprised
To find themselves alone with one another,
Still waiting for a third to turn the page.

All this was long ago, and I imagine
The girl herself septuagenarian
Hardly recovered from her first surprise
Doing the church flowers with her long hands

And knowing no-one in the congregation
Of the too-bustling village she had found
Far from the parish where she left her rector
To turn to dust in the appointed ground.

The Broken Willow

It was an old willow with a dark
Hawthorn bush underneath its leaning stem.
(The bush was dark not because of shadow
But from the rustling silver of the willow

Poring over it like an attentive head.)
Over the stile and to the river-side
I went to examine this conjunction.
It was no girl poring over a lover

Or comforting a child dark but her own.
It was an old broken sexless thing
Which time had ripped open and its tubes
Rings and soft places open in their rot,

Yet more like a circuit than a man,
A control panel with the cover off,
Saving a natural grace, a contentment
Of ruin sinking into renewed life.

Blackdown

Here was a distant and remote youth
– I saw them on waking under the old apple-tree –
And a girl smudged by time but not remote,
Withdrawn that is from him but not from me:

Wind perhaps but not much against her dress,
Enough to show the outline of a girl.
I see them both against the blackened earth
– Burnt heather, it would be, from the smell.

Walking or standing, with the sky huge
About them on all sides except one
– It might be everywhere and they hung
Among the improbabilities of youth.

What was he saying? For it is his words
Which spring as from my lips from that image.
They are obscure now but they pierced the sky,
The future, but they have not reached me.

And yet I half suspect: 'There must be something
I could do' – or 'do well' – 'I don't know what.'
But 'well' was what I meant yet this was not
Ambition, you might rather say definition.

Yet it is she has become definite;
I never did. We twist and grow together
Like old trees with their attendant ivy
And it is I who am the parasite.

Night Thoughts and
Other Chronicles

Night Thoughts

I

A wall of apples towering among leaves,
The very same I left beside the lawn,
Come back and are the apples of my eye
As I lie here in bed imagining.

And who was Mr Smith? I think of him,
Sixty years back, with dark moustache and hair,
A furnace of disaster with smoked breath:
That and a seething fury were his air.

And the Miss Jellies – yes, they wobbled too,
The name was all they needed, in that flesh
Sad and encased and withered as it was:
They passed like sailing ships and sometimes smiled.

Yet to be weak was all that they desired,
The silly savage Mr Smith, the gentle
Miss Jellies: when he broke it was to thrash
His son and call it moral, while they giggled.

Ah shepherdess, the third who comes to mind!
Your husband, a commercial traveller, came
Home from his bars and girls to find you cowering
In bridal innocence, you told the neighbours.

And Mr Hardwell, butcher, with a knife
And a brisk laugh, and kind to his old man
Who, white, plump, butchery, sat on a close-stool,
Surprised himself as were the bystanders.

Ah, memories of childhood, pile them up!
Was no day happy then? Is any now?
Or is this gruesomeness the work of night?
Observe what others come out of the crowd.

There's Mr Arthur, military, small,
With waxed moustachios to frighten boys
And a long cane, pretending to be just:
Now he is shrunken and he slinks away.

And Mr Yandall, unjust, hair brushed back,
Who swung his cane over the memory
Of stinking trenches and explained to us
A German schoolmaster would have a horsewhip.

I saw these two once in a day of triumph
Carrying a screaming boy into the staff-room
To take his trousers down, as an exception
To their kind rule of caning on the hand

Which Mr Marshall practised in the hall;
Being headmaster, he had privileges
And, on the asphalt playground, we had some
– To cower or bully till the whistle blew.

Oh Greenbank Boys', mother of charity,
The home of spelling and arithmetic,
Go into night and stay there! Could there be
Friendship or love for any of your sons?

Night holds you still, and I am held by night
Which tells me nothing but my cowardice,
My shrinking and the wish to shrink to death,
The quiet when there shall be no more time.

So, in the day-time when you see me pass,
Doubtful in spite of kindness and good fortune,
Say nothing but a superficial word
Lest I should find a voice and tell the truth.

The sourest truth has never yet been told,
Nor would I try for not all truth is sour.
Root of my being! where God hid in love
– Or did, until delight hid in her hair.

The pleasures of erotic surfaces
So late discovered or so late recalled
Took from those depths the last uncertainty
And left the world in sense around my heart,

Where it remains, and none can call me now
To any other world, I feed upon
The natural benefits of leaf and sky
And fruits in season, when the mind escapes.

Peace be with all men, and all women too,
Although I have turned my back to homely ways,
Doing what must be done because it must,
The public world of green and lavish days.

For I cannot excuse, no more than reason
A will that breaks the surface of the time:
Fruit comes when fruit will come and that is all
And so I give away even my wishes

Or would do so, if I were perfect here
As once commanded to be perfect there.
Happiness seeks no answer but itself:
Therefore the earth, therefore the sky are mine.

Thus to conclude were quite impossible
Did not life of itself itself conclude:
What reigns is queen and I the only king,
Happy at last because subordinate.

A house, a garden, those that come and go,
There are enough and more for in excess
Only is pleasure and I have it now,
Too much of everything and therefore peace.

II

Muncaster and Morella were a pair
Come out of fable into history,
Hidden deep in the former as the latter;
I pulled them out only to point a moral.

It was a shallow grave and no mistake
That hid those two, although it seemed so deep
Because I simply woke up one morning
Remembering them, and there they were before me.

Muncaster saw Morella pass his shop
Each morning as she walked stoutly to work;
There he was always taking down the shutters
For all this was a long time ago.

A hat, I dare say, of unusual pattern
Or what seemed so, over a country face,
And what else there is inscrutable
In a young woman, to a young man

And above all to one who was robust
But, as Muncaster was, strictly brought up:
This Ulysses knew how to avoid Circes
But that, in truth, is all he did know

Though once in Brighton, a wicked city,
He saw his landlady bare as a pin
Standing beside an armchair in his lodgings,
But certainly she did not stand there for him.

He left next morning for the case was plain.
If he found solace, it was different
– His duty and a little spirit-rapping
Perhaps, as extra-sensory perception.

Yet one ghost came and stood at his bed's foot,
His mother, and she called him by his name,
Then vanished, at the hour the telegram
Next morning, re-affirmed that she was dead.

Had he not come out of that northern town
Where all the clocks declared the time he knew?
Had not his father died there years before
Leaving the empty streets without excuse?

And four children looking to their mother?
Muncaster was the eldest: out he went
To earn a few shillings as an apprentice.
What would you do? What would he do but work?

Father, remote, could not become a ghost
But mother could and did, and Muncaster
Looked now upon Morella with desire.
'Good morning' was all he said at first.

And she? God knows she had known poverty,
But also pride. Turned out at thirteen
From a too numerous family and a farm,
She lived in service with a grim great-aunt.

Life was not then as life has come to be.
Morella was no daughter of a hind,
No skivvy, for she served a relative,
Yet ever, ever was she penniless

Until she came to serve at Baker Bakers,
Then she could smile, but on how much a week?
Her great-aunt only treasured her the more.
But damn such servitude! She found a friend.

A Sunday necktie under a brown face
And recollection of the ancient farm:
The hay was soft and prickled like a conscience;
She did not yield but passed into a swoon.

Was it so? Was it otherwise? The grim
Unnecessary question hung like fire.
Muncaster saw only the hopeful smile
Of a girl utterly reliable,

A good housekeeper when that was a word
Which meant frugality with elegance
So far as that might be behind the shop,
Looking out on a stony back yard.

Four children Muncaster begat, and each
Declining from the vigour of the last.
I who speak to you was penultimate
When there was faith and order in the world.

Yet these were not my parents: only shadows,
They are dancing now like figures on a wall
As firelight once was, and I believe
No worse of them than I do of myself.

III

The child in setting out is innocent,
Or is he? So, I fancy, was not I,
For weakness, fear and every form of crime
Had hung around my cradle from the first.

Or so it seems. Because, in looking back,
There is no Eden, nothing but a cloud
Louring above the trees, touching the tops.
Behind that spreads the mischief of our God.

The glade or grove of freedom down below
Is haunted by this monster of despair.
I would not notice him but go my way,
Yet I had none to go, for all was still,

Listening, inscrutable, I could not move
For fear, for fear! and not of anything
Visible, but the thing which might be seen,
Unknown, untouched, intangible, obscene.

I do not ask a psycho-analyst
To give a name to what I cannot say
Or obscure further what I did not know:
I was there, he was not, that is enough.

It is I who have followed through the years
The course that leads from fear to nothingness,
Stopped here and there to smile upon pretence
And never laid my hand upon the truth.

Story and fable now are all there is
And so I tell it here, for memory
Is treacherous and can tell a pack of lies.
Do not believe me then, I am a liar.

Truth moves upon the face of other waters
Perhaps, but not upon this raging sea.
What then is history, mine or another's?
The evil whisper of a tainted mind.

There is only a cage, and I in it,
Set in the middle of a market-place
And all you people pass, or think you do
Although the tale I tell is unreliable.

Whistle then rather with the snake charmer
For there is no music in the spheres.
A tale once told cannot be told again;
The whistle whistles and it whistles still.

Stokes Croft

It was a prehistoric afternoon
With half today's light and half yesterday's
And I heard these voices: no, there was none,
Only a girl standing in a doorway.

Or was it? Seen or heard, the long mist
Ran past the stony wall, the brick wall
Along the pavement of Kingsdown Parade,
My footsteps perhaps, or the last sound,

Not here, not there, only a voice calling:
You are the clock, I am eternity
That never was, nor will begin again,
Coming for me now across the moors.

Under all this, what cover for our lives?
What is asserted loses power at once
And had none then, when only agony
Answered the affirmation: This is love.

The mind crept sideways through the streets, the body
Huge above cities, strode like Gulliver:
Stoke's Croft and Sussex Place, welcome me now.
Now comes the conqueror with the withered arm;

And now comes the dark-faced boy built like iron,
Son of a warder, prison in his grip,
And now comes Welsh Stringy fresh from a mine,
Dark, Celtic, venomous and hymn-singing;

And the white hero who as called O'Connor,
Captain of everything, suave as a knife,
Though after two years his teeth had gone,
His fingers were stained, his face pimply and sallow,

The dulness of knowledge in his eye;
And Pussy Carter, masturbator, sallow,
Grinding his teeth and crying in despair:
'Do you suppose that that one is pure?'

As she came primly walking over the bridge,
Wheeling her bicycle to be admired.
He had also lain in a single bed
In a girl's house – her parents were away –

And she came to the bottom of his bed
And sat there in her night-dress while his prick
Rose and he entertained himself with it,
Judging the girl had caught him in a trap.

No wonder that the sky hung heavily
Over this city of so little pleasure
Where youth was expended in a groan
Or winched into agony by the mind.

O corps féminin qui tant est tendre,
In theory at least and to the touch,
The lightest touch through aluminium clothes
Or winter coat that stood away the hand.

No names, no pack-drill is a pretty legend,
For I had none of these and much of that,
Anonymous even to myself
But trudging under loads of infamy.

I could name places where I stood at ease
And watched and waited and nobody came.
I could name others where the crucifixion
Nailed me to mist in spite of company.

The intervening years have hardly mattered:
Some love, much coldness, neither mine nor hers
But in an eradicable world
Placed and objective as a wall of stone.

Mr Crocker

And Mr Crocker was a lame figure,
I see now how he was regarded then
In spite of hair brushed back and dapper manner,
Affable, smart, devoted to his mum.

The leader of the Boys' Life Brigade
– Left-right, with swagger stick under his arm –
Had been a private in another war
And even, so he told us, left for dead

Under a heap the Germans came and prodded
With half-indifferent bayonets while he
Constrained himself to imitate his neighbours,
Which then succeeded, and succeeded still

As he marched with the Boys' Life Brigade.
There must have been others in like case
For one evening in the Counterslip,
On rumpled cobblestones beside the dock

I can remember their 'Into line!'
Marching off one by one the companies
Were in Picardy for the officers;
For the boys, under that romantic shadow.

Fred Crocker dreamed himself and others too:
'I'm one of the nuts from Barcelona'
Was beautifully sung by him, but best of all,
On a stage with foot-lights in the chapel hall

'Burlington Bertie': costume, grey topper,
Morning dress I suppose, and walking stick
With silver top. Burlington Bertie rose
At three and reached the Park about four,

A social splendour not allowed to Fred
Who lived with mother in Freemantle Road,
Rose at 6.30 (a.m.), laid the fire,
Cleaned up a bit before he went to work.

For Park, Fred Crocker had Eastville Park
With coats for goal-posts and him referee.
He blew the whistle and they kicked the ball:
The 'Life' in 'Life-boy' meant a lot to him.

Crocker F., your name should have been upon
A war memorial and you safely dead,
Honoured and honoured when the bugles blew
The Last Post till Revelly woke you up.

But you had life to live, a bunch of flowers
To carry round to your young lady's door,
Your best tie adjusted, grey suit brushed,
But she was on the sofa with a friend,

Perhaps somebody's uncle, the moustached
And tooth-showing salesman with gold rings
Who had a quicker way than you with girls
And strummed on them as sometimes on the piano.

It was the old bawd opened the door,
Discreet and prim as any chapel-goer,
Then shut it in his face, having explained
That Miss Rita Surface had a cold

– Or any other name she might have had.
I hope they burnt their ashes long ago,
All of them; but worst of all I think
Fred Crocker may live now as he lived then.

Granny Underdown

Muses, you are the daughters of memory;
Then let me be the son of one of you
And take a little after my grandmother
Without too much verisimilitude.

Show Granny Underdown, who had none.
Her kisses had been given long ago
And she gave others in memory of them
Now that she had become her own mistress.

A child might take them and a child had to:
Lie on your bed, shrivel your body up
Or put on your bob bonnet and go out;
There was no end, it seemed, to your aggressions.

Everything happens and then nothing more;
The violet on Gran's bonnet was half-mourning
Of how many years before, and now she
Had to prepare herself to be half-mourned.

Her quarters were in our former play-room:
Where Paphalonian armies on the floor
Had always had the better of the Gerondians
Now stood embattled her *pot-de-chambre*.

Death had to come but would not come quickly;
Old hands grew bonier, old eyes more sunk
– No visitors except a worried son
Fearful lest he should have his mother back.

One day she went. Returning home from school
I saw the ambulance stopped at the gate
And hung back at the corner of the road
Lest Granny Underdown should catch my eye.

She was borne on a stretcher, which I saw,
Also the slight shape underneath the blanket,
The men putting her in the ambulance:
The ambulance drove off and all was safe.

So I went home. My mother, close to tears,
Said: 'You should have come to see her and say good-bye.
She would have been pleased.' The hand of death
Had been close enough for my liking.

But what rankled in my mother's mind
And made her pause sometimes among her cooking
Was Gran's parting reproach, often recalled:
'You said I need never go from here.'

'I should never have promised: it was wrong,'
My mother said and bit her lip again.
What remorse, for an innocent remark!
The old farm stirred in her, and fortitude

Of how many industrious generations,
Some in the dairy, some about the house,
While toothless grandmothers rocked by the hearth
Or mumbled old advice from their beds.

But for my part, to be relieved of death,
– Or what was so near it, to my mind,
That nothing in me made the fine distinction –
Was all the care I had that holiday.

Arthur Fry

The best come out of the worst houses
Or so it seems, although it is not so,
But the explosive fires of Berkeley Street
Concealed spirits greater than any I knew.

To be drunk on Saturday night, to bawl
Was an exception to a better rule.
I think so too and so thought Mrs Fry,
Careful and grey and living next door.

The other Mrs Fry – at two doors up,
And no relation, as was pointed out –
Was a balloon that sailed past the door
Each day at lunch-time for her pint of beer

Which she bore fervently in a jug
– Mild, probably – to have with her lunch:
So reckless were some of the lower orders.
And this Mrs Fry had a son,

Perhaps a grandson, now I think of it,
But it was she was the enlivening presence
With a clout for the children, or a voice
Calling and calling till they came back home.

Arthur was this hero: four years old, and fat,
He could be seen grovelling on the road
And shouting 'I be dead' as one alive
Until collected with the horse manure

Carefully watched for when the baker came,
Or milkman: Mrs Fry, with spoon and bucket,
Took it up thoughtfully and puffed back home
Though what she did with it I never knew.

Arthur grew bigger still, a footballer
Instead of just a football, with a voice
Still noticeable. It is no wonder then
That when the war came, Arthur was reported

To be a sergeant up at Horfield Barracks,
Giving the recruits hell, as far as noise
Could penetrate their often wily minds
As well as tell the left foot from the right.

I might have joined the Gloucesters and been educated
By Arthur in my turn, but so it wasn't
And what became of him I do not know:
Perhaps he was a prisoner at Dunkirk

Or met a bullet in North Africa
While I – but I am not among the presences
Which crowd into my mind or one by one
Appear out of the unacknowledged past.

A second war, to join that other one
That hung about my boyhood like a dream
With cold steel clicking as the trench was taken:
No real death could ever equal that.

And out of how many snug houses
– Snug but impoverished as the world now is –
Had come those who returned to bear trophies,
A shell-case, polished, on the window-sill.

The Methodists

The Eastville Park United Methodist
Church – facing the park – had a high terrace
From which the worshippers came down on Sunday
Like angels descending Jacob's ladder.

Yet I cannot have seen them, for I was
One of the company, not in holiness
But in my Sunday suit or maybe jersey,
The best I had, respectable certainly.

To get outside was more than the word of God
The minister with the bald cranium
And floppy side-pieces, prayed in confusion:
His prayers were preachings and his preachings prayings

And what he prayed for was the unemployed
Who came in person to the Men's Bright Hour
Just round the corner, in the afternoon;
When I was old enough I went to that.

The Leader was a military man
Who wished that he had been an officer
And made up for it now with his moustache,
His brushed-back hair and natural stocky build.

The men whose hour was said to be bright
Sat round morosely, but they sang out loud
Approving the statistics in the prayers:
'O Lord, who hast all this information.'

A local journalist talked about Gogol
– He had not read him but neither had we:
'Our speaker this afternoon.' Men looked
At their frayed cuffs and waited for a hymn.

'These things shall be, a nobler race,' etcetera.,
'Than e'er the world has known' would soon arise.
Meanwhile Praise God! – but with conditions –
And woe to any man who lost his pride!

A wan packet of Woodbines in the pocket
Was fingered by the noblest, going out.
They said: 'Never light three from one match!'
– The old superstition from the trenches.

And if one should die, the cemetery
Lay ready at the end of Gloucester Street.
– Wet acres of clay! – I knew them well,
From which there could be no resurrection.

And once, on a remarkable day,
The minister came to lead a coffin out
From our dark dining room: he touched my shoulder
But I would have no comfort from that man.

His touch only precipitated tears
For my dead sister gone beyond recall.
What had his putty hand to do with her?
I shuddered, lurched, and moved a foot away.

So all sorrow ends in sorrow now.
The only comfort is when we forget,
As we forget, and are forgotten too.
So much mercy there is: no doubt of that.

Montagu House

He was a poet that I had admired
When I was fifteen or thereabouts
And borrowing books from the Fishponds Library:
Umberto Wolff, the old papers said,

As I discovered when, seven years later,
I went to work in Montagu House
And he came floating down the marble steps
In a cape and raised his broad black hat to me,

Ironically, no doubt. I was the least
And most unsuitable of the recruits
The annual harvest had brought into Whitehall
– No notion of anything, shy as a rabbit.

Humbert – as he had been long enough –
Was clever, suave, dramatic and remote
And sat in a great eighteenth century room
With a door open to the ante-chamber

And there, behind a paper-loaded desk,
The young man who was his secretary,
Polished, but talkative and affable,
A dark Irishman who moved dartingly.

Wolfe at his desk within was darker still
And darted faster when he had a mind to.
He visualised telephone numbers on the wall
Brilliantly, and admitted they were wrong.

The great man wrote in the Sunday papers,
On files, and in the *Strand* magazine,
Acted the poet with his floppy hair
And courted ladies who were not his wife.

My principal, in a remote room
Far from the centre, took my case in hand,
Explained with donnish elegance and a giggle
Everything a provincial could not know

– More or less everything, you might say.
A soft Sherborne man from something, Oxford,
He explained how files worked, French was pronounced,
And how one raised one's hat, passing the Cenotaph.

I gathered Wolfe was a better poet
Than Yeats: and my incredulity
Was not well received: but I was received
With tact, understanding and despair.

Into the vivid world of better people,
One quiet morning, Mrs Wolfe arrived
To face the private secretary's refusal:
'Mr Wolfe has a meeting at the Treasury.'

A baffled wife paused and then looked
At the open door. Suddenly, from within,
A roar: 'Moriarty!' She swept past
The secretary, who fled like a hare.

But old De Boos, with whom I shared a room,
Dug two spits in his garden every year.
A silver man who had failed years before
Filled up his time by doing chess problems.

So were they then, the high and the low.
Outside this fastness, unaware of them
And waiting for their dole, the unemployed
Huddled and queued along the chapel wall.

In the Raj

He was a tight-lipped devil and a rigorous
Company sergeant-major, I recall
Under the sweaty sky of Barrackpore,
Where all was sweat, where clothes were never dry

And Bengal rot started between our toes.
The sun of Asia! So it seemed to us
And the dead rotting by the Ganges shore
Where melons grow huge but taste of nothing

And the poor lie all day upon the streets
While the exquisite Brahmin minces by.
The air-conditioned and American
Left us to treason and the Queen's red-coats,

Quiet and moderate men, you might say,
Shipped out there, packaged, waiting for our turn
And doing nothing with expiring hope
But drive the kites off from our stinking food.

CSM Birt was adept at all this,
Long enough resident to have prepared
His own devices for a happy life
Or, if not happy, one he could control.

It came first like a rumour in the dark,
There in the sun, that something was amiss:
The CSM glowered and said less
And what the sepoys said I do not know.

I was elsewhere, a thousand miles away,
When an explicit story reached my ears.
CSM Birt had been under arrest,
Then court-martialled. What the swine had done

Was to sell army pistols in the bazaar.
So far, there was only curiosity.
But then the tale came out. One night the guard
Of Indian Other Ranks had been turned out

While Birt said he would check the weapon store.
He took the pistols and accused the guard
– Such turpitude behind those foxy eyes
Which seemed dishonest, abject is what they were.

It was some two years later I saw Birt
And at a depot far from Barrackpore.
With three stripes on my arm I stood outside
The sergeants' mess and Birt came slinking past,

Abashed, silent, shorn of his insolence,
Looking at no-one and his face was dead,
The first day out of gaol, a cowed man
Waiting a posting where he was not known.

Different was Curly, now inside the mess:
A rough, soft-spoken man, I do not know
What his crime had been when, years before
He had done time in a military prison,

Running in circles in the blazing sun.
The NCO in charge threw boxing-gloves
And any man they hit must fight with him,
A bruiser with a pair of bruising gloves.

'Never no more,' Curly would say, 'never no more,
They won't get me again, happen what may.'
He drew a long breath and turned aside
Into the racket of the gramophone.

It was a servile life, the only dream
Was white wings over the fucking cliffs of Dover.
Roll on that fucking boat. Get up them stairs.
And some of the fucking officers was shits.

But one especially, as I remember,
A jumped-up quarter-master, regular,
Who wired a hut to spy upon the men.
It was a round-faced corporal who refused

To obey orders while the wires were there
And in a flash was put behind bars
While sympathetic mates did guard outside.
I do not know the end of that story

Except that two days later he was out,
The wires dismantled and the adjutant
Putting the best face on it that he could.
And I remember other men, six or seven

Years out from home, promised a break at last
Then told they could not go, whose passion would
Have torn the camp up and yet nothing happened,
So impotent was rage against that rule.

Ah servitude! We who have been in chains,
Accepting bitterness for every day,
Now walk as free as any men can be
And know that every pleasure ends in death.

The Pleasers

All that remains to tell is how, later,
I became a top person in my way
But did not reach the top after all,
Because I had not the right sort of mind

Or because, when Fortune's smile was half-formed,
I did not keep a civil tongue for her
As certainly as the best people do,
Who otherwise would never be the best.

No matter now. No matter, really, then
Though then it seemed a matter of importance
That scurvy characters should win all
– As so it seemed, and so in part it was,

As was the case no doubt in other courts
In other times, and so it always is.
The most expensive thing is innocence
Which I half-had, yet not more than half;

For who can walk in the raging world
Without fury or fear or, worse still, hope
Which is the poison which endears us most
To fortune and betrays us most at last?

We work the world we live in, and so I
Whom other times and places would have made
A different thing – as all of us are made
By times and places which we do not choose –

Wanted the vanities I saw around me
And not the good of ordinary work
Which someone has to do and which I did
My share of, I suppose I may say.

But honour, now given another name
Though not another substance, drives us on:
Ambition can take our sleep away
And it took mine, although I knew better

And know it better, probably, than you
Unless you too have known camps and courts
Or some contemporary equivalent
Where men push for distinction as defined

By the conventions of an enterprise.
It is an unfashionable confession
– All true confession is, for anything
More or less fashionable is always right.

Yet those enemies that I remember
Were silly men enough, though clever men,
But what they had which others did not have
Was more than any poison I had drunk

Which turns to bile and sometimes to anger.
They had a self to love and loved a self
Illusory as any of my own
Yet believed in without intermission

– A picture of greatness in the mind
Which convinced them before convincing others,
Or else a cynicism which betrayed
Everything but its own skill in betrayal.

So one knew how to flash beautiful eyes
And talk like a book on any subject;
One sneaked and lied because lily-livered,
Dreading all that might keep him from success.

One dreamed of triumph and enforced his dream
On any weak enough to let him have it,
For triumph needs subservience and that
Can generally be bought with promises.

The other had no strength to spread his lie
So told enough truth to please his friends
And, falsifying records when it suited,
Made sure that no critic should come near.

And both fawned and flattered when they saw
The possibility of any benefit
– The darlings of their betters, till too late
Those betters found they too had been betrayed.

But so the world is, and to complain
Is only ignorance of what must be;
Whoever seeks salvation in it for
Himself or for his friends, should take a knife.

For My Brother

John Sisson 1908-1983

The little cat, the night before she died,
Took four steps from the door and then she fell.
I thought of that, John, when Molly told me
That you had gone into the garden and fallen

– Out by the French window, as I imagine,
To look down where the elms used to be
Though it is several years since they went,
But nothing so dramatic was your end;

It was simply that you did not have your stick
And so, exactly like the cat, you stumbled.
It was the next day when you departed,
Sitting in your arm-chair and closing your eyes

For the last time on the television screen,
I hope to see perhaps the west country
Where you and I had walked long ago
Out of the mean streets and the seedy city

– Snuffy Jack, Cromwell's Encampment, Moor End,
These were places, there were many more
And you, if you remember anything
Will recall how we walked to Cerne Abbas

Thirty miles and arrived in the rain
So that the Giant which we saw for the first time
Could hardly be seen: and it was next morning
When we looked out through the workhouse window.

'You will not be overlooked,' the ex-police-constable
Had said, showing us into the bare room,
A dormitory in which we were alone
With the row of windows and the night outside.

No more were we, but when the morning came
We looked over the slope of Giant Hill
With sunlight pouring on it, and there he was,
One truncheon hoisted and the other covered

– Somebody's notion of propriety.
Not everyone stopped at Cerne Abbas then
Or belted past: a county where the roads
Were still walkable, where cottagers

Still kept pigs and looked hard at strangers
From, as it seemed to us, Celtic eyes.
All that is in the past and now you with it,
The closed book, after so many pages.

O gentile Engleterre, a toi j'escrits
John Gower

God Bless Karl Marx!

Read me or not: I am nobody
For myself as for others, and so true:
If only it were also so with you
Every accommodation would be easy.
But so it is not, for what we see
Assumes as we look the mask of who,
Doing convincingly what others do:
So you become yourself without falsity.
Or so it seems. But when delusion stirs
It dreams of a mask, of his or hers,
And so must you. Where is the truth in that?
And you who read me read nothing or, worse,
What you make out for yourself, some borrowed features.
Who is what you say but I answer, what?

Vigil and Ode for St George's Day

Déjà il ne cherchait plus le bonheur
RENÉ BÉHAINE

What is the cure for the disease
Of consciousness? The cures are three,
Sex, sleep and death – two temporary
And only one that's sure to please.

In sex the circles of the mind
Close to a point and disappear
And that is something, till we hear
The world again and are not blind.

Sleep closes round us from without
Until it has us in its grip
And then the pincers start to nip:
It tells us what to dream about.

And death? Then all is gone, or so
There is best reason to believe.
In manus tuas: what we leave
Is certain, and enough to know.

For we are stone, or so they say
And how should we have ears to hear
Any objection, we who are
The treaders of the obvious way?

Either the truth is what we see
Or else it is not to be seen.
No more is it, perhaps; that green
Is grass, that tall thing is a tree.

But what else is it cunning men
Invite the suckers to believe?
All manner of follies weave
Their ways past us with if and when.

Yet there is truth which we assert
And I myself would die for one
If there were need, as there is none:
Better the world should be inert.

There is a time, it is enough
To know, there have been, will be times
And places when and where the crimes
Habitual to mankind, grow rough.

But we can rest in comfort, no
Mind need assert what all betray.
We in the light of common day
Without concern watch the light go.

So must it be, that only death
Relieves us at the sentry-box;
The guard comes marching up, the flocks
Of augurs' birds catch at our breath.

I watched them once, when harmlessly
They flew as martins near the house,
Dipping and soaring, and could rouse
No trouble but in memory.

A line of sceptical recruits,
Myself among them, waited for
What fortunes there might be in war
But no-one found the one that suits

Because no fate is suitable
To any man who hopes for more
Than comes his way, or comes before
He has decided it is well.

For fortune like the birds that fly
Takes its direction from the wind
Which no man changes or holds pinned
And which blows on us till we die.

The first, the bitter lot of all,
Is to be born, for so it is
As time and place and parents please
Or rather, as their fortunes fall.

Then come the choices: none is right
For none is as the birds allow;
By Aldebaran and the Plough
They pass, we into darker night.

That much is tolerable, but that
The same should swallow up our land
May not be borne, and yet the hand
Points to the hour that we are at.

The time that bore us runs away,
The place must follow, the extreme
Edge of the world is here, the dream
Breaks on another homely day.

The strong will always be unjust,
The weak will cringe and run away
Or find their comfort in a day
When they will do as all men must:

And who would dare to boast of that?
We who survive, though not for long,
May envy those who do most wrong
Yet soon enough they too fall flat.

And who is he who in the end
Loves life more than he longs for death?
Does not the most exulting breath
Turn at last to the only friend?

The spirit which was proud to be
Collected in a little earth
Finds what the privilege is worth
And in that knowledge he is free.

Fortune which holds us in its grip
Does not change, though it seems to do,
The same for me, the same for you
Whatever words are on your lips.

For what we say and what we are
Are different things, and we console
Our patience when we take a role:
Only one voice will carry far.

Christ comes to all, because belief
Is necessary for our peace,
The world cannot give it, release
Can only come by way of grief.

The Man of Sorrows is the one
Who represents the way we go:
He is the only one we know
However furious our fun.

For he knows better than the most
Experienced practitioner
Whatever comes to him and her
And that their pleasure is a Ghost.

And of death too he understands
The comfort and the mystery;
The secrets of mythology
Lie always open in his hands.

The bark of Charon and the bite
Of Cerberus, are jokes to him
Yet in his mind no single whim
The pagans have, is lost from sight

For all is laid upon the cross,
The auguries, the sacrifice,
The marching armies, every vice
And virtue, every gain and loss.

There, all was nothing to the God
Who was inside the man, who was
The man and all was all because
He died where Adam first had trod.

The intervening years were gone:
All this he did for Adam's sake
And so the future reeled to take
Another face from that time on.

The face is sorrow, like the Man,
The underworld no longer waits
To have our shadows and our fates
And where our God hung, others can.

He has gone climbing out of space
And time, yet taken with him all
That we have here, the world is small
Beside his new appointed place

Which also leaves him where he was
Before he came, but with a new
Body which he already knew
From his intent to visit us.

Our bodies too, so lifted up,
Will shine as his does, so they say,
But that is for another day
When we have also drunk the cup

Which will not pass, and when we leave
The world we credit now for one
Invisible under our sun
And in which none of us can believe.

So glory, laud and honour, all
To the impossible, and most
To Father, Son and Holy Ghost
And let our own pretensions fall.

They may, but only if we love
No other as we love our end.
The night comes down upon our friends
As on ourselves, yet still above

Their graves, the grass grows and the sun
Shines upon others as on us:
The fieldmouse and the weasel pass
And do not ask whose will is done.

But we, who saw our friends depart
Into the shadows of the moon
Leave others, as it may be soon,
Glad we are gone or, in their hearts

Holding our tiny memory
A moment till that too goes out.
Why not? For we can never doubt
The comfort of mortality.

Yet may Time's treasure still remain
Until it quietly ebbs away
Beyond our knowledge, England's day
– I cannot help it, for the pain

Of her demise is more than all
The mind can suffer for the death
Of any creature that draws breath,
And should her time come round again

Our dust will stir, not to a drum
Or any folly men devise
But to the peace which once our eyes
Met in her fields, or else in some

Of her best children, from the first.
All this is folly too and yet
Rather than any should forget
Let this sad island be immersed

In raging storm and boiling seas.
Let no man speak for her unless
He speaks too for her gentleness
And it is her he seeks to please.

Waking

May has her beauties like another month,
Even June has her pleasures. I lie here,
The insistent thrush does not trouble me
Nor the slight breeze: a tree stump looks like a cat.
Yet all is not altogether well
Because of memory; crowd round me here
Rather, you ghosts who are to drink of Lethe.
Who else would go back to the upper world
Or take again the nerve-strings of the body
Or will to suffer grief and fear again?
Once I did: and the echo still comes back,
Not from the past only – which I could bear –
But from the young who set out hopefully
To find a bitter end where they began
And evil with the face of charity.
I have seen some such and do not want
Ever to pass along that road again
Where blind beggars hold out their hands for coin
And saints spit in their palms. This I have seen
And shall see if I wake from sleeping now.

Another Waking

Was it a cat squealed or was it metal,
This grincement I heard as I awoke?
A cloud in the sky and a cat under the bed,
Both perhaps startled by my waking.
The cloud steamed forward, lumen de lumine,
A puff of white travelling over the blue.
The cat? There was an impact in the bushes,
I saw it no more than uncertainly.
Incident? Hardly. Machination, dream?
What else is there? Things are what they seem.

Cotignac Again

Cotignac is full of spies
– Not one but tells lies
Or whatever interests him;
Not one but looks out
To enquire who's about,
To mark him down and take his name.
The windows may be high, the wall
Blank, it does not matter at all:
Nothing is impervious
To the man who is callous.

Cotignac is full of thieves
– Not one but leaves
Footprints everywhere. How can
We hope to find the right man?
How believe what is said
By a man who may be dead?
How know if we are known
Or can be, by such a one?
How escape certainty
Which is of all pleasures the least?
How know what we know
When we dislike it so?

False amour where truth is found
There is none around:
The imaginary point
Puts all out of joint
– Lies, lies and lies.
So, the imaginary
Point recedes and the fact
Formerly exact
Loses reality.

Dead man, you are a lover
In the spaces of hell, either
Racketed by images
Or tendentious ghosts.

Satan in all his pride is
More complacent than most:
You mop and mow
Among the least,
Up and down, around,
Fabulously misplaced,
Erroneous, king of error,
Queen of yourself or
Mere bath-water running out:
Do you not hear the gurgle?
Follow the circle,
An ape with others, holding hands.
The supreme exit is at hand
– City of rascals, the
Infernal city
Where every inhabitant
Is imaginary.

The Absence

How can it be that you are gone from me,
Everyone in the world? Yet it is so,
The distance grows and yet I do not move.
Is it I streaming away and, if so, where?
And how do I travel from all equally
Yet not recede from where I stand pat
In the daily house or in the daily garden
Or where I travel on the motor-way?
Good-bye, good-bye all, I call out.
The answer that comes back is always fainter;
In the end those to whom one cannot speak
Cannot be heard, and that is my condition.
Soon there will be only wind and waves,
Trees talking among themselves, a chuchotement,
I there as dust, and if I do not reach
The outer shell of the world, still I may
Enter into the substance of a leaf.

Song

Others shall live instead of me
The old say, with a silly grin.
What pleasure in a withered skin!
The real life is all within.

And then the others? God, they stink,
They sweat, for they live normal lives
But when they suffer, nothing thrives,
They drink all day or beat their wives.

If others live instead of me
I'd have them do it tidily
Not bothering the old at all
– So wide is human sympathy.

What Do You Know?

Not all the reasons that they give
Will ever make their actions live.
　　　Reasons, ha, ha!
You think you have them when you say
Some words that you learned yesterday.
　　　Ha, ha!

What takes the sun across the sky?
What makes you cough or spit or sigh?
　　　Reasons, ha, ha!
You do what you must do, you do
What seems because it seems to you.
　　　Ha, ha!

Mirrors flash everywhere, before,
Behind, which makes your reasons more.
　　　Reasons, ha, ha!
Election, with a touch of grace,
Can save your independent face?
　　　Ha, ha!

Perhaps the course of history
Will turn out dialectically?
　　　Reasons, ha, ha!
So that's the shape it is? Ah well,
So you know that! How can you tell?
　　　Ha, ha!

The swindle of the world, the mind
Visited upon humankind,
　　　Reasons, ha, ha!
You may be sure, is never sound:
Take a look at the whirling ground.
　　　Ha, ha!

The Description

Ne dites pas: la vie est un joyeux festin;
Ou c'est d'un esprit sot ou c'est d'une âme basse.
Surtout ne dites point: elle est malheur sans fin . . .

Do not describe human life at all,
Any description is a load of rubbish:
Live it – as you can not avoid doing
And therefore you can make nothing of that.

The descriptions, whether gloomy or enticing,
Are comforts of a kind, to their inventors,
But the world spreads out underneath them
Inscrutable as ever, like lands in flood.

No word covers a square inch unharmed
But what the harm is, we do not know
Nor do we know what the knowing would be
If know and harm are the right words.

No word is right, that is the long and short of it,
No saw is true, though it is nice to think so;
Even these verses wobble in the making
And yet I have brought them to an end.

The Hare

I saw a hare jump across a ditch:
It came to the edge, thought, and then went over
Five feet at least over the new-cut rhine
And then away, sideways, as if thrown
– Across the field where Gordon and I walked
Talking of apples, prices and bog-oak,
Denizens of the country, were it not
That denizens do not belong, as they do
And the hare tossing herself here and there.
And I? If I could, I would go back
To where Combe Farm stood, as Gordon's stands

Trenched in antiquity and looking out
Over immense acres not its own
And none the worse for that. You may say
It is the sick dream of an ageing man
Looking out over a past not his own.
But I say this: it is there I belong,
Or here, where the pasture squelches underfoot
And England stirs, forever to hold my bones.
You may boast of the city, I do not say
That it is not all you say it is
But at the Last Judgment it will stand
Abject before the power of this land.

On the Prayer Book

The empty bucket, sound, clangs in the well
And draws up nothing, banged against the wall.
Was meaning down there? It is dry now
And all around the well-head chirrup and mow
Empty figures of silken Why and How.

To His Grace the Archbishop of York

*with recollections of his contribution to the BBC 'Sunday' programme,
30 December, 1984*

A shepherd in a northern town
Saw angels just above his head:
'They look like geese to me!' he said
And took his bow and shot one down.
'That will do, as I am a sinner
For Mrs Joseph's Christmas dinner!'

He seized the bird and dragged it round
To where the happy couple slept:
'My dears, take this.' And as he stepped
Inside the stable, there he found
A baby with a brilliant future.
'It shows,' he said, 'in every feature.

'Why, bless my soul,' he added laughing,
'Mary, they said you were a virgin!
The truth, I said, is just emerging.
By God, and here it is! A passing
Joke but I mean to keep it up
When I am made an archbishop!

'By mirrors and prevarication
I will proceed, they will like that;
The creed is rather awkward but
It works, in the imagination.
None the less I put more reliance
On stinks and elementary science.

'God, I am sure, won't touch my minster;
He only works in images,
They're harmless, aren't they? What a wheeze!
As soon suppose he'd make a spinster
Into a mum, as that he'd trade
In medals for the Fire Brigade.

'Pull up the ladder, Jack, the rungs
Are words I used in my ascent.
The Word is nothing different
And earlier ages got it wrong.
After all, Athanasius
Can hardly count as one of us!'

Thoughts on the Churchyard and the Resting-Places of the Dead

FROM THE GERMAN OF ANDREAS GRYPHIUS
for Kurt Ostberg

1

Where am I now? Is this the ground
In which humility may flower?
Is there refreshment to be found
For those who knew in busier hours
The heat and burden of the day?
And bore the frost of bitter nights
And in the midst of hurts and slights
Took up their share of care and pain?

2

Where am I? Here are the narrow plots
Which hide within their pregnant wombs
What has been sown there by the God
Who can wake corpses from their tombs.
Where some see splendour, I see fear.
Not for me the Hesperides
Or Babylonian luxuries;
I see the best of gardens here.

3

Although here no seductive scent
Streams from the jasmin and the rose,
Although no tulips here present
Their brilliant military shows,
Though here no cultivated land
Grows pomegranates or such-like fruit
It bears here what I long for but
What the world does not understand.

4

O School, in which the best instruction
Is given to us mortal men!
No pages full of false deductions
And no delusive apophthegms.
While I have passed in vanity
The wasted treasures of my time
The hours spent here instead define
The straight way to eternity.

5

O School, which utterly appals
Those whom the world regards as clever,
Which those for whom repute is all
Or money all, regard with terror.
O School which terrifies the mind
That knows the lot and has no conscience!
O School which offers no emollients
To cut-throats claiming to be kind.

6

O School, which puts men in a sweat
And makes their hair stand upon end
When they are near the judgment seat
But nearer their lascivious friends.
O School, which makes a man's knees knock
And his limbs tremble, cold as ice,
Because with all money can buy
He knows his mind is closed to God.

7

I go to school with you and long
To fathom where true wisdom lies.
Examine me! There's nothing wrong,
You will find, with my ears or eyes.
What Socrates once taught me, now
Is nothing, and the Stagirite
Has quite collapsed. There is no light
In Greek philosophy I know.

8

Who is there now that will explain
The subject that I want to master?
Set out the principles and main
Conclusions that I should hold fast to?
Or can I here and on my own
Sit down and work the answers out
That will put paid to every doubt
That troubles me? No, not alone.

9

What's happening? Is the ground I stand on
Reeling? And is that roar the trees?
Is the earth tearing its mouth open
So as to let the roots get free?
Do I hear dry bones rattling? Say,
Do I hear clamorous human voices?
Is that the south wind getting boisterous?
Or heavy stones, rolling away?

10

I stand and stare. A bitter cold
Freezes my veins, my heart, my lungs.
From my brow streams of sweat have sprung.
I am glued where the ground still holds.
The whole field has become a grave
And all the coffins are revealed.
What dust, brick, plaster once concealed
Is open now and plain as day.

11

O last but still uncertain house!
The refuge into which we creep
Whenever the clock tells the hour
And the rose pales upon our cheek.
That palace, which the world once gave,
Swearing that it would last for ever,
That same world, once our life is over
Destroys to assail us in the grave.

12

You for example were wrapped up
In tin and you perhaps in copper.
And you perhaps once had a flood
Of liquid lead to line your coffin.
You were rich, no expense was spared;
This one, now that I think of it
Had gold and marble in his pit.
Then how is it I find you bare?

13

Ah, greed and fury have not scrupled
To open up the grave's dark night,
And what I sought in pain and trouble
Lies patent in the deadly light.
Ah, lifeless men, no robber's hand
Would have intruded on your rest
Had you seen proper to entrust
Your bones in plain boards to the sand.

14

For even cedars shrink at last,
The rotten pine-boards go to nothing
And the oak's strength is quickly past,
The grave is her grave, no escaping.
Why do you value the light fir?
The joints will always crack and split.
The narrow box will go to bits
However hard you caulk and hammer.

15

God help me. Coffins open wide,
I see the bodies in them move.
The army of the once alive
Begins to exercise anew.
I find myself surrounded by
A host death has deprived of power,
A spectacle which forces showers
Of burning tears from my blank eyes.

16

O spectacle which makes the world
And what the world most values, stink.
I feel my arrogance desert me,
My courage and my folly sink.
Are these the men who ruled our land,
Defied it, knocked it, held on tight,
Who sharpened daggers, swords and pikes
And held it down with bloody hands?

17

Are these the men who mollified
The Father's heart with sighs and prayers?
Who, though distressed and mortified
Dared face his anger with their cares?
Who bewailed nothing but their faults
Though money and possessions vanished,
Though anguish left the body famished,
The oppressed spirit nipped and gnawed.

18

Are these the men who put aside
All trace of decency and shame,
Who brought from hell into the daylight
Abominations without name?
Who piled up crime on crime, who slit
Throats for fun, poisoning the world
Until the hour when they were hurled
With thunder and lightning into the pit.

19

Are these the men who were not stained
By pleasure in their pleasant youth,
Whose young minds were early inflamed
By passionate desire for truth?
Those who now sing before the Lamb
The joyful song not many know
And walk in garments white as snow
In endless peace before I AM.

20

Are those who once strutted round
In purple, silk and gold, and these
Those who crept on by on humbler ground
In hunger, nakedness, disease?
And these those whom envy so roused
They begrudged others even breath?
Whom no land could contain? In death,
In what packed quarters are they housed?

21

Where are the miracles of grace,
Beauties who captured souls by storm?
Of their delights I see no trace,
Only some ghastly heads, deformed.
Where are those whose store of knowledge
Astounded everyone? Who were
Honoured as great philosophers?
Time has demolished the whole college.

22

Now for the most part all I find
Is bones from which the flesh has slipped,
Skulls with no cover of any kind,
Faces without noses or lips,
Heads missing skin or maybe ears,
The brow and cheeks have gone to nothing
And where the lips should be hanging
Only a tooth or two appears.

23

The bones that once made up the spine
And neck, still somehow hang together
But nothing now keeps them in line,
The ribs stick out and they will never
Again hold heart and lungs close pressed;
The chest's as empty as can be,
The contents eaten, similarly
The double pleasure of the breasts.

24

What use now for the shoulder-blades?
The arms have now lost all their strength.
What served the man in all his trades,
The hand that had the management
Of tools and achieved mastery
Of sea, land, air and dared such feats
Of heroism, is in pieces,
Deprived of all activity.

25

The belly empty, hip and shin
And foot are nothing now but bones,
Hollow, misshapen, yellow green,
Broken and dry like shards or stones.
In thousand-shaped deformities
Deformity is recognised.
Here every quality's disguised,
Young, old, poor, noble, lovely, wise.

26

And these are they against whom time
Has fully carried out its sentence;
There is no trace of flesh or slime
Mortality could take from them.
Far more repulsive are those here
Who wrestle still with putrefaction,
On whom decay pursues its action,
Those who were with us till last year.

27

The pretty ringlets fall away,
The plaits begin to come apart.
Where the moist flesh still has its say,
About the temples, movement starts.
And the unseeing eyes begin
To be unstable, as the worms
Inside the head hatch out and stir,
Wrinkle the nose and break the skin.

28

The lovely cheeks crumple and shrink,
The chin and tongue and teeth show white.
Upon the coral lips black ink
Spreads blots which put colour to flight.
The forehead splits, the snowy throat
Becomes earth-coloured, as if the sun
Which shone above it, had begun
To melt the frost and the soil showed.

29

What whisper comes out through the wind-pipe?
What is that hissing in the breasts?
It seems to me that I hear vipers
Whistling their music with the rest.
What an intolerable vapour
Rises into the frightened air
Made heavy by the poison there!
So is it by the Avernian lake.

30

So steams the marsh of Camarina,
So smoke the yellow dragons' dens.
The tortures of the Japanese
Do no worse to half-strangled men
Than the plague striking from the mist
Which rises from the popping corpses
Bathed in sweet oils not long before
And incense brought from lands far distant.

31

Filth from the guts breaks through the skin
Where the maggots have bitten through.
I see the guts dissolving in
Pus, blood and water. It makes me spew.
The mildewed flesh that time has left
Is gobbled by a snaky mob
Of bluish worms which do the job
As if they revelled in the mess.

32

What is the use of aloes now?
They cannot keep beauty in shape.
What about myrrh? It has no power
To stop the youthful limbs from ageing.
Is what came out of Palestine
Asphalt or flesh? There is no knowing.
We cannot tell, of all these bones,
Which went with which in former times.

33

What use now is a splendid dress
Embroidered with a golden thread?
And is not all this silk now pointless,
Embellishing the banished dead?
See how the purple loses colour
And all that work becomes unpicked,
How quickly patters are unfixed
Which once cost hands so much endeavour.

34

You dead! Ah, what I learn from you!
What I am, what I shall become,
A little dust that the wind blew
Is all I carry to the tomb.
How long will my body persist?
How soon shall I conclude my years?
Say good-bye to those left here
And go where time does not exist?

35

Shall I be able to prepare
Thoughtfully for the long journey?
Or shall I have no time to spare
When I am called whence none returns?
Do not be sudden, Lord of Life,
Or send for me without warning!
But be with me on that last morning,
Protector, guide, my Way, my Light.

36

Where shall I leave my lifeless body,
Entrust it to the final grave?
How many, thinking to make ready,
Have their tombs built, but yet in vain!
How many lie in unknown sand?
Who can guess how chance may fall?
How many has the ocean rolled
To throw up in an unknown land?

37

It does not matter very much
Whether I'm married or lie alone,
Lord, so long as I may touch
Your garment, pleading at your throne.
I see the appointed hour like some
Tremendous prelude with great crashes
Of thunder and great lightning flashes,
And soon eternity will come.

38

When, amidst prodigies and trumpets,
We hear God's final battle-cry
Echoing through every land in triumph
Announcing death itself must die,
When marble, copper, metal, stone
And Pharaohs' tombs from their long night
Deliver to the air the light
And re-invigorated bones;

39

When the sea gives up its dead
Casting up thousands on the shore
From its deep gulfs and tangled weed
The bodies that the Judge has sent for,
When what the north wind blew off course,
What tigers ate up in Morocco
Of flames devoured in Persia,
What rivers that were sown with corpses;

40

What the Brazilian cannibals
Ate, wilder than their own wild beasts,
And those whom appetite for gold
Buried beyond hope of release;
When what Vesuvius overwhelmed
With burning ash and blazing sparks,
What Ætna buried beyond help
Or Hekla spat at in the dark;

41

When what time winnows in the air
Will suddenly be whole again;
Prisoners, however deep they are
In dungeons, will become free men
To see the Son of the Most High
Come in glory and put to shame
His foes, and in his Father's name
Sit where all causes will be tried.

42

Now hear how the Judge will pronounce
His principal and final sentence,
He who himself was judged here once
And bore it for me with all patience,
Who gives new light from heaven above:
How he makes earth dissolve, and breaks
The heavens asunder! Here stand and quake
The Jesus-haters, the Jesus-lovers.

43

Those whom I see here now without
Distinguishing one from the other
I shall see (as I cannot doubt)
Plunged into joy or sorrow, either
Into joy more than sense can know
Or sorrow such as none felt before,
Into delight for evermore
Or everlasting loss and sorrow.

44

Joys that the world cannot contain,
Sorrow before which Hell will reel,
Pleasure that destroys all pain,
Sorrows none here could bear to feel,
Pleasures that will drown all cries,
A sorrow that is pure despair,
Bliss which leaves no place for care,
Sorrow so keen it never dies.

45

Then I shall see you in your skins,
Free from corruption, with full veins;
All that before was hidden in
The grave, will be alive again.
I'll see you, but how different!
Transfigured some, O what delight!
Others disfigured, terrifying!
Joy! I shall shout, and then lament.

46

I'll see you shine with more brilliance
Than would be in ten thousand suns.
I'll see you and avert my glance
From those who have no consolation,
See some more beautiful than beauty,
Some uglier than ugliness,
Some finding comfort, some the darkness
Pregnant with ghosts and devilry.

47

Many the world called good and great
God's sentence designates as lost.
Many spat on and reprobate
Are chosen for the heavenly host.
Never mind how the marble reads,
Epitaphs may be pitched too high.
Corpses however cannot lie
Nor this Court ever be deceived.

48

The corpse shows that you must decline
In rottenness and stink to dust,
That nothing in the world's too fine
To go to ashes when it must,
That though we are not equal here
In death there is equality.
Go and prepare your case and be
Wide awake when the Judge appears.

49

He alone knows how to distinguish
In the confusion death has brought
Who will depart to endless anguish,
Who find the peace that they have sought.
He ensures that no single speck
Of dust from bodies shall escape him.
Air, wind and water keep from him
Nothing, in spite of time and death.

50

You dead! Ah, what I learn from you!
What I was, what I then shall be!
What is eternal, what is true!
No more the world shall trouble me.
Oh you who lie there, teach me so
To stand, that when I end my days
And take leave of the world, I may
Leave Death, and find Life where I go.

Toys

The brightness that things had, at one time!
When the curtain went up, everything was there,
Brilliant, alive, coloured. These two bricks
Recall it, but I cannot live again.

Miscellaneous Notes

1

Imitation silver and gold
Is all the money we have nowadays but since
The currency is only current and runs
Away anyhow to what it represents
Better not bother about the original metal
Which is only secondary, after all.

2

Better not go in for too much kissing,
I think nervously at one of those parties
At which old people greet one another effusively.
False marks of affection! as I would think,
Remembering kisses of another complexion
And not wishing to profane Aphrodite Anadyomene.

3

If things seem not to be as once they were
Perhaps they are as once they seemed to be.

God Bless Karl Marx!

A centre in a kingdom is absurd
You say? And where else would you find a word?
A theory, like a skein of mist that covers
The sacred members of a pair of lovers,
Mythological giants strewn by the way
Of history? The proletariat, say,
Reluctantly embraced by the middle class
Or some such dream? I at least
Prefer the ground under the two-backed beast:
Wet or fine it is less phantasmagorial,
You may even get a damp touch of the real
Or so it seems to me. Not only giants
But field-mice, rabbits, creatures more compliant
With grass and molehills – even human beings –
Shaped and sized more conveniently for doing
Whatever moles and men and women do,
Live in that terrain, having private limits
Less subject to the theoretical gimmicks
Of Marx and others living in a library.
Their words and noises are the things we see
Or hear or touch or smell, the mist that swirls
Around them is not everything in the world,
Just one delusion butting against others;
They say their piece and then their life is over.
If history rolls on they are not with it,
They understand for only half a minute
And then go blank. But the great sage Abstraction
Flies like a pterodactyl, with an action
Appropriate for imaginary millennia
Before or after there were any men here.
Here? Yes and now. Enough past for a man,
Some sunlight, moonlight, changing clouds that can
Be caught for a moment in an eye
Which must wear spectacles and then must die.

Looking at Old Note-Books

It would seem that I thought,
At that time, more than I ought;
I noted the reflections
Of those for whom perfection
Came in a sudden phrase:
How one should behave,
How others did, the wise
Remarks of men in difficulties
Or who observed others
Making a great pother
While they were easy themselves.
All this should have been useful
To a young man rising twenty,
Yet one finds that at thirty
He was still floundering.
If he understood anything
It was by way of suffering
For his first incompetence
Or third or fourth inability
To do anything sensibly.
How much had the wise helped?
They could do nothing themselves,
Being dead, buried in books
In octavo or folio, works
In several languages
And always, phrases that pleased.
What price then Schopenhauer,
Throwing a woman downstairs,
Fénelon, Proudhon,
Goethe in Eckermann
Or Plutarch in the North?
I might add, 'and so forth'
– Out and around
The world but all bound
In antique leather,
Mercure de France yellow
Or the elegant brown or black
Of the *Insel-Verlag*.

There was the London Library
Doing its best to confuse me
– Then back to Valéry,
Antoine de St-Exupéry,
Barrès, Cocteau, Jouhandeau
And what d'you know?
On oriental customs,
To confirm my observations
There was the Abbé Dubois
Or the Japanese school reader
For children of five.
It can cause no surprise
That with such learning
For half an hour each morning
And a supplement at night,
I knew my way all right.
The world opened before me
Like a speck in memory,
I grew in wisdom
Like a mastodon
Or other inept animal.
Behold me now, in old age,
Seated in my cage,
Pulling through the bars
What leaves can be reached from there.
Naturally I advise
The young who would be wise
To follow my example.
They should all read examples
Of the philosophers, I recommend
The moralists of course and
The epistemologists,
There is a long list.
They are not to reject
The theologians, I expect
They will find them illuminating.
Imaginative writing
Isn't all it's cracked up to be:
Take it cautiously.
Avoid writing poems, a frequent

Cause of discontent;
You may read one occasionally
And that is all
– And all I can tell
You about how to live well.

Things

It is unbuilding now,
All I have to do
– Down down and down.
It did not matter, no.

A man should have a thought
Or so I thought
But why did I think that?
I suppose, caught

By time and place,
By a name or by a face.
Why not? For then and there
That was my case.

Things rule, O.K.? The mind
Is left behind:
Dazed and amazed, numb
Not, alas, blind.

Epitaph

His full folly he would not confess to:
He could not judge what showed his better sense;
His vices – he was reckoned to possess a few –
Were, like his many virtues, a pretence.

Conclusions

*

How superficial is the mind of man!
Unhappiness, which I see everywhere,
Comes often from the thought those things are true
A momentary culture entertains,
While underneath the pull and thrust of pain
Savages those who do not understand
But have to live. Oh, how we have to live!

* *

It has gone, the old mystery
And I stand bleakly before the rain:
The church-tower sinks among trees;
Only mist remains
– Cloud fallen upon us
O let it be
Heavier than earth upon us.

* * *

All things askew: the wind
Blows from a distant forest
Composing Sibyl's leaves.

The thought is aloft, carried
Contemptuously above tree-tops
And cannot look down.

Below in the woodland path
There is moss, there are scuffed leaves.
Who walks there, rat-face?

* * * *

Now I am back in my own fen
And night has fallen, I peer through the willows
At no-one approaching across the water.
I let my past slide from me like the mist.

The ghostly people pass, of them at least,
Their bodies gone, only the shadows stay
Of ghosts that passed them, in other times,
Themselves made of shadows, and of what?
Ilot or island, home of the blest
Or of no squeaking figures but of the trees,
Bulrushes, sedge, from which the snipe emerge
Saying they have a thought, but they have none.
I have it. And yet I cannot grasp
Any except that their course is crooked.
So life ends without even a farewell:
Uncertainty remains the end of all.
The loved join the unloved, the violent
The gentle, even beauty is everywhere
And night falls stunningly, soon to be day.

News

They live in the excitement of the news.
Who is what? What is that? And is the noise
I hear from an important quarter? When
Is what to happen? Who is what, finally?

Finally nobody is anything.
That is the end of it, my busy friend
And just as what you hear has no beginning
It has, assuredly, no certain end.

The end that comes is not the end of what,
The end of who perhaps, and perhaps not;
The rattle and the flashing lights are over,
Death is overt, but all the rest lies hidden.

Think of what you will, nothing will come of that,
What you intend is of all things the least;
As you spin on the lathe of circumstance
You are shaped, it is all the shape you have.

On a Marxist Litteratus

I expect he sees the Revolution clearly,
I expect he intends to be there early:
So much to lose, so much perhaps to win
If he is only the first man to be in.
Smart in his Russian overcoat, and with fame
Still polishing the buttons in the name
Of an imaginary working class,
He really could be the first to surface.
Is he a rock? Is he a heap of pebbles
A storm or even a tide or two could level?
Is that the sea or just a plate of mist?
What makes you think that such people exist?

Conscience

For any man whose words are sold
Will sell his conscience with his words:
The more he sells, so we are told,
The more the rascal should be heard.

It may be so, for humankind
Loves a cheat at a market-stall
Rattling his wares, although it finds
The goods are worth nothing at all.

Up the Arts!

Shall we make legends of our silly selves?
The lies invented by the semi-great,
By Yeats for example, cut no ice:
After a few years the truth shows through
And where is folly or invention then?
The folly heightened, the invention fallen,
The bright surface cracks, and underneath
The muddy water slinks away to sea
Or lurks still to be lost below the weeds.
All nature will resume her homely sway;
What grew will grow, what was invented, die.

For the Primate of All England

The Archbishop of Nothingness
Blew up a bag of wind one day
In place of a sermon, more or less,
At least, that is what people say

For he would preach at politics
As hard as some might hammer texts
And if one did not like his tricks
– Why, there was a great prelate vexed.

'I may not know,' he said, 'the truth
About what happens here or there
But I must give a line to Youth
Who love explosions of hot air.

'So there am I at this committee
Or speaking at that institute:
I pour out pints of verbal pity
And kill the country at the root.

'Item, I find the Church of England
Is much too narrow for my mind.
Shall my myopic eyes look inland?
No, rather at all humankind.

'The more myopic, the more distant
The objects I prefer to see;
The more I fluff, the more persistent
I like my discourses to be.

'What happens in the heart of Africa
Pre-occupies me day and night,
Yet half a glance at South America
Enables me to put them right.

'Then why is England such a muddle?
What every Christian child should know
Is, if the bishops there are fuddled
It's I who helped to make them so.

'I told the Queen they spoke a language
That anyone could understand:
Now bus-conductors talk like bishops
And there is Babel in the land!'

In the Var

1

Yes, it is certain that all is gone
With the winter weather, as on
Mountains snow is replaced by green;
Under the blue sky nothing that was
Recently apparent, remains because
Everywhere the fresh spring is seen.

All that is gone is not lost:
Water into rivers, the frost
Melted to uncover red earth
Sweating and glistening between vines
Like cloves in a ham, mathematical signs
Concealing what all is worth.

The dormant branches come too
Into leaf; over all the blue
Sky replaces the travelling grey.
All is not lost because what
Was here yesterday, now is not.
It is death that makes the new day.

2

Adam and Eve, the prime pair,
Not stript because the air
Was always about them from the first:
The fine woman and the strong
Man they were, but not for long,
For their birth was curst

Or, not being a birth, there was a flaw
In their heredity, or else they saw
Things as they were but the presiding
Manipulator did not approve.
Be that as it may, love
Which united them, was dividing

And their mutual reproaches
Had the effect, as you may guess,
That they grew old and hideous
To one another, their bodies decayed
With the evil that made them afraid:
So much for being lustrous.

3

What is it the blue sky
And the lost darkness signify?
Nothing but the usual change.
It happens that in your case
The profound evil has taken place,
The light has gone out. Nothing strange.

For of evil there comes the good,
Not as usually understood
But different, that is all.
The new world comes, the old
Has no mind further to unfold
So that the end is fatal.

Yet not so neither for after spring
Summer infallibly comes racing,
The grapes swell and turn colour,
Autumn is here, the juice
Pours in cascades through the sluices
And then it is winter.

4

Unending, unending, or if
There is an end, the gift
Of the immutable and so
Without end or beginning.
It may be so, that is something
I do not want to know.

The horror of the world is enough,
The permanent evil, with love
Cast as the occasional good.
That this too should be permanent,
Free as it is of all intent,
Is possible. It is Christ's blood.

Credo quia impossibile
Or not at all, the light of day
Promising what it cannot perform
Or not to be credited.
Accept nothing that can be said
For to lie is normal.

5

But what of the lying light?
The shadows, under the bright
Sky the subservient Maures
Crouching between us and the sea?
The dazzle we do not see
Lapping the murderous and corrupted shore?

What of the Bessillon
Where so much murder was done?
Where were the hostages shot?
Of the dead – all the dead, for me?
It is calm now, let them be:
They are happy who are not.

Not or not, the choice
Rides over the speaking voice
Into unperceived distances.
No effort that does not creep
Under a blanket and sleeps
As the light grows less.

6

Implacable enemy, time, change,
Always the new and strange
Come to my door which is
Open to all strange visitors:
Yet, if I ask for more,
Death then to all occurrences!

– Death which is tiredness,
Neither more nor less,
The clanging angels
Are too noisy, the light
Wherever it comes from, too bright.
In change and death all is well.

To a Satirist

Leave Swift out of this;
You are paid for what you say.
Every dog has his day:
Bark like a journalist.

What you think is what they pay:
They cry 'Halt' and you desist.
Leave Swift out of this;
You are paid for what you say.

The Voyage

Happy the young man who disregards
The siren who conceals herself in words,
Stopping his ears but seizing on the flesh
Which will serve his intelligence the best:
What seas must he sail on, what strange lands
Visit before he claims to understand
What song the sirens sang or other such
Matters which do not matter overmuch.
It was not so with me: I sought to find
What errors might be in a human mind
And to embrace them all, the skimpy ghosts
Who flee like shadows when we need them most.
Yet the bold sailor comes to the same port
As I who lived on charts and false reports.
Observe the wisdom that I have today!
Which others have, who had it on the way.

Ellick Farm Revisited

The design on the ground, there it is:
Ellick Farm, Gadshill Road and 468,
As it was, as I wish that it had been,
Folly in retrospection, then as now.
As I drove to the yard, past the pond,
Or where the pond should have been, the crack of shot-guns
– A clay pigeon shoot – and there was Laurence
Coming towards me with a broken gun
Over his shoulder; but he was pretending.
I was pretending too, the old house
That was never mine, the untampered lintels,
'1689' over the door, but not William,
Not William and Mary and the Dutch bankers:
Built out of memory then, it might have been
Eighty years before, James I,
Elizabeth not far behind, older time,
Older time still with Laurence Minot crying:
'Jesu for thy five wounds,
Help us to have peace in Ingland now.'

Words

What is that we make as we obscure
Each one our sight with words?
What starts within the mind, what voice sings
Uncertainly across our doom?

The autumn mist falls: somewhere under it
Figures move, our own, silent.
We call to one another, we are many
Yet each voice is lonely.

Forgotten fathers' voices, forgotten mothers'
Speak through our own.
Is there any man who is not a cousin
And whose voice is known?

But who they are, and who we, or whether
Is settled only by a twang
Here and there, in the darkness perhaps
Among the trees.

An ocean of voices perhaps, but whose words?
Nobody owns them perhaps, they blow away
Over the flat fields to the low hills
At break of day.

Sisson's Good-Night

Goodnight, and hang me on a tree
Or lead me to the firing squad:
Say, he pretended once to be
The patriot and the friend of God.
It is not quite so bad as that,
But once I dabbled in the Creed
And England always has my love
– Two eccentricities indeed
But hardly capital offences
One would have thought, though there are those,
Certainly, whom they do not please
And the displeasure rather grows
Than lessens, in this world in which
I find myself septuagenarian:
Politics side with poor or rich
And all the Christians are Aryan.
What did I say in all that ink
I spilt in poems, in novels or
The prose in which men say they think?
What was all that effusion for?
Hard to say: if it has a meaning
The words are there, you can find out
And you will find the author leaning
To too much hope or too much doubt
– Sometimes, they say, to plain despair;
More often, I would say, observing,

Quite simply, certain things are there
And that is more or less deserving
As others think they are there too
– And that includes the dead, as well
As critics A and B, or you,
And how right you are, time will tell.

On the Edge

Now that I have come to the edge of, edge of
The grass is so thin, nothing more
The air is thin too, and the birds forget
Their augurial purposes, and fall.

So the wide sky stares back at the questioner
Blankly. 'Bring what you can
Of meaning,' it says, 'if you want any.
Here is none.'

Taxila

There is a rail-head at Havelian
– Or was, for I was there long ago –
Around it a sweet plain circled by hills:
This was my Greece, the only one I know.

It was a ghost of olives that I saw:
I had not seen the Mediterranean light
Where it falls, but I had dreamed of it.
I who had not been born woke to the sight.

Rus in urbe, urbs in the dazzling grey
– Or was it green? – green, but so grey and brown,
A spot of light in the surrounding darkness:
Taxila was the name of the town,

The heart of all I loved and could not have;
And in that limy track, as I approached,
A child with bright eyes offered a coin.
It was a bargain that was proposed.

Would I, the soldier of an alien army,
Neither the first nor last to come that way,
Purchase for rupees certain disused drachmas
Left by the army of an earlier day?

Alexander himself came down from those hills,
Over the mountains beyond them to the north
– Far lands, the boy said, but mine was farther
And longer ago still my setting forth

For my exile burned me like the sun.
I should have bought that coin, I often thought of it
After that time, and in far different places:
It would have carried me over the Styx.

I would have returned, but there is no returning.
Yet you may rise, ghosts, or I sink to you.
The world is in my hand, breathing at last
For now I know, only the past is true.

On Reflection

I sit in an unfurnished room,
Leaning my back against the wall;
A large grey sky looks in, and I
Stare back, in case the heavens should fall.

They will not: over seventy years
They have stood up and nothing now
Will bring them down, or lift me up
Further than gravity allows.

I made the journey and came here
And had my reasons on the way.
They served their turn: each step I took
Met some occasion in its day.

The long string of occasions now,
As I look back from where they led,
Appears to be so tightly strung
That no-one could discern the thread.

Juxtaposition is enough
To hold in place the days gone by,
Snug between after and before:
But how then does the future lie?

For lie it must, or not invent
A reason for the course it takes:
So the day ends in truth or sleeps
To hear no reasons when it wakes.

Et Praevalebit

When all retire within themselves,
Each to declare that what he has found
Is nothing to anybody around,
Then friendship cracks and each one salves
His stupid conscience as he may:
Or so it seems to me today.

Only a gust of social wind
Can blow a spark into a flame
And still the heat is not the same:
The former smile becomes a grin.
Old men are grinners, and they know
Enough to think it should be so.

Then: 'Leave the exit door ajar,'
They think, 'for I must soon escape.'
Better too early than too late
For that at least because there are
No expectations of surprise,
No cures for one another's lies.

But truth is hungry, we no doubt
For it, but it also for us
And it will eat our frowsy dust
Before we know what it's about.
It's possible that that may be
The lesson of theology.

A Dedication

Better that you should forget
Everything I ever said,
Everything I did
Should be hidden,
No-one ever know
That I was so:
But I have vanity
And you must read me.

Antidotes

Aller Moor

And now the distance seems to grow
Between myself and what I know:

It is from a strange land I speak
And a far stranger that I seek.

A heron rises under my nose
And into the flat distance goes.

The thoughts that follow her grow less
And vanish into emptiness.

But I am I and I stay here:
Who and where I am is not clear.

And if I spoke, as I must not,
World that encircles me, then what?

No-one could find me, no-one say
On what sad drove my journey lay:

From where to where, which makes the who,
Cannot be visible to you,

Nor I, here walking, can declare
What lies beyond this open air.

Beyond all touch the cities lie
In which so many gasp and die

And make the words which seem to run
From mouth to mouth, as once my own,

Yet what runs with them is no more
Than I well know has run before:

So I resign me to this space
Which neither knows another face

Nor mine, and where no answer is.
If one should ask, the answer dies.

The Quandary

Within the closet of my mind
There dwells a body, not my own.
What ghost, what image left behind
By other days, and timeless grown?
Or is this the unspeakable,
Because unspoken, hope I have
Of an attendance in the grave
Where, so I fancy, all is well?

No hope, no promise, lives in me,
For I have found that hopes are dreams.
Though not awakened yet, I see
The endless folly of what seems,
Seems for a moment, and is gone
To other mists and distances.
Can faith presume the things that please
And so assert what no man knows?

For, as the yellowing hand of time
Seizes on the most beautiful
And turns the smoothest flesh to slime,
So every promise must be null,
As dream will follow dream until
We dream no more, the engine gone
Which drove our apprehensions on
To flatter an imperfect will.

The child wet from the womb will sleep
Into the world of consciousness,
And fill its members with the deep
Nutriment of the sights that press
Upon it from the earth and sky
And every trace of taste and sound
Accepted from the world around,
Not knowing yet that it will die.

So what we see will pass away,
Thunder will cease, the lightning fade,
The argument that won its day
Will vanish with the noise it made.

Significance is not for us
Who place it in a word or two,
Not yet for those who thought they knew
That silence could be marvellous.

If there are marvels, they are not
In anything that we assert
Or silently embrace, one jot
Of us in them will do them hurt.
So stand aside and let the stars
Circulate as they surely will,
And let the wind blow on, until
It blows against the isobars.

Grow, body, from the little shred
Of flesh without a thought, to one
Who tosses on the marriage bed
And has through all delusions run:
The youth, the beauty that amazed
And gave the mind its vanity
Were not designed to make you free
But to leave you and others dazed.

At last you creep into the shell
Of others' minds, and in your own
Hovers a truth you cannot tell,
Too complicated to be known.
The nothing that you are is clear,
As I am nothing, and for all
Only the universal Fall
And what we afterwards hold dear.

The only hope the living have
Is Christ, and never mind the dead,
They are in peace: the fortunes of
The world by them taken as read.
The arms and legs and other parts
The living have, are useful for
Movement and noise, and what is more
Than that does not come from the heart.

They whirl around. Image of God,
Where are you in this dreadful din?
The flying word, the wink, the nod
Are only attributes of sin,
Once recognised, but now denied:
Self-will, complacence, are the best
That words can reach to, and the nest
Of infamy is built with pride.

Even the patient world of sense,
Which registers the things we see,
Receives no other recompense
Than thanks for what it does for me.
The light and quiet of a day
That shimmers from a staggering blue
No more discover what is true
Than any word that I can say.

I seek reclusion from the years
Which have brought nothing but the lack
Of what I wanted, even tears
Are not worth shedding, for the pack
I bear is light, a nothing that
I trumpet like a treasure found
After long search. Is the world round?
The one I walk upon is flat.

And so the bread that I would take
As body, turns again to bread,
The wine, which should be blood, will slake
No thirst of mine, though the words said
Are His who made the world, for I,
Filled with the sights I love no more
Than any pebble on the shore
Am conscious only I must die.

And yet my heart will not stand still
Or fill with what I know is there,
The love which interrupts the will,
The glory which the heavens declare.

I long for silence, yet desire
The words to speak what is absurd:
The confidence to touch the fire
Lit once and no-when by the Word.

The Residue

All that is past, whatever attitude
Was struck, what words pretended to be spoken
Were not, or else were so frivolous
I hate them now: whether the attitude
Which showed the appropriation of some thought
I could not have now, or else the words
Pertaining to a role no longer mine.
What then is left? Either the friends I had,
Lying in dark places far away
Or, here, the luminous sun upon the moors
Ever before my window, and the birds
Uttering their phrases not to be construed,
In this or that tree, here in the garden.

Fantasies

The time for hope has gone,
The coloured world remains;
The retina flickers still:
What happens in the brain?

In that recess the heart
Reads as upon a screen.
And what am I who watch?
What have I ever been?

What moved from a to b
And now is fixed at z?
Pore as you will, there is
No answer in the head

– Only another lie
As once there was in youth:
Then, that the body spoke,
Now, that old age is truth.

On Reading Old Memoirs

Not what the wind said but what solid people
Have said at the height of their delusions
Or in the middle of a tough campaign
When choices filled their minds and nothing else:
These are the speeches I can listen to
Although my own delusions may be different,
My choices formed by a quite different world,
Or world my own delusions have made different.
The naked figures running in the rain,
They are the stuff, ideas are the form
Which made them wheel and dress and be polite
– And that is human life, the finished article.

Fifteen Sonnets

1

The minutes have gone by, the hours, the days,
The years have counted themselves up, and now
That little piece of time, a life, is proud
To show itself complete: 'fini' it says.
Yet I who speak for it in so many ways
Cannot say this: the when, the where, the how
Must be determined first, and who knows
Less well than I what may be the delays?
To be on the outside and yet to speak
Is not a thing the mind of man can compass,
Yet inside I am inside something else
Than the completed life and cannot break
The circle of it to see it as it is
Even now, at the end even less.

2

No other language but that of the Creed
Will serve to say the things which must be said.
And what things are they? All things, I said:
Or did not all things come from the same seed
– The seed which is unsowable indeed?
When we name that, we say what we cannot know,
Much less express, the inexpressible, so
Beyond our every thought or word or deed.
So no word counts which is not beyond speech,
No action but what is beyond our reach,
And if we rest, it is in mystery.
No explanation touches us, no word,
Once spoken, is not more or less absurd:
Why then, not *quia impossibile*?

3

Why should one write poems when one is old?
Not, to be sure, in hope of reputation
Which has either come, or else will escape one.
In hope of love perhaps? But what is told
Now, will not strengthen anybody's hold
On me or mine on them: the time of truth has come,
And yet I lie as I have always done
And leave myself and others unappalled.
Poets are liars, yet no more than others,
Those who are not their sisters are their brothers,
All of the same lying family,
Children of Adam, fond of all evasions,
Blaming, beguiling on the least occasions
And to the last, and so it is with me.

4

Of all that can be said silence is best
In which God can be heard and none but He,
But that silence has not come to me,
Rather I lie and babble with the rest.
Quiet may come, but in it can be guessed
Voices like shadows which I hear or see
Hunched in a courtyard under a great tree,
Dark and faint, with nothing clearly expressed.
Then words come, or else shapes, and what they say
Is nothing to the torture of this day
Which is all cloud, above me and without.
Or maybe like lunatics they rush
Out of the gates of reason and so flush
The mind not knowing what they are about.

5

To look back is to look back on a thing
Which never was, because it then was *is*
And I was going forward in a mist
Which cleared without revealing anything
– For what showed then at once disappearing,
Another scene flashed, another, this
With no sign that what is seen exists
Beyond the blind instant of its coming.
Even the hour does not contain the minute,
Much less the day the hour, the year the day.
How, in the end, can anybody say
That his life had this or that thing in it,
Or that it failed or succeeded, caught,
As all time is, in multiples of nought?

6

More is what they say, what I say is less,
And so, naturally, will each of us be served.
Do we get our wishes then? No, our deserts.
Asking there must be, for happiness,
Yet one may ask for it and find distress;
Door after door closes, the right words
Are never spoken, the wrong silence observed.
Who is responsible for all this mess?
It is not a mess: the end is always found,
The young go roaring over new ground,
The old come to a stop. So it should be.
The world must either grow or shrink, or seems
So to do, for life is only dreams
For time to wind up in eternity.

7

The only dream I had did not come true
And we are to believe it never does:
Dreams are like that, they represent the fuzz
Of what might be beyond the things we do:
Integer vitae is the way you grew,
Sceleris purus is ridiculous,
And every other character no less.
What makes you think that you are really you?
No names, no pack-drill, and the simple act
Amounts to no more than a pile of fact
No-one can know unless you lay a claim to it.
Truth is in action, but your words will lie
Until, escaping into truth, you die
And then what might be and what must be fit.

8

All such excitements are illusory.
How prove they are more illusory than most?
They are not illusory, more than a ghost
Or any ordinary thing daylight can see.
What makes the difference, it seems to me,
Is that they are so entirely lost
– Some careless Rubicon having been crossed –
They are a past which is a past completely.
Such an excitement I had on the way
And often think of it: and what is thought
Except a finding of something we have sought,
Which, being found, has nothing more to say,
Or, being said, must then be changed for new,
Thoughts being many and the truths but few?

9

'What?' said the World, 'You come to beg from me?
Where are your papers then, who are your friends?
Will they serve me? I love a man who bends
To every whim I have, and I have many.
Here come the cohorts of the wise who slily
Swerve when the word goes round, whose common ends
Waver to suit my smile, tend where mine tends,
Constant only to instability.'
They are in the right of it, for well I know,
Nothing endures that any man can say,
The lips that spoke the words will fall away,
The words precede them or else quickly follow.
But what in this can ever hold a man
As the impossible Eternal can?

10

When time stands still, it is you who have stopped,
For time goes on and leaves you standing there
And crumbling, for as long as you breathe air
You are mined, and your little growth is cropped,
Like a field tunnelled and yet grazed on top,
And soon the empty surface will lie bare.
You stand? You lie. Lie still, time will repair
Your pride and see your last pretensions drop.
And if time moves again, what do you see?
A hurrying world in which you have no part:
Either way you have lost the fruit of time,
Which was to live as if you had been free
To choose some other error which your heart,
Always deluded, would have turned to rhyme.

11

The world in which I wander on my own
– For who is there? To whom can I speak now? –
Spreads like a terror round me, and I go
As one to whom no mercy can be shown
Across the acres of a shadowy down
Over which clouds determine all I know.
While barrenness flavours the earth below
– So impervious to hope has my age grown.
If through the darkness there appeared a rift,
A streak of moon-light, a square inch of blue,
If there were any breath to start a drift,
Real or imagined, or if one blade grew,
I would rejoice, and stretch a living hand
To touch the surface of this once loved land.

12

To cast off, as a boat that puts to sea,
Is difficult, the eyes are fascinated
By all that lies ashore. It is too late
Now to enquire the meaning of what I see,
The little houses, the great rock, the trees
Standing against the hill, the tempting gate
Leading into the fields. And those who wait
Idly beside the lane, what are they to me?
If I had taken that turning, found them there,
Exchanged a word or else a look, what air
That I did not draw in, should I have spent?
Was this land my land? Or I made of it,
As part and parcel of its growth and grit,
Incapable of being different?

13

As the mind shrinks, the body withers too.
And whither does it wither? To the ground,
Where at once nothing or else all is found.
But the poor mind? It flies into the blue,
And who knows what is there? A plant that grew
Cannot grow rootless, and in heaven abound
The principalities and powers, while here around
The earth the lingering air holds nothing true.
So the faint voice of fame is only lies,
Misprisions, misapprehensions, and the heart
Moves silently, or not at all, is lost
As memory vanishes and no-one tries,
Though generations flow past and depart,
To reckon up the little that it cost.

14

What I imagine is the least of things,
The less than nothing that I call my own
In place of what might actually be known,
The world beyond me and the gifts it brings,
Colour and size and shape – no, trees and limbs,
What else God knows, all that his art has grown:
Knowledge can count only what stands alone
Beyond the harm of my imaginings.
If there is truth I need to look at it,
Well knowing that my mind will never fit
Even the objectivity of sense:
So back to images and back to me,
Who cannot trust the slightest thing I see,
Much less come to the edge of penitence.

15

If love and death are one and the same thing,
As Ronsard said – others have felt it too –
Yet neither he nor they can make it true,
Nor anything, by mere imagining.
Whatever evidence the world may bring,
The mind fills like a pond and what looks through
The waters is the sky's cloud and blue,
But what have images to do with naming?
The names of love and death we have from far
But who can say what their originals are
Or whether the names they have are their own?
When we sail into that unexpected harbour
The moment of trespass beyond words is there,
All freshness and newness begin, or nothing is known.

The Christmas Rose

A spray of myrtle and the Christmas roses
Come from the garden like a grail of light.
They climb out of the mist into a hand
Which holds them till they flower in her sight:

Myrtle for Myrtilus, who died for treachery
And yet found a place among the stars:
The Christmas rose for peace and chastity
– Old stories both, if any of them are.

Yet love remains, although I cannot see it,
The myrtle berries hovering among leaves,
Dark for sorrow, white petals of the rose
Straggling from the gold centre to grieve.

Rapacity and lust will not forbear
And there is no retreat from injury
Except one: *amor vincit omnia,*
And rose and myrtle float in the same sea.

Myrto a woman, Myrtos an island, the Mare
Myrtoum where the rival of Pelops fell.
What light now plays across the sea?
Is there any? O Christmas rose, Noël!

A Dialogue with Maurice Scève

SCÈVE

Free was I in the April of my years,
Without a care, for in that adolescence
The eye did not yet know the force of tears
But saw itself surprised by a sweet presence
Which by its true exalted excellence
Astonished so my senses and my mind
That love pierced me with arrows of such a kind
As took away both liberty and breath:
And, as on that, so to this day I find
In her beauty is both my life, and death.

CRITIC

'Amaritude': the word was quickly lost
And yet remains, as if beauty should say:
'I defy you to say that all is past
Of what touched you in a now distant day.'
And what girl passes who does not portray
The faithful image of your young desire?
As underneath the ashes lies the fire,
So in her voice, her walk, and in her eyes,
Under the shield of ordinary attire,
Ignore it as you will, nakedness lies.

The Birth of Venus

So she stepped naked on to the shore and broke
Into a thousand pieces as she awoke
To life in sunlight, and forgot the sea.
The spray blinded all to her symmetry.
Imagination saw a pearly flesh;
The hand that touched it found it cool and fresh,
And moulded it, complete from top to toe.
A liar then asserted that it was so.

In the Apple-tree

The mistletoe is back
Among the knitted twigs
Of the old apple tree.
And what is that to me?
My pruning hand still digs
And the old branches crack.

But where the bunch first grew
Is a great skeleton,
The berries and the leaves
For which my heart still grieves,
All, all are gone;
And so I love the new.

How rare now that I can
See new replace the old,
As, on the neighbouring bough,
I see it now!
The pleasure must be told,
And I am still a man.

Thurloxton

Was silence the best they said?
Was it? For no
The answer was, from the dead.
How should they know?

'You who stand by our graves
And vainly boast,'
They gravely said, 'are slaves,
And more than most.

'Our words are gone and done,
We have no use for them:
You, in the rain and sun,
Move towards Bethlehem.

'Presenting gold and myrrh,
The fine, the sad,
You who are where we were
Have what we had

'– Thoughts which do not return,
Flying away
Over the trees which learn
Nothing to say.

'Their whisper still remains,
And nothing leaves
No traces of our pain
But the fall of leaves.

'Look then at the cold side
Where the half tower still stands.
Those stones,' they said, and sighed,
'Were set there by our hands.'

I long for sleep, which comes,
But only to bring dreams:
The sleep I want runs
Deeper than dreams,

Runs under everything
Which has or has not breath,
A mountain or a starling:
But do not call it death.

What runs under the tide
And is lost in the sand,
You will know, who have died
While I hold up my hand.

The vacant figure drifting
Along the vague sea-shore,
Is it I, or the mist shifting
Where I was before?

Where you lie buried
I do not seek to lie:
Let none remember me
When I die.

No stone mark a spot
To say, He was,
I who was not, am not
Even a voice.

A voice must speak a word
And I spoke none,
And a voice must be heard,
But I, of none.

When they say, He is gone,
As they will say,
The air will be lighter
On that day.

We would not wish him gone,
But could not wish him here:
Let him fly with the rooks
He has watched many a year.

Let him cry with the pee-wits
High over Aller Moor,
Melancholy, observant,
He could not wish for more.

Christ came to him, and left him,
Half-spoke, or he half-heard,
And all his understanding
Was the incarnate Word.

The root has grown and withered
That now is dead today:
The silence that has followed
Is all he had to say.

The Test

There is no body but the body of
The person who is offered up to love:
Rare body and rare person, for without
Extreme love every person is in doubt.
Where there is none, the scavenger desire
Will still find the material for his fire:
He lacks only the metaphysic twists,
For who can be, if no-one else exists?

Appearance

Silence cannot be broken
Without a lie;
Word-perfect where none is spoken,
You and I.

Ah, I appreciate
Your speechless line,
Yet I must hesitate
To utter mine.

Appearance, though I love it
Is not another mind;
If what I see, I covet,
It is myself I find.

The Begging-bowl

It cannot matter much how I grew up,
Housed in this body which is now so thin
A parapet for me to lean upon.
Fall I must: and with me will go down
The entire empire of my former days.
Look, sun, upon my last, and so you be
The Light which made the world, I have my part.
It is a public country that I want
And so indeed it was, the world I had,
Growing from nothing to the edge of doom.
But what was in between?
The hope and love I had in fields and moors,
In hills, in waters lashing round the coast.
The coast of where? And where but you, O England,
Which name has gathered all my hopes and loves.
Changed like a dream, the land that never was
And yet to which I gave my dearest wish
Which contained all the wishes that I had,
The contents of my begging-bowl, perhaps,
Into which time had thrown so many things,
So many persons, a few held most dear,
A many who had helped to make them so,
Either as tributary to the stream of time
Or my companions as I swam along
– Given rather than chosen: it is as a gift
We love those whom we love, and not by choice,

For choice is but our own, and what we love
Is other, other which we inly crave,
Not to be what we are or who we are
Which is the nothing that we brought with us,
The nothing that we take out of the world.

Minerva

If silence were enough
I might well have it here,
And yet the word will puff
And blow until I hear

As it climbs the vast hill
From the dark pit where none
Can apprehend it till
It sees the distant sun.

In the pit only sleep;
In the sun only death:
One moment on the steep
It draws a waking breath.

I go to meet it where
It touches life at full:
'Salut, *mon fils, mon frère*,
Touch hands, but do not pull.' .

You pull, and I go down
Where silence holds me fast.
I pull, and with a frown
You mutter and push past.

Only a moment's poise
Gives us a common mind,
Mere silence and mere noise
Shown up as being blind,

As when, before a form
Containing all I seek,
I recognise a norm
And do not try to speak.

Address

You whom I never loved,
You I shall never touch
Live in my mind as if you proved
A thesis about other such,

Which is, that firm and tender flesh
Is medicine for an ageing man,
As if one body could refresh
Another as it never can.

The crook of age, the spring of youth,
Are equally the work of time;
What is in common is the truth
That age is age and prime is prime

And that both quickly slip away
To other hours, or none at all:
Whatever words the ghosts may say
It is the bodies take the fall.

Pretence may entertain the old,
The young may answer with a lie,
But neither old nor young can hold
The same illusion till they die.

I look on you, you look on me;
For both, to speak no word is best.
I contemplate your lovely youth;
You cannot bear to think the rest.

The Blackbird

Blackbird, at my elbow,
When I address you
It comes from the heart, I allow,
But can I speak true?

Not so, for I imagine
Only your attentiveness
– A nodding head, a knowing grin,
A beak that says yes.

So am I with my friends:
Age keeps its track;
The old eye glints, but sends
No message back.

Uncertainty

The future is the only thing
That makes for thought, the past is past:
It brought its presents, had its fling,
But what it flung could never last.

The future has not lasted yet
Even the second that it can
And so is good for any bet:
It is the guessing makes the man.

Human uncertainty is all
That makes the human reason strong:
We never know until we fall
That every word we speak is wrong.

Looking

Look, looker, if you will,
But what you see,
That shape, that colour, still
Is no-wise me.

So beauty is a dream
And ugliness the same:
To seem, to seem, to seem
Is all that's in a name.

Azure may Fade

Azure may fade and then the moon appear
To trick the watcher with her slippery light,
Shadows more real than death steal on the lawn:
The fox peers from the shrubbery, his sharp nose
And bright eyes suddenly extant. O fear!
Dream on, not in myself but in the night.
I feel no trace of it, but when the dawn
Shakes itself, day herself is in the throes.

What must be, will be, and whatever grows
Moves on a pace to death, the moon which hangs
Over the red of east, to nothing goes.
What can the church bell then do but jangle
Its solitary note? – and, as it clangs,
The door is shut before the day begins.
Hope no more: it is the loser wins.

Endymion

The world darkens, everything grows old,
Yet all is not lost for treacherous youth
Continues at its play, blinking the truth:
Nothing is lost until the sum is told.

Youth is a victory, age a defeat,
And victory will dazzle while it can:
The game is blinding to the growing man;
It is the growth which fosters the deceit.

Hope and intention will accompany
The body which grows strong and beautiful:
It can what it could not: the moon at full
Forgets her light is borrowed. She can see

And so comes down to stroke Endymion
As if she were the queen that made the light,
And so they struggle in a double night,
A double dream of false dominion.

They wake to morning and the usual scene:
Neither is subject to the other's whim;
He observer her coldly, and she him,
And they are both what they have always been.

The ocean mirrors her, for it is still.
'What breasts I have!' she thinks, and takes her dip.
'No goddess that I want gives me the slip!'
He thinks, following her in, of his own will.

And so youth flatters hope, but it must sink;
Greed and ambition change their objects, which
Can now be satisfied by being rich:
They magnify themselves with power and drink.

But nothing works. The body grows more mean,
The mind recedes, imagination dies.
Each dresses in a coat of many lies,
Yet naked as the weather they have been.

The body blazes in the height of noon,
But once was nothing, crouching in the dark:
It is the interval that makes the mark:
Its end will be another nothing soon.

A Fossil by the Sea

There is no need to think, to be human,
Surely? The lithe girl stretches up a hand,
An arm, and elongates her whole person,
Pointing to what she does not understand.

Curiosity and science give the excuse,
Connived at by the young man watching her:
The flowing body has another use
Which they ignore, and learnedly confer.

And so it is what floats upon the mind
Is not the breath that makes the body go:
It moves because it must, and can be kind
With no more sense than lets the sea-weed grow.

Another time; another pair repair
To the same beach a thousand years before,
And she holds up her arm, loosens her hair,
And uses other words which mean no more.

O done, done, done the task they came to do,
And from that moment nothing is the same:
It needs only wisdom for the two
To find love in the hollow of the game.

What else may be found in fifty years
Which wait for them, they neither know nor care:
Yet time is patient and, when it appears,
The thought that passes them scatters in air.

On the Departure
a sequence of six poems

1   DEEP-ROOTED FEARS

Deep-rooted fears
– Should not fears have deep roots? –
And terrifying love
Send their pale shoots above
The surface where no other growth appears.

Expect no more,
Though other men will live, and women too,
To see out time and witness its distress
And what in us grows less
May grow again as it has grown before.

O barren age! whose trust is all in lies;
Others have known what you no longer know:
Hope backwards, you may find
The speed of a slow mind
Dawdling eternally before surprise.

Wonder there must be which is not short
Or long, nor has any dimension.
Can you find that? I say
That there in night shone day
Although I know it only by report.

Leave hope, leave fear, attend to what is,
The smallest thing that is is better than
The best that can be said,
And a man dead
Finds more than we in our short silences.

2 THE SOW'S EAR

The sow's ear
Is now more valuable than the silk purse,
Nature than art, the silk-worm than the silk.
The breast now swelling with tomorrow's milk
Signifies hope, and the young eyes averse
From any fear.

So the bud too
Promises silently the future flower;
The chrysalis in winter in its sleep
Marks out the place of wings. Nature may keep
Her undertakings in another hour:
So may not you.

The race which came
To Eve by Adam has another plan:
Corrupt the garden and destroy the seed.
Its work is almost done, and former need
Translated into all that pleases man.
The hunted game

Shrinks and the leaf
That once hid Adam's shame dies on the tree.
The rivers die, the seas are empty now.
The fish lie stranded and upon the bough
The fruit is only shadow, and we see
Our time is brief.

3 MUCHELNEY ABBEY

The quiet flood
Lies between hedges and turns back the light,
Black and blue like the bruises of the time
– Sheet after sheet of record where the crime
Is lost beneath the water. Rushes write
Illegibly in mud

And willows point
Downward without weeping, or else raise
Flourishing heads topping gigantic trunks.
Uneasily the shadows of dead monks
Move past an abbey in which no-one prays.
Who will anoint

The wounds they did not,
More than we do ourselves, attempt to cure?
Grey evening behind which the sun, unseen,
Sets to the sound of church-bells, which still mean
No more than echoes: and, for sure,
Nature will rot.

O come away
To death O human race! Accept no more
This watery world in which the fox and hare
Have lost their scent, in which the livid air
Promises nothing on this wasted shore
But closing day.

Yet spring may come,
Who knows? with drought and terror, or else flowers,
For time may circle back, once more pretend
A grammar of renewal without end,
A summer with its vacuum of bright hours.

4 NATURE IS MERCILESS

Nature is merciless,
Tears at the roots and murders out of habit,
Yet all is well they say, you say, we say,
And saying so makes for the less distress,
Not in the broken tree or in the rabbit
Executed each ordinary day.

The same kindness shows in every act
We do to please ourselves, though we pretend
Love and superior reasons for our fault,
Mistaking inclination for the fact.
Trust no man, nor no woman, though they bend
To do you pleasure, hunted or unsought.

Only God, out of the desolate sky,
Comes to renew the pattern we have spoiled,
Walks for a moment in one or another as
He walked before when he came here to die
Our natural death, and it was so he foiled
Our bleak intention with unnatural solace.

How hard it is even to recognise
His presence in the tempest of the world!
Yet there are words which shadow forth the Word
Which may not be, but Is, for all the lies
We treasure so and praise, as we are hurled
Headlong into the arms of the absurd.

5   THE TURF

What fever is
Burning under the shrunk turf of our days?
The sky is dark with winter, but what rises
Smokily from the heap distinctly says:
Here is fire: and yet a thousand ways

Promises chill.
A vast uneasiness shifts in the air.
No-one can name it, and whatever ill
It brings forth forebodingly cannot declare
Itself. Is then nothing but nothing there?

Nothing perhaps
Is what it is. Evil walks up and down,
Prince of this world, emptying the future's paps.
What drains the mind will soon empty the town.
The smiling earth now shrivels to a frown.

6   THE GEESE

The turmoil of the geese,
Plodding across the sky with heavy wing
Is in the heart – not theirs, but yours and mine.
We see them pass, and by their flight divine
Our going too: and their diminishing
Tells us our own decrease.

Westward they go,
And where they vanish, there they will be fed.
But we? One tale, if true, would feed us too.
Yet we look backward on the way we grew:
Those who engendered us were left for dead
And we must follow.

Fly with the geese
Who go without the prick of consciousness.
Knowledge is out of place, and speech betrays
The very thought it forms. Then end your days
In the security of nothingness,
And so fly loose.

In Other Words

Words fly like birds across the sky,
And how they go is also why;
There is no other reason.
It is the wind and temperature
Which sends them on their way, for sure,
As suits the changing season.

Words do not come from any mind
Which might belong to humankind,
Or might imagine choices:
They have their sounds and histories,
Adjustable to every breeze,
But they are words, not voices.

The human engine works away,
Begins and lives and ends its day
As best it can, and nothing
That words can add changes its plight,
Nor do they ever change their flight
To give it better ending.

What wonder then if, when we talk,
Although it may affect the chalk
The cheese remains the same?
The words pass by across the sky;
The flesh does not reach up so high,
And so, what's in a name?

So action goes as action must
With noise and pother in the dust,
But oh! our fine pretensions!
Accept no cheques on verbal banks;
Reality returns no thanks
For any man's inventions.

The Sands of Dee

Since Mary called the cattle home
And left her body in the flood,
Horizontal, her skirt spread out
Where the tide left her in the mud,
Others have licked the salty foam
And left their purposes in doubt.

The body tells forensic lies,
If it can manage them, the tongue,
However, once the body's cold,
Does not remain so loosely hung:
And no girl any longer cries,
Or laughs whatever tales are told.

So silence. Yet the world around
Begins to chatter and deplore
And act the human part
Which she, at least, can play no more.
It is not she whom they have found,
But folly in the human heart

– Their own, not hers, for she is free,
And they, alone with ignorance,
Multiply their inventions, which
Expatiate on time and chance
To make a pleasing tragedy,
Enough to make her body twitch.

It does not, twitching time is done
And she no longer sleeps or wakes.
Time has divided her: they move
A body which no longer makes
Any heart glad, yet their thoughts run,
In self-defence, past death to love.

It was for love she died, perhaps,
And yet they turn from death to live.
All our defences are in vain,
In vain every alternative,
For any choice is a relapse,
And every pleasure finds its pain.

She asked for Death to take her hand:
He quickly took her by the throat.
Did she like that? Are lovers kind?
There is no record of the kiss
He gave, her body was afloat,
And Death no longer on her mind.

It was those others who sustained
A lesson in necrology
And saw her drifting in their dreams.
Her harbour was Reality,
There is no other to be gained:
All there is is, and never seems.

Waiting for Charon

Waiting for Charon, looking back on figures
Crowding the world still, I stand dismayed.
Who are these who are now escaping the lures
Of what seemed worth while once, though since decayed?

Where was reality, in tissue-thin
Shadows or less than shadows which they saw
Once as the meat of life? Could it be in
The amber of the flesh, or in the raw

Spirit inhabiting that tiny space
Fixed by a name to be unfixed by time?
In the fair face of nature, or a grace
Not to be burnt away by any quick-lime?

It was not known. What is? We pass away
Through seen to unseen, through the flaming crowd
Claiming to live, bright in the light of day
As if beauty and movement spoke aloud.

Perhaps they do. Or perhaps nothing speaks
But what they can be is intrinsic in a word:
That not for long: it whistles as it seeks
Its meaning, but afterwards it is not heard.

The spirits gabble, but they come to stand
Where I do now and cast and backward look
With Jean Meschinot, and my blind land
Fills with the shadows other ghosts mistook.

A Renaissance

Now that the theories of Freud
Are recognised as null and void,
The dialectic of Karl Marx
No longer gives out any sparks,
Time to return to simple fact
Which has all theorising whacked.
The human race is always wrong:
The evidence for that is strong,
And has been, ever since the day
When Adam first had his own way,
Which was, however, not his own.
The Tree of Knowledge was full-grown
When he began his foolish quest
For what he thought would suit him best.
The best was there already, he
Had need only of eyes to see.
Few are content with that, preferring
Ideas to set the head-piece whirring.
And then the mouth: how nice to hear
One's own inventions made so clear.
His first idea was smart: he told
His Maker he was not so bold
As to be naked in His sight:
Surely God would think that was right?
But God knew everything, which makes
It difficult to pass off fakes.
This trouble has persisted since

That day, and still it makes one wince
To think that nothing can be thought
Which will add up to more than nought.
Instead of thinking Adam found
He had to dig the stubborn ground,
While Eve had babies in a row
And sorrow too, they hurt her so,
And both were peeved to find that pleasure
Extinguished their accustomed leisure.
Too bad that disobedience
Should count against people of sense!
They thought, and soon their vanity
Infected the whole family,
Till Cain killed Abel and so ended
The notion man could be befriended
By other creatures of his kind
– Or should have done, but that the mind,
They proudly thought, could put that right.
Philosophers sat up all night
For generations after that
To prove that the round world was flat,
That people were born free and could
Find their own way out of the wood.
God had foreseen that too, foreknew
The silly things that they would do,
And, as intended, sent his Son
To throw new light on everyone.
Some such solution was expected
But vaguely, and what God projected
Was not a human thought at all.
Men thought God's story rather tall:
Conception without human help
Which yet produced a human whelp.
Absurd! God did it to reprove
A misconception about love
Which was endemic from the first.
So bang! Another bubble burst.
Christ walked in all humility
Upon the earth, and man was free,
Or could be, if he did not find
The reason in his own poor mind.
God! What a God! So great and small

Must bow before Him after all!
A likely story! All the grand
People refused to understand,
As well they might. It was not funny
To be assured that power and money
Counted for nothing. But the Son
Went on His way, God's will was done.
He put himself upon a cross
To prove that gain was only loss,
And afterwards everyone said
He could not come back from the dead.
But that is what He did, and few
Believed the story could be true,
And yet it was: the Resurrection
Was not a human insurrection
(They always fail), but He who rose
Went to His Father as He chose.
The Devil sneaked around and said,
As is his custom, God was dead,
Or up to tricks which he, the Devil,
Thought not entirely on the level,
He took the side of humankind:
The human will, the human mind,
Slightly adjusted, could devise
Reasons for everything, first prize
For everybody, and a place
Far better for the human race
Than that old garden where all knowledge
Grew on a tree, not in a college.
So man grew wiser, theory
Replaced the things we touch and see,
And language in the end referred
To everything without a Word;
Number came in and counted all
Hitherto thought innumerable.
The world became a counting-house.
God saw it all, and then a mouse
Squeaked, a cock crowed and so a man
Remembered how it all began.
Back to square one. A human heart
Popped up and made its owner start.
Worse still, the world again had Art.

A Variation on Eustache Deschamps

You who live in this brilliant world today
And live in blazing strength and confidence,
Have you forgotten death, so trusting sense?
Those who preceded you have gone away,
Dust true to dust, false only to pretence,
You who live in this brilliant world today,
Have you forgotten death, so trusting sense?

Think of it now, for you will soon be grey,
And cold before you spend your life's last pence;
Your end will be in naked indigence.
You who live in this brilliant world today
And live in blazing strength and confidence,
Have you forgotten death, so trusting sense?

The Mind of Man

The mind of man is nothing but
A repertoire of what is not,
Never was, and can never be:
So, at least, it is with me.

For Thomas à Kempis

*ne amore visibilium trahentur
ad infirma*

Old monk, I cannot drain the world of sense,
Nor despise beauty, which says everything,
For use says nothing, and there must be praise
For all created things, and recompense,
Surely, in all that world which, vanishing,
Leaves marks upon the squalor of our days?

Even the human body, not immune
From beauty or from kindness, touches us
With splendour which was found in Paradise
Eastward of Eden, and may still attune
Our instant eyes to catch the marvellous
Which is not anybody's greedy prize.

The fine proportion which is in the deer,
And everything that man has never made,
Corrects the mind which watches silently.
Contemplatives? They are found even here,
Where the mind registers the light and shade
And even flesh may teach humility.

So, Thomas Hemerken, you should complete
Your praise of nothingness with praise of all.
The girl dressed only in her falling grace,
From perfect shoulders to as perfect feet,
Lacks nothing, and her beauty seems to call
With one design in every track and trace.

Image of God, for so she is! He chose
So to portray desire of union
With the invisible, to which all tends.
The spirit clothed in flesh cannot disclose
Itself, whatever other will is done,
Except in what it wears for human ends.

All is concealed, indeed, unless it speaks
The language of the flesh and speaks in love,
Counting itself as nothing lost in all.
And so, through ordinary days and weeks,
We may see everything, around, above,
The oak-tree's rising and the acorn's fall.

And yet the whole green world cannot prevail
Upon the mind love has discomfited,
For speaking there must be, another voice.
Who hears? Who speaks? If, indeed, meaning fail,
The spirit is unreading and unread,
Cannot despair and can still less rejoice.

Flesh understands, or spirit cannot teach:
The Devil has no way but emptiness.
Beware, Thomas à Kempis, Hemerken
Can know no more than human sense can reach.
All is in balance, neither more nor less,
So just, in Love, but singular in men.

What and Who

The Mendips

The stream that runs
Under the earth and is the stream of death
Is also that of life: without
Its sombre, unheard flow
What pulse would beat here or what ghost
Re-visit? Where
The sparkling shapes come tumbling from the mouth
Of that dark cave into the light of day,
The living are, and see
The splash and laughter of their ecstasy:
No sound. Imagination only made
That single figure dancing in the shade,
Naked as air, and it is she who slides
Into the mind and eats the heart away.
Turn back the spring
Which feeds the torrent: let the stream flow back.
The falling water mounts and disappears
Into the cave-mouth. All is quiet now.
The eaten heart goes with it, and the man,
Empty of grief as hope,
Watches the sunlight on the glinting rocks,
The tufts of bracken and the scattered flocks
Upon the hill-side. Age has come again,
And found its victim patient and at ease
Upon a world that has no power to please.

The Wind

The wind is rising, and it takes me past
Houses and gardens. Do I have a face
Any would recognise in this known place?
Is knowledge possible to be held fast
Either by me the merest breath can lift
Or the familiars who see me drift?

They still may know the living world, but I
Am perhaps not perceptible, or seem
Less than the emanation of a dream,
Recent but lost already in a sky
Too blank for definition, which is what
The others see who think of what is not.

I who look inwards see that nothing now:
They who look outward see me as I am.
This common truth, that leaves no room for sham,
Rejoiced nobody, and that is how
Life ends, whose days promised us all, at first,
More than is found within the last and worst.

Et in Arcadia ego

And in Arcadia never have I, Charles Sisson,
Passed a day, my days have been otherwise:
I am the old Adam, in another garden,
Driven by tormenting angels from my prize.

The living days are over, and I remember
Only where I have failed, as any might,
On this or that occasion, with him or her,
When almost could perhaps have turned to quite.

So ends a journey which was hardly necessary,
Or so it seems, but what is done is done:
Fact has replaced illusion and I see
With what ineptitude the course was run.

Steps to the Temple

What is belief? A recognition?
Who knows of what? If any say
He knows, he lies.
Who knows what never was begun
And will not end? God is a way,
And a surprise.

And in that way we cannot choose,
For choice deceives us, as it must.
We live in sense,
Certain at least that we shall lose
That urgency, for we are dust.
Our recompense,

If any, cannot be to find
That beauty and that bitterness
Again. A new
Perception must await the vanished mind
– Or none, and which of these we cannot guess.
That much is true.

So here, we who are fallible
As shifting sands, may feel the tide
Flow over us, or in, or out.
If in, then all will then be well;
If not, then we should feel no pride
Even in doubt.

I talk from distant times

I talk from distant times,
An empty voice, perhaps,
Or perhaps not. The past
Moves as the sun climbs,
Shadowing the present, maps
The future to the last.

None can escape its goad,
Boast though he will
Of the new light he bears.
He did not choose the road,
And travels still
With the familiar cares.

The contents of the skin
Contain all mystery.
Dress as you will, the mind
Sums all that is within,
And neither he nor she
Knows more than flesh can find.

Yet what it seeks is more
Than words can ever say:
All words that ever were
Haunt all that ever pour
From the dumb lips today
Of every him and her.

The two, who seek to eat
Each other, never can
Consume their prey, or speak
The hope that would complete
The woman or the man,
And therefore flesh is weak.

Language is all a lie,
And every utterance
Always extravagant.
Do not presume to try
More than the gift of chance:
The only word is Want.

Holà

Words do not hold the thing they say:
Say as you will, the thing escapes
Loose in the air, or in the shapes
Which struggle still before the eyes.
Holà will run upon its way
And never catch up with its prize.

Three Sonnets

from the French of Jean-Baptiste Chassignet

1

When old age enters we are well repaid
For the excesses of our youth; from one
Hearing, and from another strength, has gone.
The fittest stumble, by their eyes betrayed.

Our senses, each in turn, begin to fade,
Except the sense of desolation:
Disease grows stronger as the time goes on.
What a poor coffinful the corpse has made!

There is no part of us inhuman Fate
Does not mark as its own before due date,
Knowing that we grow weaker all the way.

Enough, everything dies in us but vice
Which, subject to a greedy avarice,
Living on death, grows younger every day.

2

Make sure you stifle your concupiscence,
Tearing the world's temptations from your heart,
But choosing your own moment to depart
Is something for which you are without God's licence.

The Christian leaves his earthly residence
When his due time is up: to flee in fear
From this pained body before the time is here
Offends the God to whom we owe obedience.

You must not hate your days too much, nor yet
Love them too much, for always there is set,
For one and the other, an appointed day.

God has determined that we are to fight
Here in the body till he sends the night:
The chief commands, the soldier must obey.

3

O great, amazing, strange affection
Of our Redeemer, whose avenging death
Not only saves our souls while we have breath
But saves the body for resurrection.

Formerly corruptible, in incorruption
It will live again; although sown in weakness,
It will rise again in vigour and in prowess
To live in glory, rescued from confusion.

Made in an animal body, it lives again
In a spiritual body, not serving men
But for the Lord, glorifying his name.

So life is alive and death itself dies
Because the second Adam bought this prize
And it was for this vivification he came.

Esperance

Meaning is what is lacking. Size
And shape are nothing in this room
Where there is neither light nor dark
The usual servitude of eyes
Condemned to see the world in bloom
Is lifted, and it leaves no mark.

'Was somewhere once' is all there is,
Yet cannot be because it was,
By that precluding presence now,
For, in the last analysis
The past is only there because
The present lives to show it how.

This loss is more than all. I brood
On nothing but the vacant hour
Which slips away unregistered.
Language, be still. Do not allude
To any comfort in time's power:
Imagery has become absurd.

Yet there is spring, which breaks upon
The world without the help of man,
Subduing every living thing.
No emptiness can settle on
The mind it speaks to. Nothing can
Avert the meaning it will bring.

And though it seems that I must live
Beyond communication now
Of any wilful word or sign,
It needs only beauty to give
The light she cannot disallow
And every certitude is mine.

The Trade

The language fades. The noise is more
Than ever it has been before,
But all the words grow pale and thin
For lack of sense has done them in.

What wonder, when it is for pay
Millions are spoken every day?
It is the number, not the sense
That brings the speakers pounds and pence.

The words are stretched across the air
Vast distances from here to there,
Or there to here: it does not matter
So long as there is media chatter.

Turn up the sound and let there be
No talking between you and me:
What passes now for human speech
Must come from somewhere out of reach.

Explaining

All we can build is built on love
And everything we de-construct
Is merely an attempt to prove
That every flower is better plucked

BY US – professors, Ph.D.s,
And all who think intelligence
Cannot be shown by those who please
Only by holy negligence,

As, growing on a bank, or finding
A word by accident, and being
Indifferent to computer-minding,
Preferring hearing, smelling, seeing

The evidences of creation
To human ingenuity,
Convinced that any explanation
Is somehow less than what we see.

On living rather long

What wind blows now? For all is still,
Yet somewhere, certainly, a breeze
Assaults the summit of some hill
And carries foliage from the trees
While I, whom nothing now can please
Accept my stationary position
And cannot change my own condition.

Youth is a time when an event
Is bound to happen or impend
Without our knowing what is meant,
And ignorance is then our friend,
Giving us hope that, in the end,
Either we move on to despair
Or learn to relish the hot air.

And middle age is for design:
We think we know what we are doing
And where it's best to draw the line,
Content that we are not renewing
The follies of our youth, pursuing
The good we know until we find
That it was only in the mind.

We stand impeccably aloof
At last, and see the empty plate:
The eating was the only proof
The pudding could excogitate
– And that will always be too late
For hungry men, and when they're full
They find the appetite grows dull.

So listen for the wind, without
Asking what quarter of the sky
It comes from, what it is about,
Or either how it blows, or why.
It blows. However hard you try
You cannot mitigate its force,
Still less deflect its final course.

Ascendant Lines

'Time: half-past nine, morning,' Wilfred Sisson,
Born to doom on the 13th, a Sunday;
The month was July, the year 1878:
I only perhaps remember him now.
Unravel yourself, past, and tell how
One born so early is remembered so late.
He had no son or daughter when he went away,
And it is only I who am bound to listen.

To me he is still audible. But regretting what?
I cannot decipher anything he said
Except this recording of his first moment
– Particulars he cannot have been aware of
When he crept into the world and found love
Not as reported, perhaps, for he went
Early to take his place among the dead,
Wilfully, as it is thought, rightly or not.

Vague ghost, who left no trace, except these:
Second-hand copies of a number of poets,
Not those of the moment or only of his century,
But Herrick, Wither, and several Mermaid dramatists:
These are the relics by which his spirit exists
And by which he spoke so unmistakably.
He could not evade the musical voice which sets
Beauty in the mind more painfully than prose.

That was his secret, rather than possible suicide
Or other adventure beyond which was thought licit.
The ancestral voice touched him. He recovered old furniture,
His great-grandfather's desk, and on the fly leaf
Of his grandfather's gardening book wrote his brief
Farewell, may be while he was still unsure
What his life would be or how he would take leave of it,
And what stars ruled his coming he could not decide.

Anyway he died, I do not know how old
He was when he fell into his last error,
Or where he went to seek his only relief.
I who have lived nearly eighty years have found
Some way farther in spite of the trembling ground,
Not finding either any secure belief
And stalked as he was by unnameable terror,
Certain only as he was it could never be told.

Another candidate for recollection
Is Charles Worlock, surely from my mother's family,
For they farmed in Gloucestershire since who knows when
– Perhaps since Saxon times there on the marches –
And he embarked under the shining arches
Of North Star and Plough, 22, fair, 5ft. 10,
No further away than Bristol, for where he would see
The blaze instead of southern constellations.

He did not sail there for astronomy
But altogether against his better judgment:
The judgment was that of a judge.
The jewels he stole were bacon and potatoes.
His gaol report was bad, but when he put to sea,
Good: whether the waves and sky gave him contentment,
Or merely left him without an immediate grudge
As the hulk rolled and the stars fell and rose.

Once in the Antipodes his conduct was not impeccable.
I will not record the full roll of his crimes:
One was to make 'five pairs of boots on his own account,
Without permission.' Was he not a shoe-maker?
That, certainly, had been his trade in Bristol,
In what he had not then regarded as happy times,

As perhaps they seemed on the purgatorial mount
Where he slipped so often on his way to his Maker.

He married Ann Wilson, an alleged widow
And a fellow-felon, who escaped from her wash-tub
And 'pretended to be free' – another misdemeanour.
In '59 he was insolent at the man-pushed railway,
Perhaps pushing it himself. In '67, they say,
Pardoned, he did not reckon that he could rub
His record clean and, maybe, thought that his behaviour
Would not do in Gloucestershire,
So, free to return whence he came, he did not go.

Sonnet

I well remember what it was to be
On the outside of what I was inside,
An office where the competences tried
Were not those which came naturally to me.
I had no notion of the fantasy
Entertained by the colleagues at my side;
I had my own – a solitary pride
Which drew me to the well of poetry.

Now old, I wander still and lack the light
Others can see by; nearly but not quite
Is still what others read as my device
Which either, blind, I cannot read at all,
Or for a moment dazzles, and I fall
Outside the in or through the slippery ice.

April

Exactly: where the winter was
The spring has come: I see her now
In the fields, and as she goes
The flowers spring, nobody knows how.

The Traveller

I have come far through a strange country
Where dead trees stand above the yellowed grass.
That was not all I saw, for further off
Snatches of green showed through the emptiness.
Sometimes I touched a leaf or felt the warm
Skin of an animal beneath my palm.
Yet the abiding desert was my tutor,
Strange that the love of beauty should so end,
And all the radiant world:
I dissolve into ether and am gone.

The Lack

All is past that is not now:
How long ago it seems!
What was, when life was, is remote
Beyond the reach of dreams.

The life was in the wants we had,
And now what do we need?
Less every day. True riches are
In hope, intent and greed.

How we fared in that starving time
Is less than the starvation
Which gave the future all its worth
And negatived negation.

But now, we only lack the past,
And now is less than then,
Less even than the direst lack
Which will not come again.

Eppur si muove

1

People I have not known enter my head,
Clear a room for themselves, and sit down,
Knowing that I shall welcome them, and the living
Are not likely to intrude while they are there.
Why so? Is this then a cavern for the dead?
Has it become so because under the frown
Of death there is no hope or forgiving,
Or in the hope that all there is fair?

The kingdom of the dead is no farther
Away than the centre of my mind.
It is there that the vanished speak, some word they said
Lights up or darkens my own vacancy.
It matters little enough what ghosts are there,
There is always some pain or folly to find:
The folly is mine and not that of the dead,
Who nod together, and in their nodding agree.

2

I who no longer circulate
Where people think they think, or do,
Know there was never yet debate
Where either *pro* or *con* was true.

What statement ever was? What act
Rested on more than movement?
And, on the simple bread of fact,
Is butter an improvement?

3

We who seem to others not what we are
But what they think we are: we the old,
Plausible travellers who have come from far,
Remember others of whom strange tales were told.

So generations find no secrets out;
The traveller came from nowhere after all:
The bold advance of thought became a rout.
It is some time since Adam had his fall.

4

Where is God's image? Deep within the brain
Or in the form he took and we have too?
The brain is addled and the world talks on,
But to some purpose beauty still is seen
Striding by, unconscious of herself.
What purpose? For the movement of the world.
Forget all else, for still the world will move,
Whatever meaning we attach to it.

To a Garden Asleep

Sleep, garden, in your beauty now:
You may, nor fear a meddling hand
Will dare disturb a single leaf.
Be what you are, your time is brief:
Do not attempt to understand,
Or wonder when or why or how

This moment will disintegrate.
It is, and while it is, you are.
The day is windless, and it seems
To hold the present fast; our dreams
Vanish into a distant star
Insensitive to human fate.

Extended leaves and petals fit
Exactly into the still air,
And neither proffer nor refuse.
The quiet is complete. No clues
Suggest another time will dare
To force your beauty to submit.

Thinking of Politics

Land of my fathers, you escape me now
And yet I will in no wise let you go:
Let none imagine that I do not know
How little sight of you the times allow.
Yet you are there, and live, no matter how
The troubles which surround you seem to grow:
The steps of ancestors are always slow,
But always there behind the current row,
And always and already on the way:
They will be heard on the appropriate day.

The Rake's Progress

The continuity of man
From before birth till after death
Is necessary to his kind.
Either the womb contains the mind
Which carries on to the last breath
Or history never began.

The baby who at last appears
And drinks his mother with her milk
Is clad already in the past:
Spinning and weaving hands at last
Achieved his gown of sack or silk,
As voices made the words he hears.

And there is nothing that he sees
Which ages have not modified.
The very smile his mother wears
Reflects how she conceives her cares:
The terms, slightly transmogrified,
Have been in use for centuries.

The clever men of Babylon
Who had ideas about the stars,
The Christian Fathers who could prove
That everything was made by Love,
A world of condoms and of cars,
Have brought their contribution.

The mother thinks, the child imbibes,
Then talking comes and carries thought
A generation further still
Without much effort of the will:
Words have more meanings than are taught;
It is the outside speech describes.

The world is found by bumping heads,
But also by analysis.
So theory mixed with bumps will give
The best instruction how to live.
The child grows up and soon he is
Full of invented hopes and dreads.

Most likely he will have ideas
– New ones of course, they always are –
But those damned words will not allow
Him liberty to work out how
The world of sense stands off so far
And does not fit his panaceas.

Then love comes, and ideas go:
Imagination fills the gap.
The body takes its rightful place,
Conceptual as the human face,
And he no longer cares a rap
For an abstracted to and fro.

He shrinks into himself, a squid
That quickly disappears in sand:
He has become a universe
In case he should find something worse
Than the delight he has in hand,
From whom, however, all is hid.

She cannot share the loveliness
He sees, for what she sees is him,
And there is not a perfect trade
Between the offers they have made
Of concept, promise or of limb;
Each gropes alone for a caress.

Both trundle through the course of time
But shapes and shades are all I see,
And sounds that fall upon the ear
Are all the persons that I hear.
The ghost of others is in me;
My ghost sticks somewhere in bird-lime.

Or are you empty, world? The birds
Gathering in autumn, are alive
And twittering too. We may depart
With half a word upon our heart,
To climb and circle or to dive
And scatter like the words.

Peat

If I could only return to where I am
From where I have been or from the vague reaches
Passing imagination saw, but not I,
The darkness would softly occlude the sky
And all sound faint before the barn-owl's screeches
Or the cry of a solitary lamb.

The sum of everything would be the peat
Which runs cool and dark between my fingers.
It is night itself, a peaceful shower
Which not one minute falls, not for one hour,
But endures while consciousness lingers
And follows it into its final retreat.

A Storm

O rain and wind, O wind and rain,
I not interpret what you say
But understand as if I were
A talking element myself
That speaks more faintly with each hour.
Yet every word and all intent
Loses itself among the wind,
Denounced under a flattening rain:
Presumption disappears, as best
Becomes the lips which might have spoken.

Beside the River

Two figures on a river-bank:
A full-grown man, a child of three.
The river passes them, yet stands
For all its flow, as still as they.

River! Exact and noiseless time
Passes as you do, and the two
So fixed there now, are not the same
As when your surface caught their eye.

The river holds their gaze, but they
Flow away into emptiness.
Or where? Who knows? Or who can say?
It is not time, but they, who pass.

Trees in a Mist

The mist is so thin, the world stands still
Before my eyes: there is no vanishing.
Dead figures ape the live ones which before
Breathed and were blown about by wind or will.
The winter cold embraces everything:
Death is the country I must now explore,

Yet cannot, and my corpse is not among
The number that I count before my eyes
– Trees which another time will bud and fruit,
And do not wait for any season long,
Though time seems long under these hazy skies
And there are trees which perish at the root.

So plays the outer world with that within,
And maybe that within with that without
– Consciousness no more than an interface
Between the two, with roots under the skin
And in the natural objects round about,
Housed where it occupies no shred of space.

And as the body perishes and finds
Itself confounded by the world of sense
– Taste, scent and hearing joining touch and sight –
The mist comes and goes; the river winds
Into the darkness: can there be pretence
Where there is neither confidence nor light?

Figure

It is quite easy to imagine thought
In any animal, as in this sparrow
Hopping reflectively with his mouth full,
Or this blackbird who walks disdainfully,
And at a distance, clearly occupying
A different universe of discourse. We
Have thoughts as well as they, but we have words
To claim more for our thoughts than they deserve.
Men and women have shape and colour, yet
Their thoughts seem verbal custom more than shadows
Of movements they may make or ways they go.
But watch this girl who bends to pick a flower.
Her eyes lighten, blue as what they see;
Her arm stretches, and the fingers flutter;
Her foot arches, the sole presses the ground,
The leg braces, then folds as she kneels;
The thoughtful back and head conclude her purpose.
Thoughts without words: the word is an intruder,
So, when she rises, turns, and shows her flowers,
The whole says, *Look!* and the whole is seen.
Is there another thought beside that one?
Now add a word. O what word can conspire
Against this beauty to make it vanish?
Would not the perfect word corroborate
The whole appearance of the world, and leave
Reality intact of any discourse?
Back to the sparrow and the strutting blackbird,
And you who stand before me in your skin.

The Levels

Summer has come, with no comfort
Except the cattle munching as they think,
And green being green where they bow their heads.
The river runs low, emptying itself
As if the sky itself were going out,
Streaming to westwards as the evening falls.
When light comes again, what shall we see?
Only the ruin of this ancient land,
And hear no more the old authentic words.
Yet somehow out of silence truth is born,
Which nothing now can harbour but herself,
And so succession will make all things new.
Let autumn come, and winter fill the dykes.
Spring will succeed, and the incredible
Prove itself by the plenty that it yields.

Conversation

It is by answering one another
That we exist. How else? How else?
For none alone, without reply,
Can with conviction utter 'I',
And even talking to oneself
Has part in it of him and her.

A shower of persons patters down
Upon the cradle where the child
Lies without briefing till a splash
Bounces back, and in a flash
A watching face, thereby beguiled,
Reads in it either smile or frown.

So in illusion there begins
Such conversation as there is
Between all creatures of a kind.
The fallacy promotes a mind
Fitted to serve the purposes
Haunting beneath our several skins.

And truth? And truth! Find if you can
Its plain location, or the words
Which hold it steady and secure.
The end of purposes is sure,
But truth is like the flight of birds,
Above the head of man.

Portrait of the Artist

What then am I? How can I be
A person that is spoken to
As others are, to whom I speak?
It is the otherness I seek,
And find by looking. So, how you
Appear, is how you are to me.

Appear is, for whoever looks,
The only *is* there is. Not so
For the one who is looked at. *Is*
For that one is the precipice
He stands on. He can never know
Who stands, or what man wrote the books.

The Question

Can who be what or what be who?
The question is resolved in you,
Though not *by* you, for you will say
Your many thoughts get in the way:
You think and think and therefore are.

Before you take Descartes so far
Consider how it looks to me,
Who think you are because I see.
Admittedly I cannot prove
That what I see and whom I love
Are interchangeable and one.
Yet no consistent theory can
Displace the woman and the man,
So either must remain for other:
And what is one without the other?
A person? And what is a person
Except a metaphysical assertion?
I hesitate to make one so
Detached from everything I know.
If what I see and touch is true,
Then what I see and touch is you.

Broadmead Brook

O you haunting ghosts, I move towards you.
Could I go over these flooded plains
It would not be to any Paradise:
I came from none and I expect to find none;
It was a long journey, or so it seemed.
The scene changed, and thoughts went through my head,
But even the possibility of knowledge
– Never coveted – seemed no more than a slide
From one thing to another. First the child
Tasting the world, and finding that it hurt;
Then the youth, felled by the bolt of love,

Then labouring where the knowledge was acquired
In self-defence or else in mere ambition.
But late in time and after all deceits,
I came to stand beside Broadmead Brook
As in the very hollow of my hand.
A woman stood there who had been a child
Where in another century my mother
Had played and laboured. Now all was changed,
Yet Broadmead Brook flowed, exquisite woods
Marked her course, for in my fantasy
It was she guarded the bounding deer,
The rabbits and the partridges, and all
Who dare to dream, and be, of England still.

Into the Darkness

The woods have fallen and the countryside
Vanishes from the eyes which knew it best.
What love was that which sought alternately
The open moorland and the crowding trees?
Do *they* make love, or does the watching eye
Merely have work to do for what within
The skull, the heart, the very finger-tips
Aches for companionship and can find none
But what has beauty for a name, and kindness?
Sleep on: it is a dream. Nothing I see
Speaks to me; it is I who speak to it.
Yet words, we know, do not answer the call
Of inmost need, for that would mean reply,
And nothing speaks to me, for beauty is
A hunger, not a feast, and it is made
By wants we have and not by what we are given.
Fall, trees: I can do nothing for your growth.
Conceal yourself, beauty, before my eyes
Which bring you nothing but my hunger.
What I bring to the failing countryside
Is nothing but the failure of my need.
It is for youth and hope that morning breaks.

I who am

I who am and you who are
– If we are, as we suppose –
None the less are very far
From knowing what each other knows.

Even the curl of that curled leaf
Is not the same for both our eyes,
Much less a hope, much less a grief,
A memory, or a surmise.

Much less the whole that makes the Is
Of any living creature. I
May utter perfect sentences,
And so may you, who make reply,

But these toy structures are no more
Than any rule held in the hand,
And what your words, or mine, are for
Is not a thing we understand.

So ask the body. It alone
Knows all you know, and it imparts
Little enough of what is known
To what we call our minds and hearts.

So fumbling bodies try to make
Friendship and love as best they can:
None was ever without mistake
And lies by woman and by man.

Man lies by woman, woman lies
By man, and in a common bed.
Where is the rule which truly tries
What is done there by what is said?

On a Drawing

Toi à qui . . . You had never speech;
Only the lines on paper spoke.
No words of mine could ever reach
The silence that you never broke.

Beauty is poised in clear mid-air
And there you are, and there you stay:
For my cold words to find you there,
What silence must they not convey?

The poet and the work of art
Meet where the silence of the word
Encounters lines which have a part
In every echo that is heard.

And you who wore, and were, the flesh
These lines endeavour to translate,
Cannot yourself keep memory fresh
Of what was at that distant date.

It is abstracted lines that live,
While you must die, as others do;
A draughtsman, certainly, can give
A longer memory than you

– But not of you; the temperature
Of flesh, its movement and its thought,
Have no pretence here to endure,
Nor fleeting colour to be caught.

You see the lines the draughtsman drew
Although yourself unmade by time;
I see, and what I see is you
As others saw you in your prime

– Or so your presence is to me,
I boast, I think, I partly lie:
The poem holds you silently
And in that silence words must die.

The Mappemonde

The face, hardly issued from innocence,
Where walls of flesh held fast her feet and hands,
Is fresh as dew, and the emergent limbs,
Tiny at first, grope to achieve their shape.
She has the pulp and surface of a grape:
Do not crush her. It is a new life brims
In that soft skin before she understands,
Or senses congregate and so make sense.

Insensibly she grows, but sensibly
Takes in the size and meaning of those blocks
Of hard and soft, those loud and quiet things
Which make the world before the world begins.
Legs and arms do the work of tail and fins,
Propelling this small fish until she flings
Prudence aside, and first kneels, and then rocks
Upon unstable feet for all to see.

So is childhood begun, and consciousness
Grows like a weed within this harmless frame,
Tangled with others as it turns and twists.
You may, indeed, doubt how it can affect
The flesh in which it is rooted, or the aspect
Of that stripped form by which alone exists
All that can have a hope or bear a name.
Yet a face may be thoughtful, none the less,

And thought does not end there. The body flows
Through the slim torso, lengthening arms and legs
– And as they run, dive, frolic and be pleased,
Sayings all quickly seconded by the tongue,
Which speaks also for stomach, heart and lung
And every nerve demanding to be eased.
So every syllable the body begs
Is written in the skin from scalp to toes.

O words joined to the flesh, as once the Word,
And so when shoulders firm and arms grow round
And there is definition in the breasts.
Although the whole frame hesitates to be

The woman who took apples from the tree,
Yet time runs on, the time that never rests,
Until the first maturity is found,
The unmistakable Eve is seen and heard.

Even her smile is ambiguity;
The look and looked-at tumble in her brain
– The arms meant to assist or to entice,
The breasts are apples to the glancing eye,
The patch of hair below writes clearly why.
Yet the whole figure gives more sad advice,
That youth once lost will never come again:
The future comes, in which no one is free.

This was her mother not so long before,
Her mother and her mother, till the past
Runs into darkness. Soon, shaped like a pear,
Her body still resembles theirs, and out
Falls a small girl: the times have turned about,
But she goes, full sail, into different air:
See how her comfortable flesh at last
Rises and falls, breathing at every pore.

Then age. No body is comfortable
In that last scene. No softness of the skin
Can compensate for the receding tide,
Nor any kindness written on the face.
The arms have lost their stretch, the legs their pace
Yet still only falsity can divide
The outer life from consciousness within,
And at the resurrection all is well.

If I were accused

If I were accused of what I have said
I could perhaps answer; I should at least
Have something to say which proposed meaning
– Reason enough for speaking, although the dead
Cannot avail themselves of it, and the beast,
Even while still living, finds its demeaning.

A roar or a bark or a miaow merely asserts
Existence and essence without saying why.
They are mysterious who cannot answer back.
So let nature reign; yet mystery may hurt
The Icarus who pretends that he can fly
Too stupendously close to the sun's track.

And so this girl, in whom the vanity
Of finished beauty may occlude sight,
And she see no more than she can say.
We are condemned to words: if what we see
Can never be discovered in more light
Than they can give, there is no brilliant day;

There is no brilliant object made to fill
Brimful the mind and leave no room for speech.
This girl herself will lose the wakeful shine
Of shaped and iridescent flesh, until
Whether she sit or stand, or run or walk,
Not she, but only words, can give a sign.

Adam, who named the beasts as they came by,
Had no name for the wonder that he felt,
But we have words to hide things from our eyes.
Read what is – the birds as they fly,
The lap of waters, snows as they melt.
Only a speechless look can be wise.

In the Silence

The silence of my days
Deepens, the wind is still:
Unbroken cloud or haze
Wraps up the world until
The minds which once seemed full
Seem empty, dark and dull.

I speak, and no one hears:
I listen, no one speaks.
There is no sound of tears,
No laughter. No one seeks
The future in the past
Where it must come at last.

And is the future new?
They say so, who ignore
Adam and Eve show through
Today as heretofore.
The murder done by Cain
Is daily done again.

Celebrate if you will
The triumph of your genes:
The past is working still
– That is all that it means.
In every spoken word,
Always, the past is heard.

Perhaps silence is best,
But if there must be speech,
Then watch it closely, lest
It stretches out of reach.
The future is too far;
The past is all we are.

The Model

Certainly speech is not possible,
For what are words without the world that speaks?
Voices in air come from the solid earth.
Green fields speak of May and all is well:
It is the sea tells what the river seeks:
It is the sky which says what heaven is worth.

And so with touch and every other sense,
For what are hard and soft without a stone?
Or scent without the dunghill and the rose?
Fill up the world and you may recompense
The listener listening to the hollow tune
Of sounds without content, or mere prose.

But yet who speaks? There must be speakers too
And you may have encountered one, who touch
The strings they speak with and you listen for.
How designate the speaker, and what drew
You to that note you loved little or much?
It was the garment that the speaker wore.

What garment? If the speaker is within
It is none other than the flesh she wears,
Where all the voice holds may be touched and seen,
So what her speech carries will begin
To bear the timbre that the body bears;
The world will partly mean what she may mean.

All love is dangerous, but to regard
The body as it is, is what must be
If speech is to impart its share of truth
And carry sights and sounds, and soft and hard,
The non-numerical reality
Which billows round us into age, from youth.

The words we say are part of what we are:
All flesh is grass, and so is what we say.
Observe the people passing in the street:
The words they use come to them from afar;
The use is only what they are today,
And what they are is in the flesh complete.

And so I turn to you: the conversation
Is because you are, and I seek to know
How that frame ripples as your words come out.
Except as love and knowledge are the same,
It is not love but words I seek, and so
I hope no more than to be cleared of doubt.

The Rose

What the words carry and the things you say
Must be related, but the saying is you
And what the words carry is history
To which you add your infinitesimal day.
Sweet rose of England, nothing can be true
Except so far as words and you agree.

And how is that possible? My dear,
The tongue you speak must so become your tongue
That it becomes like kisses on your lips,
Given and received at once. Then, without fear,
Your diction answers to the clear line sung
By lutenists, which dips as the voice dips.

So, when words had the colour of the flesh,
And passed from mouth to mouth, and were not laid
Like corpses on a script or on a tape,
The fields rang with laughter, or the fresh
Cry of misfortune. Now speech is a trade,
The word congealed and all meanings escape.

Absence

Go back, or forward, to a time
When I am not here. What remains?
What is here is what I see,
For I trust visibility,
Find that I get wet when it rains
And think that sense and reason chime.

No sense, no reason. For the past,
The living stand in for the dead
And try to see what others saw,
Though disappearance is the law
For what is seen, and what is said,
Though cast in bronze, can never last.

And so one can imagine sand
Carried back by receding tides,
And yet not understand a word
The ocean said when it was heart.
The present never co-incides
With any past that comes to hand.

Go forward. I am here no more:
No word of mine can extricate
The listener from the cord that binds
Him in the twist of other minds.
Unheard before, and now too late,
My words have lost the flesh they wore.

I am not even silence, as
The rows on rows of marshalled dead
Who left no word they did not speak.
An echo that is faint and weak
Remembers me for what I said,
Happy to lose the man I was.

Casualty

It is not the spoken word but the word spoken
In silence, not directed at anyone,
But holding meaning till it spills over,
Which finds its way into the casual mind.
Poetry, ha? The bed-rock of that art
On which those few can build who lose themselves.

A Word in Time

If I knew what to say I would say it now,
But speech is at an end, the words you hear
Echo through empty halls of past decades.
Others may speak again, but not I
Who am forbidden by age and emptiness.
Those halls ring with what cannot be
Because it was, in another time.
Pass on, present, into futurity,
Leaving your husk of past for other teeth.
Who munches on that will never know
The light which falls this morning nor on whom
It falls. So, expect nothing from me
Who spoke of yesterday and what I saw,
Which now has vanished though the words remain:
The flesh has melted and the noun rings hollow.

The Pattern

The days seem long now, and life is long
Although the years hurry away to death;
No one can daunt time; the young and strong
Are weak before it draws their dying breath.

It races, and they race, and still they lose;
The beds they tumble in grow comfortless.
How could imagination ever choose,
Since out of more there comes always less?

The gangling bunch of nerves which reach the brain
From every corner of the fleshly kingdom
Collects the news of beauty, but the pain
Of memory will devour comfort's crumb.

What is remembered of the years at last
Is nothing but the folly of the wise,
Prudence too much, or too much folly past,
No calculation helps the man who dies.

What comes back is that every choice is wrong,
No action finished as it was conceived,
The body withered while the hope was strong;
No itch it suffered ever was relieved.

O mind, the frenzy of a fluttered nerve,
What did you see as you went on your way?
What do you see now? Nothing will serve
To mitigate the horror of that day

When all goes crumbling to its final end;
The end of ends was far before that time.
No purpose was achieved, nothing could lend
The colour of intention to the climb

From that first pulp which once within the womb
Lived as unknowing as the wisest man,
To reach that image-decorated room
Death wipes as clean as when he first began.

Yet the pulp rises like a loaf of bread,
The harbouring belly swells, and then ejects
A naked clown who falls upon his head;
His parents see, he does not see, his prospects.

The reason of the world is in those two,
The one that bore, the one that set the seed;
The child is what he must be, and what grew
Once in the dark, finds what it is to feed.

Before the eyes can focus, ears can hear;
A cloud of sound bursts on the sleeping brain:
Then forms take shape, hunger may come, or fear,
An ancient pattern growing once again.

Love flashes from the eyes that wear the paps;
The peace they give resembles gratitude.
What deceits on both sides! The love perhaps
Following the particle it must extrude.

The gratitude compelled by satisfaction
Unable to attribute its delight:
A blind cradle rocks, and the exaction
Returns the infant to his sacred night.

So from this darkness does this ignorant
Grow senselessly, a tree without a root,
Only his predecessors confident
These vague extensions are a hand or foot.

So words collect which have no meaning yet,
Like dross upon the brain in sucking-time;
Sights veer and cloud and are indefinite;
The child moves in the chaos of his prime.

Movement it is that brings definition,
The toe, the toy, the blow or else the fall.
Wisdom creeps in then like the Evil One
To advise how to bully and to call.

And so to play, and give to fantasy
Control of every monster in the way;
Mind like a platitude will always see
Itself victorious in the shining day.

And then to youth, certain and arrogant,
Or weak and frightened when it finds defeat,
Still groping with its stream of youthful cant
To find a proper use for hands and feet.

The feet which lead him to the proper prize,
The hands which seek for softness once again;
The conjugation mastered by the eyes
Inflecting what until it turns to when.

To climb upon the body that he chose,
Yet did not choose but willingly obeyed,
Those breasts, that belly, that imagined rose
Blooming under the bush which marks its glade.

The bed of love declares itself supreme,
Yet not the love but only the desire
Which finds its solace there, is the true dream
Throwing itself upon its funeral pyre,

That desire which must flicker and then blaze
So often in what seem long years ahead,
Twists itself into many shapes and plays
Far subtler games than any in a bed.

The conqueror is happy on his horse,
The politician revels in acclaim,
The petty thief approves his clever course:
The hope that drives their movement is the same.

Justification in the eyes of men:
The lies crowd around the winner and he laughs.
And when he fails, as he must fail? Ah, then
He lies to please himself, and laughs and laughs.

So the word grows upon a tree of nerves,
To deceive all who take it for the fruit.
What fruit is there? The dying body serves
At last to stultify it from the root.

It came first rather as a bird to perch,
Twittering perhaps upon an utmost twig:
The dying body leaves it in the lurch,
The structured growth solid and gaunt and big.

The twig has lost its sap, the word its meaning.
Can it fly after that? The flock that fell
Bird after bird from nowhere, and sat preening,
Rises no more, and has no news to tell.

A twitter here and there is taken up
By other birds, perched upon other trees:
Then silence: other mimics fill the cup
Of the surrounding world, and seek to please.

And other movements bustle and are lost,
Of other bodies moving as they must,
For no word suits them, and their hopes are crossed
As others were which now compose the dust.

If any came, it was the only Word
From the beginning and beyond the end:
It was made flesh – which you may think absurd –
And if it was not, no man has a friend.

What mind is that which floats above it all?
Histories happen, words float everywhere.
Can they find meaning? They swoop and fall,
Homing on scattered hope, scattered despair,

Where men and women clutch at anything
Which for a moment seems to promise mind:
Build then who can, and teach the voice to sing,
Help them all to resemble human-kind.

Build cities, where the busy man may hide
His hope under a heap of emptiness.
Child-birth under a roof will turn to pride:
The most presumptuous building is a dress

And those who enter it with clothes and names
Still seek the cover of a common garment;
No cloth so fine that it can hide their shames,
No tower so high that nothing more is meant.

O poverty of man, woman and child,
Wordless at first and seeking to conceal
The unconversible heart which runs wild,
The mind with shapeless thoughts, and none is real.

How can they sleep or die without dreams?
Much less move, walk here or there for reasons
They tell themselves: what is is not what seems;
Sleeping and waking, for all, feed on treasons.

Remove all cover, pull the buildings down,
Strip off the clothes, show up the naked pair:
They are not stripped enough by half, the frown,
The smile express their dream that they are fair.

The sad creation of their own conceit:
The words they learned carry the poison in,
False hopes and fantasies which they repeat
To the tune of the blood beneath the skin.

Strip off the words that they are pleasant with;
They mean what the blood says and nothing more.
The blood pumps on and they cannot forgive,
Later, the many lies they told before.

Strip off the flesh, which brought them to this pass,
And what is left? Ah, there the world is dumb.
How else does any see wind over the grass,
The flowers assailed, or hear the insects hum?

How else see blue sky and brilliant cloud,
The river passing and the swan at rest?
How speak of them and not cry aloud?
How praise what must be praised and loved best?

The words which fall like petals from the sky
Are all they have, and not as instrument,
Only as gift, which none may have who try
To turn these driftings to their own intent.

The body, yes, without it they are not,
Nothing can do and nothing understand.
The rasping mind pretends to have a thought:
It lies, and cannot even lift a hand.

The paradise of the Resurrection
Waits for its people, or else nothing is.
Choose you cannot, but, chosen, fall upon
Knees if you have them, and some certainties.

Poems since
What and Who

A Valediction

The ghosts which rustle past the world
Know no world but forgetfulness.
Their way ahead lies to the east,
While you who travel westward still
Follow only a wisp of will.
Yet who would not have that wisp to follow,
Which, going, leaves no reason for the drift,
Real or imagined? I am with the crowd
Which once was, but now haunts without intent.
Ah, we are gone: do not now stop the flow
Of those who have no meanings but your own.
The dead speak only as the living hear,
And those who tramp the final miles to death
Have nothing more to say that can be heard.
So I, who praised but did not practice silence,
Move to a realm where only silence is.

Five Lines

The splashed light on the rain-wet stones
Is in the eye, not in the sun:
Eyes dimmed, the light is gone,
And all the wonder of the world
Cannot withstand the touch of age.

Eve

The countryside is silent and the sheep
Eat, like the past, the growth of other times.
Only the young may see the past alive
And Eve who is the morning of our day.

Triptych

1

Now I am come to that strange place
Where those must come who wait for death:
We expect no familiar face,
But one who takes away our breath.

So welcome to the visitor
Who comes but once, and as a friend,
Seen only as an open door
Through which we go to find our end.

He brings release, after so long
In business and captivity,
And when we go where we belong
– *In manus tuas* – we are free

2

We live within, although we hope,
Ambitiously, to live without,
In the world where we only grope,
And see no more than we can doubt.

To be, to be as others are
– Visible, moving as a mind –
Seems an ambition not too far
Out of the way of human kind.

Yet to be other is to be
The true impossible for us:
Within, it is outsides we see,
Our own not less extraneous.

We move without but live within,
Like it or not, that is the way,
And when we move no more, the in-
And out-side vanish quite away.

The only hope is in belief
In all the gross absurdities
The Creed contains, of which the chief
Are of a kind the least to please

Abstracted and ingenious minds
Which trust in thoughts but not in things,
While he who swallows it will find
Reality is King of Kings.

3

All the estates of life are done:
We wait with alms to please the world,
Which will refuse our gifts and run
From us whose empty shells are hurled

Into the dustbin of intent,
Where meaning was, but is no more.
And how should anything be meant
When life is that which went before?

For what is now is emptiness,
Engendering nothing that can be
The object of desire or guess,
Or any future memory.

The empty plain extends beyond
All human being, into what
Lies quiet as a darkened pond,
And is is overpowered by not.

On the Shore

What has been washed up upon this shore?
To call it 'who' would be to presume an answer:
To call it 'I' starts up another question.
If I am I, I think that I observe:
Can I be he who yet observes what is?
Surely the heap that lies upon the shore
Is object more than it is consciousness,
And consciousness is the extent of me.
Blind self, which still is conscious of its blindness,
Is not the sturdy matter that we know,
Made in six days by God as heaven and earth.
What He made in his image is mysterious,
Yet Eve remains for Adam all the same.

Olim

It is no longer I who speak:
There was a man who spoke, but he is dead.

Tristia

1

It is because of exile I am here,
The utmost tip of the world, for old age
Brings one to the edge of what one lived among.
Before departure I was of that race
Which passed the time but thought of something else,
But now time fills the whole horizon:
Not what yesterday was or what tomorrow
Will bring, for what it brought is dead,
And what it will, will never come to life.
When will it pass? is all I have to ask.
No-one is implicated in that question

But I who now no longer live among
Even those who see me now as I do them.
But 'as' is not the word I should have used,
For age has given sight its own blindness,
And no impression is conveyed to me
Which tells me it is here that I belong.
I am the utmost tip of what once was,
Beyond which there is nothing but the sea;
The stationary Pontic cold holds all.
I look towards it, not to those I know,
Though casual bodies hurrying in the street
May hold the eye enough to make a glance,
But where they go is not where I will go:
I turn back to the water and am lost.

2

No-one will speak to you, nor you to any:
This is the end of all communication
Which was the hope which brought you to this end
And served delusively to coax you on.
The road that leads to death goes single file,
And so it always was. Though each in turn
Surrounds himself with dreams of other minds,
The bodies which should hold them have no voice.
The voice of every lonely traveller
Is loud with silence as the company
He sees around him as he passes on.
Why then these verses? Nothing can be heard.
But speak on as you will, you who are young.
Collude with one another on the way:
Proximity may do what words will not.

3

The hollow name of Love sounds through the streets,
The newsboy crying while the city burns.
The lack of any purpose of my own
Cries louder, and the city is consumed.
The state denies the Church, the Church the state;
The promises of neither have come true,
Or so it seems, here at the door of death.

4

The past is only past which never present was:
Nor is there present now but that vain show of past.
Reality has faded into dream
– A dream without cohesion or event.
Oddities now show nothing but oddities,
For meaning has escaped. Where purpose was
Is nothing but consecutive array
Of matters past which do not matter now.

5

The day is over and the night begins,
But what is day which so resembles night?
Forgetfulness and sleep are of a piece.
The tail-end of the world: and here am I
Pledged to a narrowing prospect. I stand here
While the world fails or falters in my eye.

6

Here on this promontory by the sea,
Speech has no meaning, yet we use it still:
The flagged signal, the gesticulation,
Serve better to elicit a reply.
Yet we talk on, dazed and with hollow voice.
The empty shell you see is what you hear:
The tolling bell will tell the truth at last.

7

The crystal world that was, when I was there:
The broken morning and the silver eve,
The flashing woodland and the dew on grass,
The moon lighting up what the sun has left.
Such a world must be somewhere, but not here.
Even the sea breaking upon the rocks
Crashes no more, but laps this final shore,
Soon to be frozen. There is wind,
But only hissing as it sidles by.
O send the blustering past in new array,
And let me find the quartz within the stone.

8

The naked person is the only one
Who speaks within the chatter of our speech:
There is no truth in reason or abstraction.
They are the garments that the body wears,
The chatter of the magpie, not the bird
Which walks before the eye in black and white.
The body gives direction to our speech,
As to our thoughts: your shape is what you are,
And what you are is what I seek to know.
The brilliant knowledge which escapes me here,
At this far tip of the world, is what the mind
Can take immediately from what it sees,
Plain without any need for explanation.
So strip before my eyes and speak in tune
With what you are, and that will be the truth
– A momentary revelation
To clear the clouds which else envelop me.
But if you think cloud is where I belong,
Pile on your clothes and chatter in the words
The magpie uses and the world applauds.

9

Speech cannot be betrayed, for speech betrays,
And what we say reveals the men we are.
But, once come to a land where no-one is,
We long for conversation, and a voice
Which answers what we say when we succeed
In saying for a moment that which is.
O careless world, which covers what is there
With what it hopes, or what best cheats and pays,
But speech with others needs another tongue.
For a to speak to b, and b to a,
A stream of commonalty must be found,
Rippling at times, at times in even flow,
And yet it turns to Lethe in the end.

10

I am the place where I belong,
For other self or place is not:
The horror of the world extends
Beyond that bourn and never ends.
No friend, no other haunts that space
Which, empty as infinity,
Means no more to me than myself.
Send me particulars and limits,
The tactile and the visible.
Here only nullity is left:
What was lost has lost its place
– No, place has gone as time has gone,
And I have never been, nor am.

Necessity

It is necessity of speech
Which drives a man, though he is dumb,
As he descends and gropes his way
Along the ultimate stone paths of age.
To speak, to hear, these are the plenitudes
Required to fill up human emptiness
And give a shape to what is called a mind,
Which has that need as much as any body,
As anybody has the need of both.

The Best Thing to Say

The best thing to say is nothing
And that I do not say,
But I will say it, when I lie
In silence all the day.

Estrangement

No hope or purpose haunts my days,
Which are estranged from me because
No hint of future colours them.
The distant past which led to them
Was in its time a present too
And in that time a future beckoned
Delusively, and hopes were there.

The Media

1

The world is fabricated by
A gang of entertainers who
Have replaced God Almighty.

The universe, made in six days,
Is re-made every day by those
Who hear all that the newsman says,
For whom fact is replaced by gloze.

2

The air is full of noise,
The screen of caper:
Reality enjoys
No inch of paper.

The most expensive lies
Flourish in every home:
Great gulps of froth and foam
Win the first prize.

Go to the quiet wood
To hear the beating heart:
Leaf fall and breaking bud
Will play their part.

And so the truth is out
Which only quiet tells,
And as it does, its voice
Sounds like a peal of bells.

The Verb To Be

Nothing comes out of the forest of my mind,
So what can be? There is the outer world.
Or how should I know if there were to be
A fight of dragons or a shower of rain?
For I stand at the entrance of the world
– Of my world, of the only world I know,
Or can know – I who am limited.
There is one God who made the world complete
And all the little worlds, beetle or man,
Who see as much as their small natures allow.

The Way

Not because of where you are when you arrive,
But for the way you go before you do:
The way is truth, but history is lies.
The way is also life, and that you live:
You live each moment once, and then no more:
Even a memory is a novelty,
And never is what was, as it pretends.
Only the way you go count count at last,
Beyond which there is nothing but the truth.

Indefinition

As death approaches, I look back –
Même pas, for I see nothing.
Nothing is what it was, for what is now
Is nothing – or so tenuous
As not to lead a purpose by the nose.
Indefinition reigns, and who am I
Who, after long ranging among things
Which summoned words to say that they were definite,
Am lost in nothingness which now I am?

Poet, sergeant, Under Secretary:
Were those necessary?
The dogs have had their day,
But the three seem to lack
Coherence as a pack.
Now all are far to seek:
Three days don't make a week.

All the flatwater of the world
Is spread before my window-pane,
But my own world is small because
My mind shrinks every year I live.
The hugeness of the universe
Is not what troubles me the most,
But who or what and how or when
– The ordinary affairs of life
Which is not life unless we live
Among the meanings of the world.

Finale

Nothing means anything now:
I am alone
– My mind a vacant space,
My heart of stone.

A tuneless thing I am,
A broken lyre.
I cannot even boast
A flameless fire.

There is the work I did
– Paper and ink –
I have no part in it:
There is no link

Between the man who wrote
– And more, was once alive,
And this relic for whom
The end does not arrive.

Although the life has gone
There is no corpse to show:
When others find it, I
Alone shall never know.

Appendix:
Poems 1931-5

I wrote the following poems between the ages of 17 and 21 – that is to say, between the time I first became an undergraduate at Bristol and the time early in 1935 when, as a post-graduate student, I left Berlin for Freiburg. The poem in Berlin was to be the last poem till, in 1943, I resumed the practice of writing such things on a troopship off Freetown – although, to be exact, there was a small breach of the peace in verse during my earliest years in Whitehall, with the two lines 'On a Civil Servant', published originally in *The New English Weekly*.

The nine poems here reprinted appeared in the Bristol University student magazine, *The Nonesuch*, the first in autumn, 1931 – my first term. The great impact of 1930-31, so far as I was concerned, had been the poems of Eliot, although I had to wait until the prize-day after I left school to acquire my own copy. On that prize-day I also received (like the Eliot, by my own choice) James Joyce's *Chamber Music*, and this must account for the use of four-line rhymed verse in the first piece here. The second poem, 'A Prince in Prison' – with its epigraph, significantly, from Donne – is clearly the work of a young man who had read 'The Waste Land', and to me there are signs of my encounter with Spender in the 'Invitation to Suburbans' and with Auden in 'Address to whom it may concern'.

The first four poems were signed 'Colin Clout', the second two 'Clout', and the final three (with comparatively brazen publicity), 'C.S.'

C.H.S.

Homo Sapiens

The mirrors change. Earth does not falter
   Nor sky rush dark about my eyes.
For the convolutions of my mirrors
   Earth has no surprise.

I have put reason before beauty
   And beauty, till the mirror reels;
And the lidded stars watch me and watch me,
   And none but I feels.

Colin Clout

A Prince in Prison

'Else a great prince in prison lies.'

I.

There is no symphony
between sound and colour:
colour is still while the sound runs;
hard and extraneous, jangling the senses
while sound runs with the river.
Thin fir-needles, fallen,
make the ground seem hairy where they lie
mixed with dead leaves, the cynical yellow
of old age.
The light slants on me and upon the stream
where there swim
(without design as in a dream)
sick trampled leaves, ghost of one dead.

II.

After the long watching on stone faces,
after my seeking for some understanding
echo that would show trace of recognition,
after the slow drip of a thousand seconds,
after the, after,
I turned to climb upon the pyre of voices.
thinking another flower of beauty withered;
when I had come to break your letter open –
some faint apology I said and cold –
I found the echo there.

Coldly, over teacups
whence aromatic incense swings and rises,
chilled like the clatter of spoons –
that I expect will be our meeting.

Yes, Donne was very sensual for a dean.
And yet I would be seen
cling to your body as we went together
out of the world of light,
cutting into darkness proud and amazed.

There was a cold clatter of spoons,
and then a moment
like a child's poignant shame, imparting
pattern to chaos;
hat and fur and face swinging
into form.

              Colin Clout.

The Age of Reason

I say I love you; you contract
  And your smile crystallises, thins:
Impregnable, a cataphract,
  Your brows start out like cocoa tins.

Dearest, could you not formulate
  Some sense of a contrived disdain,
In cruel keen words to propagate
  The orthodox poetic pain?

One agrees, passion is so crass,
  Its subjects interesting, unclean,
And one concludes the middle class
  Is self-sufficing, epicene.

              Colin Clout.

Invitation to Suburbans
  'Couvre-toi de gloire, Tartarin;
  couvre-toi de flanelle.'

Will you not march out with the crass winds
that cry against your torment of repose,
climb the thin road, the secret rose?
Scanty winds that caress your garden gate
flatter the fulness of your bourgeoisie,
high-class confectioners, pet littérateurs.

Ship-shape and Bristol fashion are the laurels
whose leaves no wind will lift.
From the warm rooms bay-windows
watch the drift
along the streets, of cynical men.
Will you not march
against the sour hours with your drums and colours?

Colin Clout.

Tourist's Love-Song

Carrying a candle through a gusty house,
I think with pleasure, I will have a guide
In those locked rooms, to say:
'In that four-poster Queen Elizabeth slept;
There was a brace of princes strangled, here . . .'
Let me in, let me explore, interpret
The murmuring feet in the long corridors,
And let me bear my candle through the rooms
Despite the shuffling caretaker who tells me
The rooms are empty, shutters up the door.

Clout.

Two Poems

I.
Horses like sea-crests running main afloat
Against the wind beat, horses of Chirico;
From the kerb watch stamp tramp and use of curb
The dream-corroded boy and hazy lady
Whose thoughts like slow fish move behind their eyes.

II.

Extend your charmed boughs, expend
Music and green flames with what mastery
Of traffic and arc lamps you can command.
Fair, out of air, brightness falls,
Out of wind out of sky and whipping boughs.
To-night is no obfuscation, coruscation instead
Of night with stars, memory with distinct images.
Now rock-bottom's reached, I move among the corals.
I feel the shape of the rocks, a blind man
Tracing with devoted hands the lineaments
Of the offering face. Nose, now I have it,
Now cheek, now lip. This knowledge
Leaves me high and dry, the ideal spectator;
Pity and terror tug, I am glad of the conflict,
Admitted by this to high company.
Useless to reflect at this moment, impossible
To weigh each against each grounds for persuasion
To whatever politics or mode of prayer.
Dearest, you are mistress of your shape;
Your body contains you, supple like the flail
Of the boughs bending under which I stand.
I have thought too much of the wrong problems,
Whether in me lies the control of speech,
Authority over action. Shape into which this,
Belief under which, compulsion or what not,
This objectless faith should be reformed, is not known.
It has broken rocket-wise, hit the stars,
Spat at the dew, circled like the flail
Of the trees, like hail tintinnated
Against the window-panes or the near clock.
I am sick of this. I am half-baked and nineteen.
Given faith in progress and five hundred a year
What redirection may not occur?

Clout.

Poem

I cannot take the sun out of the sky
Which day by day screams from the horizon
A burnish'd shield. White parched and cracked and barren
The earth beneath it faints. A blue-wing'd jay
From an acacia laughs and fliest away.

                                                            C.S.

Two Poems

I.

Beat about the bush
                    in a mad dream:
Beat about the bush
NIGHTMARE
                    Lasts
                              no
                                   long-
                                         -er
Than the night.
                    Or does it
Drift within the skull
          behind the eyes
                              all day?

II.

Why should this
                    or
                         that
                              man
                              march?
But altogether, five by five,
          pack on back,
                    revolver holster
                    and ruck-sack;
Why should they march?

But up and down
        all day long
The whole town
        salutes in order
All the soldiers
        sing one song
All the officers
        have one face
All troopers
        go at one pace.
Wirklich hat das kein Zweck.
                 C.S.

Address to whom it may concern

Sirs of the army on the march,
No dance will do; we always watch.
Sirs, we shall act while you are at
Your flattening of the policeman's hat.
To your outrageous morning shine
We shall oppose the ancient mien.
Cover your ware-announcing drums:
Study the art of being dumb.
We are instructed by our bones:
Those who will know have always known.

Berlin, 1935.
                                              C.S.

Bibliography

Angels and Beasts (Westhouse, 1947); included translations by CHS of four stories by Jules Supervielle.

The Curious Democrat (Peter Russell, 1950).

An Asiatic Romance (Gaberbocchus, 1953).

Versions and Perversions of Heine (Gaberbocchus, 1955).

The Spirit of British Administration (Faber, 1959; second edition, 1966).

Poems (Peter Russell, dated 1959 but not in fact available until 1961).

Twenty-one Poems (privately printed by The Westerham Press, 1960).

The London Zoo (Abelard-Schuman, 1961).

Numbers (Methuen, 1965).

Art and Action (Methuen, 1965).

Christopher Homm (Methuen, 1965; Carcanet, 1975; Carcanet, 1984).

Catullus (MacGibbon & Kee, 1966; Orion, 1967; Viking, 1969).

The Discarnation (privately printed by The Westerham Press, 1967).

Essays (privately printed by The Knole Park Press, 1967).

Roman Poems (privately printed by The Westerham Press, 1968).

Metamorphoses (Methuen, 1968).

English Poetry 1900-1950 (Rupert Hart-Davis, 1971; Carcanet, 1981; Methuen University Paperback, 1981).

The Case of Walter Bagehot (Faber, 1972).

In the Trojan Ditch (Carcanet, 1974).

The Corridor (The Mandeville Press, 1975).

The Poetic Art (Carcanet, 1975).

Anchises (Carcanet, 1976).

The Poem on Nature of Lucretius (Carcanet, 1976).

The English Sermon 1650-1750 (Carcanet, 1976).

David Hume (The Ramsay Head Press, 1976).

Selected Poems of Jonathan Swift (Carcanet, 1977).

The Avoidance of Literature (Carcanet, 1978).

Some Tales of La Fontaine (Carcanet, 1979).

The Divine Comedy (Carcanet, 1980; Pan, 1981; Regnery Gateway, 1981; OUP, 1993).

Selected Poems (Carcanet, 1981).

Philip Mairet: Autobiographical and other papers (Carcanet, 1981).

Anglican Essays (Carcanet, 1983).

Joachim Du Bellay: The Regrets (Carcanet, 1983).

Collected Poems (Carcanet, 1984).

Selected Poems of Christina Rossetti (Carcanet, 1984).

The Aeneid of Virgil (Carcanet, 1986).

Britannicus, Phaedra, Athaliah of Racine (OUP, 1987).

God Bless Karl Marx! (Carcanet, 1987).

On the Look-Out (Carcanet, 1989).

Selected Writings of Jeremy Taylor (Carcanet, 1990).

In Two Minds (Carcanet, 1990).

16 Sonnets (privately printed by H.C. Laserprint, 1990).

Antidotes (Carcanet, 1991).

Nine Sonnets (Greville Press, 1991).

English Perspectives (Carcanet, 1991).

Is There a Church of England? (Carcanet, 1993).

The Pattern (Enitharmon Press, 1993).

What and Who (Carcanet, 1994).

Poems: Selected (Carcanet, 1995)

Collected Translations (Carcanet, 1996).

Index of Titles

Index of First Lines